# A SPY FOR GOD
*The Ordeal of Kurt Gerstein*

*Pierre Joffroy*

# A SPY FOR GOD
## The Ordeal of Kurt Gerstein

TRANSLATED BY NORMAN DENNY

\*

COLLINS
ST JAMES'S PLACE, LONDON
1971

First published in France under the title *L'Espion de Dieu*

ISBN 0 00 211791 6

© Editions Bernard Grasset, 1969

© 1970 in the English translation by Wm. Collins Sons & Co., Ltd.

Printed in Great Britain
Collins Clear-Type Press
London and Glasgow

TO MY MOTHER

# Contents

# Prelude

EVERY man is unfathomable. There was a man unknown to me whose life I thought I could unriddle in a few weeks. I worked for two years and eight months. With very few exceptions I studied all the documents and interviewed all the witnesses, some on the verge of death and some of whom have since died. (I also knocked on the doors of the dead, and turned away in despair thinking that they had taken secrets with them, although later research generally showed that they would have had little to tell me.)

I interviewed priests, soldiers, diplomats, working men; and former members of the Gestapo and the SS with whom I talked over a drink. In my search for persons who had fled, or were lost in the darkness encompassing the war years, I advertised in the press, consulted directories, checked hazy memories against the evidence of incomplete documents. I was ten times in Germany, where I visited Belzec and Treblinka. I went to London and Geneva; and to Venice in search of a man who had never been there, but where a trace of him was to be found. I neglected scarcely any clue; and yet I am convinced that ten years would not have enabled me to complete my task. Kurt Gerstein was like the rest of us: the whole picture cannot be drawn.

Memory swallows the event, lives on it and transforms it; and it does not, as our bodies do, cast this nourishment out of the system. The recollection lingers, even in the mind that seeks to deny it, saying, I cannot remember, it was too long ago. My business was to bring back the memory of things not deeply felt at the time, or which indifference or ill-will sought to keep hidden. And again, there were witnesses who talked freely, so that names and dates and miscellaneous impressions came pouring out which I then had to store in my own memory, from fear of alarming people who would not have talked to a man with a notebook. My worst enemy was not the twenty-five years separating me from the event but the reactions of the individual —conscientious scruples, remorse, sometimes mistrust; above all the desire of every speaker to depict himself as better, stronger, more high-minded than he really was. For all this I had to make allowance.

This book is full of unavoidable gaps which I have not attempted to fill or even to indicate, since in any event the picture could never be complete. It may, indeed it must, contain errors, but I believe they are minor. I have not juggled with facts or with texts, and I have accepted as essentially true Gerstein's own account of his situation, having verified most of the details. And since I was writing about a profoundly religious man I have been careful not to intrude upon that field, which is not my own.

Shortly before his death Kurt Gerstein said to a Dutch friend: 'Write down what you know about me. One never knows . . .' This book is an attempt to fulfil his request.

That there is a true link between the flesh-and-blood Gerstein and the man depicted in this book is something of which I am convinced. It is inconceivable that if they were to meet in some other sphere, the man himself and the image conjured up out of his memory, they would not know and be drawn to one another, despite the gulf that separates them.

When Rama the Victorious asked his ally Hanuman, the monkey god, what he desired as a reward, Hanuman replied: 'Nothing, except the right to live as long as your story is told.' That is why, according to the *Ramayana*, Hanuman still lives.

Kurt Gerstein will continue to live so long as men tell the story of the great holocaust.

# Chapter 1

# PRELIMINARIES

*25 October 1946.* Telegram (not to be sent *en clair* by radio): '... Kindly inform me of the whereabouts of Kurt Gerstein wanted as a war criminal by the US authorities.'

*10 June 1947.* SHAEF representative of the French deputy Prosecutor, to the Garde des Sceaux (Keeper of the Seals): 'The United States Public Prosecutor considers it desirable to hear the testimony of Gerstein, Kurt. I am informed that he has spoken on the radio from Lyons.'

*10 September 1948.* Director General of the Baden-Baden High Court to the Commission for the Investigation of War Crimes: 'My attention has been called to a certain Gerstein, Kurt. This person was transferred elsewhere in November 1945 by ORCG, Lindau. Please inform me of present whereabouts.'

Letter from Ernst Zerrer, formerly employed by the Gestapo, to Kurt Gerstein, *8 December 1946*: 'Dear Herr Gerstein, ... So many bad things are being said about me. I am writing to beg you to help me by testifying as to my conduct during the war.'

From Frau Irmgard Eckhardt to Kurt Gerstein; Berlin Schlachtensee; *22 February 1947*: 'Dear Herr Gerstein, I have often thought of you, and I have now learned by chance that you were mentioned in the *Telegraf*. I rejoice with all my heart in your rehabilitation. It is a great relief to me ... My husband has been a prisoner in English hands since Easter 1945. His absence causes me intense suffering and I am in despair at the trouble he is in. Dear Herr Gerstein, can you help him?'

SS Major Robert Weigelt to Kurt Gerstein; Arolsen Waldeck,

*4 March 1950*: 'Dear Kurt, Our last conversation was by telephone in 1944. I write to let you know that I have at length returned to our beloved German Fatherland after five years' captivity in Russia. Greetings, dear Kurt. I clasp you warmly by the hand to confirm the long-standing friendship of your comrade, Robert . . . Have you gone back to your old job? Have you any news of the former staff of the Institute? Do you know what has become of my car? . . . My very best wishes to you, my old friend and chief. In the state of utter wretchedness in which I find myself I remain your eternally grateful—Robert.'

Meaningless and fruitless letters.

\*

On *26 July 1945* (or possibly *27 July*, the date has been altered), warders at the Cherche-Midi military prison in Paris carried the dead body of a German prisoner, covered by a regulation blanket, down to the prison yard. The man was so tall that his feet protruded beyond the end of the stretcher. He was listed in the prison records as 'Gerstein, Kurt; born in Münster, Westphalia, on 11 August 1905; charged with war crimes, murder and complicity.'

Only a very small number of people, a few warders and prisoners, had seen him since his arrival at the Cherche-Midi on 5 July. He said very little and did not ask for legal aid. On 20 July, by order of Colonel Abel Sauzey, a Security officer, he was placed in solitary confinement; and on 25 July (at 2 p.m. according to the police records of the Sixth Arrondissement, and at 2:15 according to the statement of Captain Chiaramonti, the governor of the prison) he took his own life. The death certificate was signed by the prison doctor at 5:25 on the same day.

\*

A black police van was waiting in the prison yard. Funeral attendants from the parish of Notre-Dame-des-Champs had placed a 'municipal coffin'—one designed for the penniless dead —on the ground, where it stood open with the lid leaning against it. The transfer of the body from the stretcher to the coffin took a few moments.

He was too tall. His head was propped up against the end of the coffin, and one of the men bent it sideways towards the shoulder. Mme Chiaramonti, the governor's wife, looking down from a window of their apartment, reflected that she would long remember that dead figure. How could anyone be so tall?

The lid was put back on, the door of the van slammed and the prison gates creaked open. The body, with its head pressed against its shoulder, was hurried across Paris as though it were running to escape all those who had desired its death. A few days later it was transferred from the Medico-Legal Institute to the Thiais cemetery and consigned to a communal grave under the name of Gastein. Later still the remains of this 'Gastein' were dumped into the 'bone pit' in the north-eastern part of the cemetery, no one having come forward to claim the body.

Such was the end of Obersturmführer Kurt Gerstein, robbed even of his name, consigned to oblivion like any Jew embarked on the cattle-truck journey to Pitschepoï, concerning which there is an old Yiddish song:

*In dem schtetele Pitschepoï*
*Zenen di dechelech badegt mit schtroï*
*Falt a regendl, falt a schneï.*

(In the hamlet of Pitschepoï
Where all the roofs are thatched
The rain rains and the snow snows.)

\*

From Gerstein's *Report* in the official Nuremberg translation (see p. 286):

'The death's train started then, a lovely girl in front of it. They went down the alley. Everybody was naked, men, women, and children. The cripple had been obliged to let their prothesis apparatusses and went along supported by others ... I standed at the top of the slope with Capt. Wirth, between the rooms of death. Mothers with their sucklings, naked children, women and

13

men, everybody pell-mell, were toiling up. The first ones entered
the rooms of death, pushed into them by standing behind people
who were forced by the whips of the SS men ... A Jewish
woman, looking to be 40 years old, with sparkling eyes appealed
the murderers of all these innocent people be damned for their
coward crimes. Captain Wirth whipped by himself at her face
5 or 6 times; she disappeared also into the room ... I must now
proclaim what I saw there, and charge the murders.'

\*

*London, 14 Trinity Square, E.C.3. 21 December 1966.*

The Swedish Consul General, Baron Göran von Otter, was
seated at his desk. A tall man in his sixties, he still carried himself
erect. His elegant presence and gentle manner conveyed a hint of
melancholy, perhaps of sadness. I had written to him three
months earlier but had received no reply, although he was the
most courteous of men. If I had not known that the ghost whose
story I was trying to write had the power to silence tongues, I
should not have thought it worth while to attempt the task. I
came to London without an appointment and telephoned the
Baron, feeling sure he would receive me.

While he talked he played with a paper-knife, as though,
within sight of the trees and lamp-standards of Trinity Square,
he were using it to disinter the memories of a distant past.

'We were on the train to Berlin. When anyone went past us in
the corridor he glanced furtively at them and stopped talking,
laying a hand on my arm. I could feel that he was very agitated
and depressed. Physically he was tall, about as tall as I am, a little
over six feet. He did not look like a typical SS man, more of an
intellectual, although not exactly that either. Anyway, a man of
education. He told me that he was religious, but he said very little
about his personal background. There was a queer look in his
eyes, not abnormal, I don't mean that, but a look that was not
ordinary.

'That was in 1942. I was Secretary of the Swedish Legation in
Berlin, 36 Tiergartenstrasse. I was thirty-five. My Minister had
sent me to Warsaw to interview two Swedish businessmen who

had been arrested for helping Polish clandestine organizations. They had been sentenced to death, but the sentence was commuted thanks to the intervention of the King of Sweden. My mission took me only a day and I caught the Berlin express that evening. It was summer, 20 August. The train left at seven, and I remember that the sun was still shining.

'Despite my diplomatic passport and special permit I had been unable to get a sleeper. I asked the guard if I could stay in the corridor and he agreed. There was an officer in SS uniform who seemed to be having the same trouble.

'He kept glancing at me, but I got the impression that it was from personal interest, not because he had me under surveillance. After travelling for about twenty minutes the train stopped at a station and I got out to stretch my legs. He followed me on to the platform and asked if I would give him a light. I produced a box of matches of the kind that were issued to us, with the words "Swedish Consulate" printed on it, and while I was lighting his cigarette he murmured: "I want to talk to you. May I come and see you in Berlin?"

'I don't remember if he said he already knew my name, but my Swedish accent and the matchbox would have suggested that I was in the Diplomatic Service, and of course the guard would have known from my passport. I said that we could talk on the train. We had the night before us.

'And then—we were still on the platform—he suddenly burst out, as though he were on the verge of tears:

' "*Ich habe gestern etwas Furchtbares gesehen*—yesterday I saw something appalling."

'I asked him what he meant, but now he was weeping and he could only repeat, "—something appalling."

' "Is it to do with the Jews?" I asked. Rumours were already going round about the extermination of the Jews.

'I don't think he answered. We couldn't go on talking on the platform. We got back into the train and sat on the floor at the end of the corridor. He had got himself under control, but he didn't know where to begin. I helped him with one or two questions, which served incidentally to confirm what he had to tell me. The train was blacked out and the corridor was very badly lit, but there was enough light for me to read his identity papers and instructions.

'So then he told me what he had seen the day before, the appalling thing, the crowd of people being thrust off the train, made to undress and driven into the gas chamber. A wonderfully beautiful young woman had picked up a child and thrust it towards him, saying, "How can you do a thing like this?" . . . "Perhaps," said Gerstein, "she saw from my expression what I was feeling."

'Gerstein's idea was that the Allied air forces, acting on Swedish information, should drop millions of leaflets over Germany, telling the German people what was going on, so that then they would rebel against Hitler.

'The journey to Berlin took ten hours, so I had plenty of time to question him. He gave me full details, names of the people carrying out the operation, and those higher up who were responsible. I think he may also have told me about the consignments of gas he delivered and his attempts at sabotage. He showed me a requisition order for prussic acid . . . He told me how he had come to be involved. His sister, or some other close relative, had died in a mental home, in circumstances that seemed to him so suspicious that he resolved to investigate further. Hence his entry into the SS.

'He also told me about a statement he made to the Papal Nuncio, although I think this was at our second meeting. But certainly he mentioned Otto Dibelius, a leading Protestant minister in Berlin who later became Bishop, and who he said would confirm what he had told me. As it happened I met Dibelius a few weeks later at the Swedish Church in Berlin, on the occasion of the installation of a Lutheran pastor. I could have checked on Gerstein if I had not already been convinced that he was telling the truth. I was very cautious in those days, always suspecting *provocateurs*. But I had found no contradictions in Gerstein's story, which in any case was borne out by rumours I had already heard.

'Gerstein smoked incessantly during our conversation on the train, which went on into the small hours. Afterwards we both fell asleep, sitting on the floor of the corridor, until we reached Berlin. I went straight home in a state of great distress and agitation, and the same day I spoke to my Minister and wrote a report.'

\*

Little was found in the prison cell after the removal of Gerstein's body: a Paris address, a restaurant bill, a sheet of writing-paper covered with names and a letter intended for the examining magistrates which later disappeared. There was also another letter, unfinished, which was addressed to a Dutch friend:

'Dear Ubbink,

'You are one of the first to whom I send greetings. To you I can send good wishes from the bottom of my heart on the occasion of the liberation of your country from our nation of monsters and criminals. However dark our future may seem at present, those dreadful people could not be allowed to win . . . I thank God that I did everything in my power to lance that abscess in the body of mankind. Will you do me a service? Write what you know about me, have it authenticated by a competent authority (a pastor, for instance) and send me two copies. One never knows. Certainly my word is believed, but after all, mine is a unique case.'

*The Gerstein dossier.* This never reached the Central Depository of Archives at Meaux, according to the head of that establishment. In its place was a card on which the Clerk of the Paris Military Tribunal had written: 'Dossier mislaid.'

*Chapter 2*

# CHILDHOOD

THE town of Münster in Westphalia, in the first decade of the century.

A glorious and fruitful peace reigned in the German Empire. Judge Ludwig Gerstein believed that it would endure; but if it did not, as certain portents suggested, he had his share of sons to defend the throne of Kaiser Wilhelm and the red-white-and-black Imperial flag.

The people of Münster strolled in their parks and gardens, sturdy, red-cheeked serving-maids pushing the baby-carriages containing the flower of the next generation. Among them was Regina, the Gersteins' maid, leading the child Kurt by the hand. The world has lost all trace of Regina, who was never of great consequence. But even a servant has her thoughts. What did she see in that solemn-eyed, five-year-old face that so insistently claimed her affection?

In Münster, all the servants were Catholics. Throughout the upheavals of the Reformation, the town as a whole had remained true to the Roman faith. The well-to-do Lutheran minority was bound to employ Catholics. It was something that the Gerstein family had to put up with, although Regina was rather too Papist for their liking. Her greatest happiness was to go from church to church rejoicing in the sacred wafer and wine of the Mass, the vaulted roofs, the bells, the bald-headed saints in the side chapels, with hands clasped and eyes upturned to Heaven. She took the little boy with her, talking to him in peasant accents of a God whose benevolence showered gifts upon man and woman—the warmth of the sun, the scent of flowers, the taste of raspberries and the interested gaze of passing gentlemen. God the Father, the Eternal, the Creator, the King of Heaven and Earth! It was in these terms, in the capital letters of Regina, ecstatically genuflecting before so many altars, that a small boy in Münster, in the reign of Kaiser Wilhelm II, was first made aware of God.

*1944.* An SS officer: 'Gerstein, if there really is a God our punishment will be terrible!'
Gerstein: 'Be sure of it, there is a God!'

God was not wholly absent from the Gerstein home, but like a feast-day He was movable. There were periods between Easter and Christmas during which one had no news of Him. He was something like the uncle from America who appeared only at long intervals with pockets filled with toys and goodies, or like the great Emperor Barbarossa yawning in his cave while he waited for his hour to strike.

'My name is Kurt Erich.' The little boy had adopted a second Christian name because he resented having only one. He had discovered already that a name is a life, which meant that two names were two lives. Kurt dreamed and Erich wept. Neither of them laughed, there being nothing to laugh at.

Bowed under the weight of its history, the Münster region was rich in all sorts and conditions of men. Water-diviners and clairvoyants abounded, and there were also bright-eyed mystics of an especial kind who claimed to see ghosts—the *Spokenkieker*. Gerstein resembled these. He was destined, with his clear, cool gaze, to see more spectres than had been seen by the whole of Münster from its beginnings.

Too many demented horsemen, prophets of the Apocalypse, Anabaptists with streaming hair, had galloped over the Westphalian plain not to have charged its air with a mystical electricity. The feet of the Archangel still struck sparks from the stony ground. And all this was lodged in the hearts of those who lived there. It was as though Chance, with his pack on his shoulder, had fallen asleep in Münster back in the distant past. Someone had robbed him of his dice, so that everything was now fixed, weighed and determined. Those who have heard the sound of the horsemen, and felt the breath of a Second Coming on their cheek, have lost the power of choice. Their lot is cast.

The head of the Gerstein household was Herr Ludwig Gerstein, Prussian nationalist, monarchist, an ardent believer in the student corps, a great walker and hunter, a lover of views and landscapes. He was a man interested in a thousand things, with his mind closed to a thousand others. Kurt was to refer to him simply as *der Mann* or *Er* (he). He never said 'my father.' Ludwig Gerstein was a judge, an august and highly esteemed figure armed with the lightnings of weighty pronouncements. Words of great weight and moment fell from his lips, and when they were uttered from his seat in the Law Courts they became words of Destiny—X would sleep in prison, Y would be dispossessed of his civil rights, Z would shed tears into the thin gruel of his children.

But although Judge Gerstein delivered so many judgements in Court, in the family circle he pronounced only one: '*Das tut man nicht*—That is not done.' To disobey one's civil and military superiors, for example, to show lack of respect for the Imperial family or for constituted authority, to marry someone of inferior status or to be on too friendly terms with Jews, although these might be quite honourable people, was not done.

None of his seven children ventured to challenge the oracle—excepting Kurt, and this only by letter and at the end of their respective lives.

*5 March 1944.*
'Dear Father,

'I am taking advantage of a lonely Sunday evening to write the letter I have owed you for a long time. In these days, unlike in the past, I scarcely ever write to you, not because I have nothing to say but because the things I would like to say so trouble me that I cannot put them on paper. At least a minimum of sincerity is essential when it comes to writing a letter. But for reasons outside my control this sincerity must at present be confined within very narrow limits. The burnt child fears the fire. Yet I must write to you, because even if at our rare meetings we were able to talk calmly together, looking into each other's eyes, as a father and son ought to do, the opportunity almost never occurs.

'You must not think I have nothing to say to you. On the contrary, I often have long conversations with you in my mind. I can well believe that you found it difficult to instil in me the foundations of a moral upbringing. I know what is good in me and what is bad. But what I find most hard to understand is why all principles, all concepts and all values should be sacrificed to a single object. It is you who taught us the essence of those values, fostering and strengthening them in us as our inalienable birthright. I think of the little mill standing on your desk which bears the eight words whose initials spell our name—Gerechtigkeit [Justice], Ehrenhaftigkeit [Honour], Ruhe [Tranquillity], Sicherheit [Certainty], Treue [Fidelity], Ehrlichkeit [Honesty], Innigkeit [Ardour], Natürlichkeit [Truth to one's own nature].[1]

'Has all this no validity for the individual? Can one hope for anything when these basic values on which our whole being depends are deliberately trodden underfoot? I do not know what is passing through your mind, and do not for a moment suggest that I have a right to ask. But a man who has devoted his life to the service of justice cannot fail to have been affected by the events of recent years. I was greatly shocked by something you said, or rather wrote, to me at a difficult period in my life, when I was wrestling with problems of the utmost gravity—'Hard times call for hard measures.' No! Sentiments of this kind cannot justify the things that have happened. I cannot believe, in the face of so many outrageous events, that this is the last word of my aging father, who must not be allowed to take such thoughts with him into the next world . . . My dear father, circumstances may arise in which a son is obliged to offer advice even to the parent responsible for his upbringing who has instilled in him the values by which he lives. The day will come when you, too, will be called to account for the age in which you have lived and the things that have happened in it. Moreover, we could not communicate at all

---

1 An admiring juryman had presented the Judge with a paper-weight in the form of the mill of Sans-Souci, on which was a plaque inscribed with these eight words.

... if it were impossible, or forbidden, for me to say to you, do not under-estimate your own responsibility or your duty to render account. The day may come sooner than we think ...'

How could the old man be expected to understand? He was being summoned to descend from the seat of justice by the son he had brought into the world, whose face, for him, could never quite shed the aspects of childhood. His answer was, 'Obey!'

Father and son died as they had lived, each in his own solitude.

Justice, Honour, Tranquillity, Certainty, Fidelity, Honesty, Ardour, Truth to one's own nature. Such was the Gersteins' picture of themselves. At Hagen, in November 1967, a female member of the clan exclaimed indignantly: 'They write about us as though we were a family of petty bourgeois, the shopkeeping class. Let me tell you, sir, that we belong to the upper middle class!' She had been on the verge of saying 'upper class,' if not more. Kurt's brother, Karl, went so far as to use the word 'patrician.' Kurt himself, it must be said, never lost the air of being born of a distinguished line, the sort of people whose linen is always clean.

The family had its traditions, its favoured callings (the Law, the Civil Service), its friends in high places, its family album going back thirteen generations to one Daniel Gerenstein, born about 1530. Kurt Gerstein often showed it to his friends—'You needn't be afraid to look at it. The respectable members of the family get several pages each, but the black sheep are only mentioned in passing.'

No family was more solidly established than the Gersteins in the world they lived in. They were industrious and economical, monarchists by instinct, natural protagonists of that happy state of affairs in which all things pursued their ineluctable, hierarchic course, with Wilhelm II at the top, God somewhere in the middle and the maid Regina at the bottom. Since religion no longer played any important part in their lives they fulfilled their spiritual aspirations by joining clubs, societies, student bodies having some theoretical connection with the world of heroism and sacrifice.

Every male Gerstein, bureaucrat or merchant, deaf or hunch-backed, was the spiritual brother of the officers of the 1914 war.

Clara Schmemann, whom Judge Gerstein married, had nothing in her head that did not reflect the stern countenance of her husband; she was his wife, his echo, his possession. The Judge rewarded her devotion by compiling (as he confessed later, for the edification of the family) a 'History of Our Love,' in twelve pages of very small handwriting, without erasures. She bore him one daughter and six sons of whom the Fatherland—that is to say, war—took half in two instalments, one in the 1914 war and two in Hitler's war. The stress of bringing up so many children exhausted Frau Gerstein's emotional resources. Only an occasional gleam of warmth emerged from her state of constant harassment and the reserve proper to a judge's wife. There was very little for Kurt, who, when she died in 1931, had not yet created any problems.

For the youthful Kurt Gerstein his father was the man in his life, but the woman was never his mother. The woman in his life was the servant known in the town as Regina-of-the-churches, the peasant woman smelling of cheap soap and fried onions. Even after he had left Münster she did not vanish wholly from his life, being reincarnated as it were, by chance and necessity, in the person of Leokadia Hinz, the dragon who guarded his door in Berlin, seeing in every visitor a potential enemy, as suspicious in her devotion as others are in hatred. When she died, then indeed Gerstein wept, as he had not done for his mother.

\*

In 1919 Judge Gerstein was expelled from Saarbrücken by the French. His eldest son, Ludwig, had died in the last months of the war and the Judge had caused the words, 'Say not that the Righteous can die,' to be engraved in Greek on his tombstone; after which he had withdrawn into a state of oppressed sadness, heavy with the thought of his lost son and his conquered nation. Defeat, his personal defeat and the defeat of his generation, could be atoned for only by austerity. The days were bleak in Halber-stadt, the night empty of dreams. While the mother knitted the father read aloud the works of Wilhelm Raabe, Gottfried Keller and Theodor Storm—all the nineteenth-century novelists—while his children yawned. The parental voice was harsh, deaf to all appeals. 'We have been defeated. We must learn to live with defeat.' And the children bowed their heads, avoiding the stony gaze of the eyes that admonished them over the pages of the book.

Elisabeth Klimek, a friend of Gerstein's (1968): 'He always referred to his father as "the man." Certainly he found the Prussian narrowness and parsimony of his home hard to endure. I remember his mocking that period of his life in a parody of Schiller: "Around the friendly light of the lamp all the shadows of the house were nightly assembled." '

Horst Dickten, Gerstein's associate (1968): 'He said little about his brothers and sister. He referred to the Judge simply as "*Er.*" He felt that he had been repudiated by his family and he did not wish it otherwise.'

Ministerialrat (Ministerial Counsellor) Karl Gerstein (1964): 'From his earliest years, and throughout his life, my brother Kurt was always difficult to understand. He was the most awkward of us all and there was constant friction between him and our parents and with the rest of us. He always went his own way, which did not make it easy to get close to him. There was something adventurous in his manner.'

(Something, clearly, that did not suit the Gerstein family, in the letters of whose name there was no A for adventure.)

Pastor Martin Niemöller, Gerstein's friend (1967): 'I thought of him a few days ago when I called upon Ho Chi Minh in Hanoi. The President said, "We have nothing against the Americans, but the Americans have something against us." Kurt Gerstein might have said the same thing and perhaps did: "I have nothing against my parents; it is they who have something against me." '

At this point I must describe how the witnesses I have quoted, giving only a name and date, come to appear in this book and will do so with increasing frequency as it progresses.

Martin Niemöller is too distinguished a figure, too well known for his opposition to Hitler and his long years in concentration camps, to require an introduction. His relationship with Gerstein was known to me, and I had only to consult the telephone directory to find him. And I did not have any difficulty in the case of Gerstein's brother. On the other hand, I had never heard of Horst Dickten or of Elisabeth Klimek. I discovered them by a process of detective work which affords some indication of how this book has been put together.

A letter written by Kurt Gerstein to American relatives in 1938 gave the name and address of a friend from Strasbourg, Robert Weiss, a chemist, whom naturally I wanted to interview. I ran him to earth in Freyming (Moselle) and found him very ready to tell me all he knew. He said, among other things: 'There's a man in Alsace who knew Gerstein in the SS. He must know a lot. Pastor Herbert Wild, in Hagenau, should be able to put you in touch with him.'

I rang up the pastor, who confirmed the man's existence but said that I might not find it easy to get him to talk—he had already suffered a great deal on account of his wartime activities. However, the pastor said he would speak to him and let me know his response.

In due course I met the man, whose name was Friedrich Geissert. He talked freely about Gerstein, and he, too, mentioned a name that took me a stage further. 'Kurt Gerstein had two brothers living with him in Berlin, the Dickten twins—do you know them?' Although I had then been probing into the story for nearly seventeen months I had never heard them mentioned.

The archives at the Kurt Gerstein Institute, in Berchum (Westphalia), contained no reference to Dickten. It turned out, however, that the name was known, and in response to my inquiries I was given the address of one of the brothers, Günter Dickten, now a major in the Bundeswehr (West German Army) stationed in Bonn.

I went to see Günter Dickten, who was friendly but very curious to know how I had got on his trail, a reaction I was to meet with in many quarters. Through him I became acquainted with his mother, Elisabeth Klimek, and his brother, Horst, and it soon became clear that these three were of the utmost importance to my researches.

In about 1930 Kurt Gerstein had actively concerned himself with the twin sons of Elisabeth Klimek, who was then a widow. The boys were aged fifteen. He took them to live with him in order to supervise their education. Later Horst worked under him in the Waffen SS Institute of Hygiene in Berlin. He had done so from 1941 to 1944. If anybody knew the wartime secrets of Kurt Gerstein it must certainly be Horst Dickten.

At the high school of Halberstadt, and later at Neuruppin (near Berlin), Kurt got consistently bad marks. He cut classes that bored him, scribbled derisive comments on his school reports, played the fool with his teachers. Karl Gerstein said: 'He was very intelligent, the brightest of us all, but he was the only one who had to repeat a year.'

At Halberstadt, in 1920, he was severely scolded by his Greek teacher. 'Gerstein, you've done no homework at all. I'm keeping you in this afternoon.' To avenge himself, young Kurt spent the last of his pocket money on a cab and so arranged matters as to arrive at the school at the same moment as his teacher, whom he greeted with a ceremonious flourish of his cap. That picture of the criminal driving up in style while his judge arrived on foot was still vivid in the old gentleman's memory after forty-five years.

Later, at Neuruppin, when he was working for his Abitur (the higher school-leaving examination), Kurt was quizzed by his classmates.

'Hey, maverick, aren't you even going to try? Aren't you afraid of flunking?'

'No. I've got a book with all the answers.'

'What book?'

'*Wie führe ich meinen Gegner aufs Glatteis*—How to Lure Your Enemies on to Thin Ice.'

The more clearsighted among them realized that this noncon-

26

formity was not just an adolescent attitude but the beginning of
a serious revolt.

Is a man nothing more than this—an obscene shape drifting
through Time, reproducing itself and dying with no more reason
than Friday's trout?

'It seemed to me that in this there was something terrible,
something evil, an unclean secret. Until I was seventeen or eighteen
no one had ever talked to me rationally of the functions of father
and mother, so that in my mind the notions of prostitution and
procreation were dangerously close.' (Kurt Gerstein: *Um Ehre
und Reinheit*—Of Honour and Purity.)

But the evil went deeper than the mere matter of sex. Beneath
the gaze of the visionary the whole sham of respectable appearances dissolved, stripping reality naked. No human action had
the innocence of which the Scriptures talked—or of which
Regina talked, listening raptly to the Easter bells. The little boy
might peer endlessly out of his window on winter nights, but he
would never see a rich man give half his cloak to a poor man,
or a healthy man embrace a leper.

What have you done to your brother?

The evil spread still further, encompassing all the future life
of this child whose eyes were as bright as those of a *Spokenkieker*.
Beyond the Teddy bears and lead soldiers littering the nursery
floor was the distant sound of cattle trucks festooned with barbed
wire, rolling towards that hamlet of Pitschepoï where the cottages
were roofed with thatch and the rain rained and the snow snowed.

It was the time of Karl Liebknecht and Rosa Luxemburg. Defeated Germany echoed with the cry of *Kamerad!* which was like
an answer to God's question, 'Where is your brother?' The
youthful Kurt did not join in that cry, because those who uttered
it did not address it to Heaven. But in the manner of his life he
was never far from it.

' All I want is sincerity. I do not stand for Christian harshness as opposed to the current Christian meekness, but for human integrity. If the human race or the contemporary world chooses to revolt honestly, loyally, without reserve, openly and without prevarication against Christianity, saying to God, "We cannot and we will not submit to this power"—if indeed they do this honestly, loyally, without reserve, openly and without prevarication—very well then, strange as it may seem, I am with them, for sincerity is what I want, and wherever there is sincerity I can be part of it.' (Sören Kierkegaard.)

Kurt entered a church and marched through it from the doorway to the high altar shouting at the top of his voice: 'Has everyone got his ticket?'

An *enfant terrible* is a terribly unhappy child.

*Chapter 3*

# THE MAN OF MYSTERIES

HE was tall, with grey-blue eyes, his temples and the back of his neck shaved in the Prussian style. A wide expanse of forehead on a narrow head, big ears that stuck out slightly, a large nose somewhat flattened above a full mouth, of which the firmly modelled upper lip seemed to crush the lower as though by an impulse from within.

An impenetrable countenance. His face was naturally inexpressive except for a kind of sombre light of disillusionment. His voice was deep, with many modulations, and this was the only element of harmony in the chaotic and unique assortment of qualities that grew up under the name of Kurt Gerstein.

To some of those who knew him—Ernst Weisenfeld, for example, and A. von Bruch—he was a rather grotesque creature: *eine komische Figur*. To others, such as Herbert Eickhoff and Herbert Weisselberg, he was impressive, endowed with a magnetic authority: *eine kolossale Figur*. Some thought him basically good-looking, others basically ugly.

The impression he made was instantaneous. Helmut Franz said in 1967: 'I was having my piano lesson one evening when he burst like a clap of thunder into the room. We only spoke a few words and then he went out again. But it was long enough for my piano teacher to exclaim: "Who's your friend? He must be a very great man!"'

Why should we seek to choose between the prince and the buffoon? Studying his own photograph, Gerstein once remarked in a tone of intense derision: 'All-German Male Beauty Contest—third prize.' He did not know what he was, or even what he wanted. He was ceaselessly in motion, arms swinging, head in air, moving towards an unknown destination of which at the best he had only a presentiment. On his way he acted. Those who came within his sphere of action, whether they submitted to it or appealed for it, never fathomed his reasons. The man himself stood out in greater relief. He possessed the calm, massive dignity of secrecy.

After passing his Abitur he decided to become a mining engineer. There may have been family contacts which influenced his decision, but it is easy to suppose that a character such as his would be naturally drawn towards things buried and obscure, things which, at a given moment, might yield a revelation. The rocky surface of the earth was of little interest, but beneath it were endless riddles.

A snapshot taken in 1928 shows him in miner's kit, carrying a lamp. He was then twenty-three but already ageless. Under the dirty cap and overalls, with blackened face and the indescribable melancholy of his expression, he was truly a man of the depths. There is a look of exile about him, as though even then he had wanted to experience the human condition in its harshest, most despairing aspects. 'The miner always carries his shroud with him,' he said at the funeral ceremony of a shift-foreman at Kaiseroda. Death and the shared threat of it were always present to the men who worked underground. One day, when he was a fully-fledged mining engineer, he went down into the pit and was so slow in returning to the surface that blasting had to be delayed and colleagues went down to look for him. To their indignant astonishment they found him seated with his back against the wall talking to a Polish miner. This was in 1939, when no Pole was considered worth a glance.

'A Polack! You seemed to be treating him as though he were God!'

'So he was,' said Gerstein. 'At that moment.'

His daily business was with the digging up of coal, salt, mineral ores; but what he really sought, above as well as below the earth's surface, was the seam of God. Above as well as below the surface he was to witness tragedy on a monstrous scale, to sacrifice Isaac ten times over, to wrestle with the Angel, to believe and to doubt. But even in the act of doubting he believed; faith was like a solid substance within him, as physically necessary as his heart and lungs. A necessity, yet so divorced from space and time that it looked like what it was—his own private heresy. His God had no true name. He was only by chance a Protestant, he might have been born Catholic, Jew or Moslem. What did earthly authorities mean to him?

'I detested everything religious and fought against it, because it could only add to my uncertainties.' He was sickened by what he called 'the craven foot-soldiers of religion,' and he mocked them, standing at street corners, by offering telephone directories disguised in black covers, and in a quavering preacher's voice urging the passer-by to take one and read it.

He searched the Bible for traces of the God he worshipped, but it was in daily life that he encountered Him, felt the weight of His presence, rebelled under His yoke. And God, alas, knew the everyday Gerstein and did not wait till the Last Day to call him to account but judged him incessantly, minute by minute. The secret man trembled under this inquisition, all his nightly prayers an apocalyptic foreshadowing in which he remonstrated with his pitiless Master.—'What have you done to your brother?' . . .

What is a man of faith without a church? Perhaps he is something like the Danish theologian strangely named Kierkegaard (churchyard). Kierkegaard's writings were beginning to be influential in Germany at the time when Gerstein was awakening to the religious life. He found in them problems resembling his own. Those two were alike in their solitude, and at many turning-points in his life Gerstein seemed to express himself through the words of Kierkegaard.

'To believe against reason is martyrdom . . .'

'In every generation there are men who are placed above others like herrings in a shoal, to protect those in the middle.'

But only Gerstein is said to have muttered one day into the ear of a fellow-parishioner: 'God does not exist.'

By the time he was twenty he had read everything: Nietzsche and the Bible, Kleist and Shakespeare, Aeschylus and Dostoevsky, whose *Crime and Punishment* made a greater impression on him than any other book, the Bible excepted. He had devoured Freud, listened to Karl Barth, studied the works of theologians, political writers, sexologists. He glanced through all the newspapers, looking for what interested him. He did not read for pleasure.

He did not concern himself with beauty, art or any outward grace, not because he was a philistine but because he was in a hurry. The most noble monuments only drew from him the remark, 'Splendid! Well, now we've seen it let's go.' He was not interested in the theatre or in music, which he dismissed as 'organized noise.' He had other fish to fry. He wanted to *know*. An irresistible, indeed almost monstrous force drew him into those twilight regions where perhaps one might find, if not the true answer, at least the right question.

He drove himself remorselessly. Eating, drinking and sleeping were time-consuming occupations, a waste of substance. This obsession gave his life a frenetic character, so that he seemed always on the edge of vertigo and collapse. He slept less than five hours a night, there was always so much to do. During a period of nine months, when he was acquiring a practical knowledge of his profession, he visited 2,325 mining concerns.

But his breakneck progress hid a calculation: 'You must be busy with so many things that no one can ever know what you are driving at, or what you are up to.' His private mystery was concealed at the heart of a whirlpool in which all things spun round him—friends, Fatherland, sex, mines, railway timetables, innumerable books, tears, silences, doorways, clocks.

Clocks! The time by Gerstein's watch was always 8:13, 9:26, 2:47, time to the minute, never the casual 'about quarter past' of the ordinary citizen.

'I was observing and listening. My watch registered everything: 50, 70 minutes. The Diesel always did not work and people in the rooms were always waiting, in vain . . . After 2 hours 49 minutes . . . the Diesel started . . .' (Gerstein's *Report*, see p. 288.)

'So far as we are able we must think of our children and watch over them. That will do for today. 9:28 P.M. You should not

end your letters with "Good night," they arrive in the *morning*!'
(Letter written in hospital to his wife, 8 October 1944.)

'Dear Friedel, After serving five weeks at Rottweil under the
military governor I am today being transferred to the region of
Lake Constance, to appear before a higher authority.' Signed:
Kurt, 26/5/45, at 10:58.

Much of his life was spent in trains or on the road—a friend
to see, a book to lend, a paper to sign. He met people, gave advice,
took decisions. He was the man who suddenly turned up. That
was how they thought of him—bursting in unexpectedly by day
or night and leaving as abruptly. No time for ceremony. As a
director of youth movements he cowed the parents with his
summary way of collecting the young entrusted to his charge. It
almost amounted to kidnapping.

'Where's Herbert? We're going to Berchum. In bed, is he?
Well, he'll have to get up.' And sure enough, Herbert would get
dressed and vanish into the night with the tall, ill-dressed man,
while his parents never ceased to wonder why they put up with it.

Elisabeth Klimek, the mother of the Dickten brothers, re-
counted the following in 1968: 'He arrived with a suitcase at our
house in Attendorn one Sunday morning in 1937. "I'm Kurt
Gerstein, mining engineer," he said. "I know your sons, I got to
know them in our Bible Circle holiday camp. They no longer have
a father to take care of them. I'd like to do it, and to supervise
their education." Then he asked if he could stay overnight. It was
very embarrassing. To me he was a complete stranger. But while
we were talking the maid had taken his suitcase along to the
guest room. She opened it and found a Bible lying on top of his
clothes. When she told me this I thought: "Well then, he's all
right. He can take them with him." '

The pressures never ceased. Eating, drinking, sleeping—these
were important matters, not to be disregarded, but time was
passing, bringing nearer the onset of catastrophe, irremediable
damnation. He must be everywhere, turn himself into ten men,
sleepless in a sleeping world. If Gerstein was not there who would

bridge the gap between suffering and consolation, misdeed and pardon, tragedy and resignation? The Judge's son (he sometimes referred to himself in the third person) was threatened with arrogance: but an arrogance justified by the state of human affairs in that half-century. As the years passed his ear became increasingly selective; he heard nothing but cries for help.

In December 1931 a car out of control ran down a group of youngsters belonging to the Gevelsberg Bible Circle, scattering them all ways, injuring several and killing one. 'On the day of the funeral we saw a stranger suddenly appear. He was determined to do something to help. He went to see the boy's family and offered to pay all expenses—he even paid for the tombstone. That was Gerstein.' (Ernst Weisenfeld.)

*1942.* A young soldier named Horst Penschuk was driving a van containing a secret radio transmitter from Nuremberg to The Hague. He allowed himself to be distracted on the way by a chance-met girl friend, and the van was stolen. Penschuk was arrested and threatened with the death penalty. From his prison cell he appealed to Gerstein for help. (What kind of man was it to whom such an appeal could be addressed?) Gerstein took the matter up. He combed the country for a fortnight, visiting railway goods yards, checking consignment notes, interviewing railway workers and clerks, bluffing and threatening with his SS pass. In the end he got the van back and Penschuk's life was saved.

*

The German countryside in the summers between the wars was filled with tents and huts. The sons of the 1914 dead travelled in open shirts and leather shorts with rucksacks on their backs. Camp fires burned in the forest clearings. The young were seeking not only fresh air but a spiritual regeneration which was slow in coming (and when it came it had a sulphurous smell). After passing his Abitur Kurt became a member of the YMCA and the Bible Circle which were carrying the torch of the Reformation in the face of atheism and Catholicism. This did not mean that he had surrendered to religious authority or allowed himself, without second thoughts, to become integrated in society.

To him the youth movements were not yet socially ossified. One could still act upon them from within, influence them without too much hindrance, make of adolescence something other than the mental disease it had been in his own case. The young whom social pressures would so soon bring down to earth could still be taught that the spirit of God was in each of them. They could be taught to live their own unique, incomparable lives—even to rebel. Gerstein always had a weakness for the rebels, the fledglings of liberty.

'It is not easy,' wrote Helmut Franz, 'to describe the enthusiasm, love and respect he inspired in those youngsters. I remember them celebrating his birthday at a summer camp at Zingst, on the Baltic. The whole camp of two hundred and seventy boys staged a triumphal dance that went on for half an hour, shouting "Vati! Vati!" ["Pop" or "Dad"], after which they carried him on their shoulders round the camp.'

How did he gain this immense influence over them, the harsh-faced, melancholy man? It is true that he loaded them with presents. He would turn up with great supplies of fruit, cakes and sweets. He paid for parties and outings, hired motor-coaches and boats. He paid all the expenses of the children of very poor parents, even for their education. The money he inherited from his mother, derived from a business in Düsseldorf, all went in this lavishness. He took over a run-down farm near Hagen, in Berchum, and turned it into a youth centre. He was always contriving new things to offer. He had a talent for giving—or, in terms more suited to the Gerstein family, a mania for wasting money.

To the young a person who showers them with gifts may be simply a fool. But not Gerstein, not 'Vati.' He was the one who answered questions, who understood, who wrote at the end of his letters: 'If you're in any kind of trouble don't hesitate to come to me'; or who demanded briskly: 'What are you looking so glum about? We'd better have a talk.'

Gerstein was that other half of the dialogue which the young so constantly lack. He got them to talk. He taught them to recognize their true status as human beings—a recognition generally withheld until, the flush of youth abating, they have lost the power to change the world.

Men of this kind become legends. In school and camp and parish his saga grew and spread. It was said that he bought himself a sports car, overlooking the fact that he had not learnt to drive; that he bought the most expensive suits and wore them till they were in shreds; that he had spent a whole summer looking for 'a pair of shorts that aren't short.' It was said that he lost a wallet bulging with notes and in five minutes had forgotten all about it. Once, when he was talking to a friend on a station platform, his train started to move off without him. 'Let it go,' he said. 'I'll walk.' And the joke of it was that he really did walk.

With all these eccentricities, he never lost sight of the things that really mattered to him, although he seldom sought them openly. Helmut Franz tells the following story:

'One day a party of four or five strangers turned up at the camp at Berchum claiming to be members of the Bible Circle, although they had not yet decided what attitude to adopt in the light of the political situation in that year, 1935. Gerstein was extremely annoyed by this intrusion. Accordingly, he held a meeting of the leading members of his troop and they made a plan. The idea was to organize a team of reliable youngsters who would kick up such a rumpus that the newcomers would find life intolerable. It succeeded so well that we managed to rid the camp of nearly all undesirable elements.'

Needless to say, the incident had to be officially reported to the head of the camp; in other words, to Gerstein himself. Pretending high indignation, he held a mock trial. The offenders were cross-examined and sentence was pronounced: a beating all round. The boys bent down and each received a tap on the bottom, after which they were made to repeat a formula intended to be comical: 'Dear Vati, I thank you for having beaten me. I know it hurt you more than it did me. In future I will do my utmost to make you happy, and Mother too.'

'This parody of justice, turning the whole thing into farce,' Helmut Franz concluded, 'was deliberately aimed at false authority and hypocritical subservience, all the sins of the spirit that were so prevalent under Hitler and are still with us.'

In Wuppertal, on another occasion, he paid an unexpected visit to a youth-group whose leader was the only one who knew him. His tall figure and sombre expression alarmed the children, who mistook him for a member of the Gestapo. He took advantage of this to stage another comedy. At lunch he pushed his plate aside and asked his youthful neighbour to taste it, as though he were afraid of being poisoned. He asked loaded questions, such as, 'What do you really do here? Don't you think this Bible study is all nonsense?' The youngsters answered back bravely, like martyrs confessing their faith. So then he laughed and dropped the pretence, more pleased with them than with himself.

The problems of his own adolescence had made him an ingenuous advocate of 'moral purity,' the theme of the greater part of his writings. Sexual education was his hobby-horse, almost an obsession.

Hans Dieter Schulz (1968): 'He invited us to visit him at Hagen. I was the youngest of the party, ten or eleven years old. He had ordered a wonderful meal for us and we were left to ourselves, free to eat as much as we liked. There was even a bell hanging from the ceiling for us to call the maid. Then suddenly he appeared and took me into another room, probably a guest room: there was nothing in it but a bed, a bedside table and a single chair. He sat beside me on the edge of the bed and talked softly with his mouth so close to my ear that I could feel the warmth of his breath, which, to tell you the truth, I did not much care for. He asked me if I knew where babies came from. "Yes," I said, "they come from Heaven." . . . "That's true," he said, "but they don't just tumble down from Heaven and they aren't carried. They grow inside the mother's body until they're big and strong enough, and then the mother brings them into the world." That was all he said, and then I was allowed to go. Later he gave us all a little book on the subject.'

The 'maverick' was known on occasions to go stealthily

about the streets of Berlin, scratching out obscene graffiti on the walls and tearing down posters that he considered salacious. He preached continence and self-control, shunned brothels and taverns, did not drink or smoke. But he attained to this pattern of life only after countless experiments and lapses. Nor was he consistent. The heavy drinker became a teetotaller overnight; but on the other hand the vegetarian of one day became a meat-eater on the next, by some impulse that must for ever remain a mystery.

In the youth camps that came under his supervision God was present without ceremony or sermonizing. He announced one evening: 'No one will tell a lie during the coming week.' The 'no one' included himself. At the end of the week he said: 'I don't think I've told any lies ... Or wait—Yes, there was one, but a very small one.' On another occasion he decreed that they were to read the whole of the Bible in a week ... He knew long passages of the Bible by heart, and his talk was constantly interspersed with Biblical quotations, always appropriate to the matter in hand.

He sent a telegram that read: 'Warmest congratulations on your engagement. See Ecclesiastes 26:13.' And in the evenings, seated with his troop round the camp-fire, wearing the 'shorts that weren't too short' (he seems to have found a pair), he would join with the boys in singing the *Te Deum*.

There were never any girls in his flock. He was always haunted by the obsession with 'purity' that went back to the mysterious lapses of his youth. 'He was ready to joke about everything except women,' said Pastor Rehling. He was always afraid of a situation arising in which his love of youth would be transformed into love of another kind, or would be interpreted in that fashion.

Considering the strangeness of the man, his fellow-members of the Bible Circle came to wonder what his wife and their relationship might be like. This is Frau Gerstein's own account of him (Mössingen, April 1967):

'I met him first during the Christmas of 1930. I was the daughter of a Protestant minister who had just been installed in Cologne.

My brother, who was a student at Berlin University, had made Kurt's acquaintance at the YMCA. I had a friend living in Wuppertal who invited my brother and me to a Christmas party. There was a long table lighted with candles. Suddenly a door behind me opened, and, feeling a draught, I turned round. Kurt Gerstein and I looked at each other. He said to my brother: "I never knew you had a sister." He sat down opposite me. He was very gay and we talked a lot. He was twenty-five and I was twenty. He was full of humour . . . Later he wrote to my brother: "I have never met a girl like her." ' '

'If you smoked,' Gerstein said to his fiancée, 'you'd have to give it up.'

Elfriede Gerstein's mother, Frau Bensch, said to her daughter: 'I think you've found yourself a madman on the lines of Bismarck.'

If a boy became sick and had to take medicine the others were made to take it too. 'Vati' often put the whole camp on a diet. He made his adopted sons drink at least a pint of milk every morning. In this preoccupation with diet he curiously resembled his future chief, Himmler, who prided himself on having made the SS eat porridge. (Later, in SS barracks, Gerstein was to encounter notices, put up by order of the Reichsführer, bearing the Nietzschean maxim he had so often quoted to his boys: '*Gelobt sei was hart macht*—Blessed is that which makes for toughness.')

There was a small boy at the water's edge, Herbert Eickhoff, who had not learnt to swim. 'Well, choose,' said Gerstein. 'You can either plunge in from here or jump from a height of ten feet.'

Herbert chose to attempt to dive, and had to be fished out. Another youngster was afraid of the dark. 'Vati' sent him at night to get a stone out of the river. He did so in fear and trembling, and still remembers it. On yet another occasion Gerstein said to the four boys he had taken to live with him, whom he called his 'sons in God': 'I'll give you five marks each if you can cycle round the town [Tübingen] in full daylight wearing nothing but your nightshirts without getting a police ticket.' The boys took the bet—what else could they do?

Gerstein's boys were all the children of rebellion, and some of them ended by rebelling against him. The following testimonies were collected in 1967.

Helmut Franz, doctor and theologian: 'When I was between eighteen and twenty years old a crisis developed in my relations with Kurt Gerstein. I had to escape from his influence because I felt that otherwise I should never become independent. He bore me no ill-will.'

Armin Peters, engineer: 'There was something authoritarian or patriarchal in his attitude. His influence was tyrannical and it took me a long time to get away from it. He had a diabolical knack of attracting people in need of support and establishing a hold over them. His concern for them was boundless, but to live with him was almost martyrdom. If he were still alive I'm not sure that I would seek his company. I often wondered if he really had a heart. He did things on such a lavish scale. To write two hundred New Year letters by hand—is that really giving your heart two hundred times?'

Günter Dickten, army officer: 'During the war, for my protection Gerstein took me to Berlin with him. He wanted me to study medicine, which was not what I wanted to do. I wanted to fight. Without telling him, I applied for admission to the SS Officers School at Tölz. He found out and turned up one evening in the little restaurant on Bülowstrasse which we called "the train" because it was long and narrow. He started to abuse me right away, saying that I was a hopeless idiot and that I was repaying the trouble he had taken over my education and upbringing with disloyalty and ingratitude. I should have learnt more sense, he said, with him looking after me! He was extremely bitter about the way I had treated him. It was the most unpleasant and angry conversation we had ever had. When later I went to say goodbye to him he refused to shake my hand. "It will be a long time before you'll win back my confidence in you," he said; and he added something that was pure Gerstein: "But you'll always be my lost son!"'

*

As the year 1930 approached Judge Gerstein was less inclined to say: 'We are defeated.' Times were changing. Kurt Gerstein worked, meditated, watched over his hundreds of children. He was patriotic in the sense that he wanted Germany to play a great part in the world, but he did not look for any change of regime. He accepted the government elected under the Weimar Republic, which the ultra-nationalists despised as a collection of traitors. Chancellor Brüning and Stresemann, the Foreign Minister, seemed to him perfectly capable of running the country—two sound, high-minded men. Kurt was occasionally active in his support of the Republic, but without having any strong feelings in the matter. One crossed bridges when one came to them; and the hoofbeats of Corporal Hitler, galloping up from the south with Thor's hammer in his hand—to shatter the cathedrals, according to Heine's prophecy—were not yet heard . . .

A woebegone figure knocked at the door of Pastor Kurt Rehling, in Hagen. He was bent double, his neck twisted, one sleeve of his jacket empty. He whimpered to the pastor's children: 'I'm a war casualty. I ask your charity.' The little girl called: 'Father! There's a beggar at the door.'

Whereupon the man burst out laughing, straightened up and thrust an arm into his empty sleeve, to the children's astonishment. It was Gerstein, whom they all knew—a piece of admirable play-acting. Although he rejected art in all other forms, he was a master of this one: the art of disguise, mimicry, concealment. Pastor Rehling, a few years his senior, considered that in this his talent was well up to professional standards.

'I asked him once,' Rehling said in 1967, 'how he had learnt to play the cynic so convincingly, when his real feelings were so entirely different. So then he told me about the espionage work he had done in the service of the Reichswehr.'

This was a secret long preserved by the few people who knew of it, among them Rehling and the Dickten brothers. 'Vati' had been a German Intelligence agent. He had carried out secret missions in France, in the region of Thionville (he spoke French quite well), specializing in economic and technical matters which came within his professional competence. Very little is known about all this, except that Gerstein was proud of his successes and considered that the economic spy should be rated top in the hierarchy of Intelligence agents, 'because he works alone, not as one of a team.'

Judge Gerstein was very much less proud. Spying was a shabby business, disgraceful by the family standards. It was another rift between son and father, another thing that was 'not done.'

Through mixing with experts Kurt acquired some curious skills. He could pick a lock with an ordinary comb, and reproduce a document by the use of gum or slices of potato. His notes were written on a particular kind of paper that could be chewed and swallowed. He learned a great many things.

Hans Dieter Schulz (1968): 'In 1936 a party of us went to spend a Sunday at Berchum. Kurt found that he had forgotten his keys. He opened a window somehow. When he was inside he manufactured a master key out of a piece of bent metal that was lying about, and then he opened every door in the house.'

When he was in the SS he illegally commandeered a service Mercedes for a trip to southern Germany, which was also illegal. The car was destroyed in an air raid. He bought another, exactly like it, and spent a whole day transferring registration plates and serial numbers; he even reproduced the worn patches on the upholstery of the original car. Then he drove back to Berlin. No questions were asked.

Espionage is a specialized trade which has to be learnt. Gerstein, with his passion for concealment and in his resolve to play a part in the world, to become a force to be reckoned with, might have been born to it. He himself was a secret which no one ever penetrated. Who could have been better qualified to understand secrecy?

Horst Dickten (1968): 'When we were dining together in a restaurant, at the Zoo, for instance, Kurt would sometimes look round at the other customers and say: "What do you think that chap does for a living?" I could never guess. He would then label them: shopkeeper, engineer, theology student. "You've got to look at the way they carry themselves, their clothes, the way they eat . . . For instance, that pig of a man over there. Look at the way he's hacking up his meat. Probably a Regular Army NCO . . ." And then I was made to check with them, pretending that I was engaged in sociological research. I never knew him to be wrong. He was a marvellous psychologist.'

Spy, visionary, forger, cheat, nepotist, swindler, inquisitor, outlaw . . . a man for whom the extraordinary, the dramatic, the perilous, the horrible and the fateful, had an irresistible fascination . . . If we are to follow mining engineer Kurt Gerstein into the subterranean galleries which he was soon to tunnel between the seas of lava and sulphur we must think of him simply as a spy, richly endowed for the task, advancing cautiously one step at a time, without a tremor but with nerves always stretched to breaking-point. Borrowing from Kierkegaard, Pastor Rehling called him 'God's spy,' or better, 'A spy for God.'[1]

1 '. . . A spy who, in the service of God, uncovers the crime of Christianity, that of professing to be a Christian when one is not.' – Kierkegaard.

*Chapter 4*

# THE REBEL

On 30 January 1935 a racist and pagan drama by Edmund Kiss, entitled *Wittekind,* was presented at the Municipal Theatre in Hagen.

Wittekind, Duke of Saxony: *Certainly the Man of Nazareth is a convenient God. You may be a villain all your life, but if at the end you repent, grace and consolation are assured you. Is that not so, Sir Chamberlain? . . . Lurking behind the quarrelsome Germans I always see a cassock. Will Germany be for ever plunged in a bloodbath in the name of this foreigner whom you call God?*

The occasion was the second anniversary of Adolf Hitler's seizure of power. The theatre was filled with leading local Nazis, members of the SA, the SS, the Workers Front and Hitler Youth of both sexes, some with blackjacks and knuckle-dusters in their pockets. The opening performance, a few evenings previously, had been interrupted by Catholic demonstrators. But tonight there was to be no disturbance, the Deputy Gauleiter guaranteed it. He had announced before the rise of the curtain that the piece was warmly recommended by the Minister for Propaganda, Joseph Goebbels, which meant, as everyone knew, that no criticism must be expressed and that everyone must keep a watchful eye on his neighbour, just in case. *Heil Hitler!*

Many of the audience, who had come because they dared not stay away, were lifelong Christians. Nevertheless the flood of destructive dialogue caused some of them a tremor of outraged delight, a stir of secret rebellion. If the right hand was tempted to rise in protest, the left reminded them that prudence was also a virtue.

Albion, Duke of Verden: *We have no use for a Saviour who can only whine instead of suffering in silence like a hero. We Germans . . .*

At which point the actor was cut short by a shout from the stalls:

'Shame!'

A man had risen to his feet, his face very pale. Heads were turned and voices murmured: 'It's the son of Judge Gerstein.'

'We shall not allow our faith to be publicly insulted without protest!'

He was able to say no more. The ring of brown-clad figures closed in on him, the swastikaed arms, the clenched fists, the voices screaming abuse. He was dragged half-conscious out of the theatre, his face running with blood and spittle. He left two of his teeth behind.

'One man cannot fight a crowd, but I will force them to fight me. If they beat me they will take notice of me; if they beat me to death they will take a great deal of notice and I shall have won.' (Kierkegaard.)

Thirty years later, in 1964, another play was presented at the theatre in Hagen. It was *The Representative*, by Rolf Hochhuth (which appeared as *The Deputy* in America) and among the characters was that of Gerstein himself, who delivered the following speech:

'Excellency, I bring you a message for the Vatican which brooks no delay—not a day, not an hour . . . I have just returned from Poland, from Belzec and Treblinka, north-east of Warsaw . . . Excellency, I beseech you to hear me . . . I can bear it no longer. I have seen with my own eyes. I see it still. The vision pursues me even into this room . . . Listen while I tell you . . .'

At the time of the production of *Wittekind* Gerstein was twenty-nine. He was a member of the Nazi Party, the NSDAP, and he wore its rosette on the lapel of his jacket. He had been particularly careful to wear it on that evening, when he invited a beating-up for the sake of his faith. Nor did he ever get rid of it. He preserved it through all the battles that lay ahead, the symbol of his strange dedication.

There was a policeman on duty in the theatre. When people appealed to him after the episode he said: 'I didn't see a thing.' He was the embodiment of Germany.

The process of *Gleichschaltung*, bringing people into line, had been going on since 1933 without serious hindrance. The Führer was reaping the fruits of old grievances, of fear and cowardice. But he was also inspiring devotion.

'He was *our* Hitler, the man the German people wanted, whom we ourselves, by our insane idolatry, had made master of our destiny. A Hitler could have arisen only in a nation seeking a Hitler. It is our German tragedy that we make exceptionally gifted men—and no one can deny this of Hitler—the objects of an hysterical hero-worship which causes them to believe that they are superhuman and infallible.' (Baldur von Schirach, former Youth Leader of the Reich.)

But the people would not so readily have embraced servitude if the élite had not paved the way. It was the intellectuals, the guardians and transmitters of the German heritage, who thrust them into Hitler's arms. They were not even sincere. When they gave the Hitler salute it was with revulsion in their hearts. But they were infected with madness by the madmen who led the dance—a frozen flock of white-collared schizophrenics.

An army veteran shakes his stick . . . A housewife stares open-mouthed . . . A green-clad policeman appears on the scene . . . What have you done? Of what crime, what obscenity, are you guilty? You crossed the street against the red light! *Das tut man nicht.*

On 27 February 1940, at the time of the liquidation of the mentally afflicted, a woman wrote to the directors of the Sonnenstein Clinic a letter which would have been inconceivable in any other country in the world.

'The unforeseen death of my two sisters within two days is something that I find very improbable. Their illnesses were

46

entirely different. You must realize that one is forced to certain conclusions when on the same day one receives notice of the death of two sisters. Nothing will persuade me that it was a coincidence. I should be easier in my mind if I knew that there was a law authorizing the putting to death of people suffering from incurable diseases. Maria Kehr.'

Your sisters may be killed. The law protects everything and justifies everything.

The Churches should have made a stand.

This Government meant them no good. But they were already undermined by the nationalist, anti-Communist, racist ferment. The concordat between Hitler and the Vatican, signed in the very early months of the regime (brought about by Cardinal Pacelli, the future Pius XII), disarmed potential martyrs. It amounted to giving Hitler a free hand—and who would want to be more papist than the Pope?

Nor did the Protestants present a more edifying picture. The Lutheran principle of submission to authority had done its work, and the bastions of free speech were crumbling. Hitler had appointed a bishop, Ludwig Müller (known as Lügen Müller —Müller the Liar), to take charge of the 'German Christians' —that is to say, of the Aryan, anti-Semitic Protestants who did not hesitate to sing the Horst Wessel Song after a Bach chorale:

Our trumpets for the last time sound the summons
And all of us stand ready for the fray;
Soon Hitler's flags will flutter from each house top . . . etc.
Allen W. Dulles, in his book *Germany's Underground* stated:

'In view of the numerical strength and ancient traditions of the German churches, both Protestant and Catholic, and Hitler's failure to complete his domination of them, it is surprising that they were not a greater danger to him than they proved to be. Unfortunately the churches were slow to realize that Nazism was not merely a "political change" but an attack on basic Christian principles . . . Bound to neutrality in temporal matters and the avoidance of conflicts with "Caesar," a cherished church tradition supported by Scripture, the churches, for a considerable time, were the victims of self-deception as well as of Hitler's cunning. After the Gestapo State was thoroughly organized, the churches, with certain notable exceptions, were relegated to the role of passive resistance.'

Kurt Gerstein had one supporter in his protest at the theatre in Hagen. This was Max Sellerberg, a Catholic Youth leader. Their joint gesture serves to underline the defection of the rest, as a drop of water in the desert attests that the desert has no water.

Pastor Martin Niemöller (1967): 'The Resistance in 1933 consisted of the Communists and Jehovah's Witnesses.'

Martin Niemöller was speaking of what he knew. A war hero and ex-submarine commander who had achieved world celebrity with his autobiographical book, *From U-Boat to Pulpit*, he was a German nationalist of the most conventional kind. The rise of Hitlerism at first gratified his dream of a German revival. Believing that a higher spirituality would sweep away the atheistic, rationalist Republican regime, and with it the unjust clauses of the Treaty of Versailles, he welcomed the coming of the swastika; so much so, indeed, that he was sometimes referred to as 'the Nazi pastor.'

But he changed his mind after the Nazis came into power, and he set about rallying the scattered forces of opposition. Young Gerstein, already well known in Westphalian circles, was among those who joined him, together with such leading figures of the period as Bishop Wurm, of Württemberg, Pastors Wilm and Bodelschwingh, Doctor Koch, president of the Westphalian Synod, and above all that embodiment of the Protestant conscience, Karl Barth. Barth, a native of Switzerland, had been Professor of Protestant Theology at Göttingen, at Münster, Gerstein's native town, and finally at Bonn. He had dared to write in a Protestant review: 'In the tumult created by certain "principalities and powers" we look for God anywhere but in His Word—that is to say, we no longer seek Him at all. The appeal to a Führer is as vain as the supplication of the priests of Baal: "Baal, hear our cry! " ' But the chorus that supported Barth and Niemöller was a meagre one, singing with mouths half closed and voices muted in the hope that God would hear but Hitler would not.

Before being expelled from Germany in 1934 Barth found time to draft the *Confession of Faith* in which the saner element in the Protestant Church proclaimed its beliefs and defended its freedom. 'We reject the false doctrine whereby the Church is held to have sources other than, and additional to, the Word of God from which it may draw testimony—that is to say, other events, other powers, other personalities and other truths . . .'

With Barth gone, Niemöller took charge of this so-called 'Confessional Church,' born of the cowardice of the many and the courage of the few. He did not abandon it until his arrest in 1937.

Amid the tumult of fifes and drums, and the glare of processional torches, the Gerstein clan passed smoothly enough into the thousand-year Reich. They had weighed the pros and cons and decided that there was much to be said for the former. The Judge was even a little lyrical on the subject: 'The wonderful time we are living in . . . Our magnificent German people . . . Our great and beloved Führer . . .' It was a pity that the old Imperial flag had been done away with, but except for this everything was splendid and Hitler as great a gentleman as any of them, worthy of all respect. Anyway, the Pope did not deny it, nor a certain German Nobel Prize winner who was a fanatical Aryan, nor the heads of foreign governments, who seemed to have made up their minds to treat him as one of themselves.

Kurt Gerstein alone in the family reserved judgement. He was watching and wondering. His sympathy with National Socialism may be said to have reached its peak on the day (21 March 1933) when Hitler and Marshal Hindenburg met in the garrison church at Potsdam and the New Germany seemed to place its feet in the footprints of the Old. After this Gerstein's belief in it steadily declined.

Brutality, grossness and paganism were what divided the new world from the old. What part was he to play in the new?

At the root of his thinking lay the fact that although not everybody was yet a Nazi, everybody seemed to be going over to their side. But he, Kurt Gerstein, was not everybody. He might leave the country; on the other hand he might do what so many others were doing and continue to live in Germany as though he were blind, deaf and dumb, devoting himself to some form of specialized research: the synthesis of ammonia and nitric acid by the Uhdet—Mont-Cenis process, for example, or the location of horizontal mining strata in northern Westphalia. Would God be satisfied with this?

In 1932, the year before the Nazis came to power, when Von Papen was Chancellor, a criminal court condemned several Nazis to death for the murder of a Communist. Hitler sent a characteristic telegram: 'Herr von Papen, I do not accept your bloodthirsty objectivity.'

Pastor Rehling talked to Gerstein about this matter, for to him it was an alarm signal. It meant that a Christian could no longer come to terms with the Nazis. It was the end of an age-old tradition of justice and ethics, an open invitation to evil-doers: 'Join our Party, think as we do, and you may commit any crime with impunity.' Gerstein was no less shocked than Rehling, but he took a less gloomy view. How often had it not happened in the history of the world that justice had been distorted for political ends? Nations had not perished on that account. Perhaps the true answer was to join the Party, precisely in order to counteract the danger. The Party possessed great powers, and how was it to be influenced except from within? A time might come when it would be the duty of every Christian to join the Nazis.

It was not the first time Gerstein had argued on these lines. He had said to people who came to him with stories about the Party: 'You're criticizing it from outside.' To him this was wrong. No man could pass judgement on matters of which he had not first-hand knowledge. You must go and see for yourself—to Hell, if need be.

On 1 May 1933, Kurt Gerstein joined the Nazi Party, membership number 2,136,174.

'If we truly desire to lead a person to a given place we must first take the trouble to go to the place where he is, and start from there.' (Kierkegaard.)

During his first months as Party member Gerstein's main preoccupation was to preserve, at any price, the independence of the Protestant youth movements. This was his private battle, a battle for the future, for the whole idea of civilization. All around him, on the streets, in factories and holiday camps, he witnessed the growing attraction of National Socialism for the German young. As a Westerner, a man shaped by the Greco-Christian world, this deeply afflicted him. His dilemma was starkly outlined in Schiller's *Laws of Lycurgus and Solon*, in which the poet gives a chilling picture of Spartan youth snatched from the arms of its family to be delivered body and soul to the totalitarian State and methodically conditioned for rapine and slaughter.

It must not be allowed to happen! As Gerstein's flock diminished so did his efforts increase; he fought and urged others to fight, circulated pamphlets and leaflets, uttered protests and denunciations. It was a rearguard action, a battle that was already lost. In December 1933 an avalanche swept it all away. Hitler's Bishop, Müller the Liar, the head of the 'German Christians,' announced that the 800,000 members of the Protestant youth movements were to be incorporated in the Hitler Youth.

Any man might have kept silent; but Gerstein joined with two other leaders in sending a telegram of protest to Baldur von Schirach, and on his own account he sent one to the Bishop that sounded like a Papal bull of anathema: 'The Church is dying at the hand of its Bishop. Signed: Gerstein, engineer, counsellor of the Church of Hagen.'

Two months later the Bible Circles went into voluntary liquidation. In his farewell speech—interspersed, as protocol required, with complimentary references to the Führer—Gerstein likened it to the scuttling of the German fleet in Scapa Flow after the last war. Like those great ships, the Protestant movement was going down with flags flying. 'It is months since the Hitler Youth openly declared war on us,' he cried, 'but we have not been defeated. We are giving up the struggle because the logic of the totalitarian State teaches us that we must rally to the State. Rather than repeat the treachery of Versailles we have taken the way of Scapa Flow.'

The treachery of Versailles was the 'stab in the back' which, as the German people had come to believe, had been inflicted on the nation by its republican leaders. But the youth movements suffered both Versailles *and* Scapa Flow.

'It may be,' Gerstein wrote to Egon Franz, 'that we shall be forced to abandon the visible Church to those others, leaving them to go through the antics of their "mass mission," while we rebuild the true Church, the Church *invisible.*'

He had not surrendered. He continued to argue and protest, to denounce by name Party members and the leaders of the Hitler Youth. But his tone was not that of a man shouting at the top of his voice; it was more like the steady growl of a watchdog seeing strangers enter the house where its master lies dead.

A Party informer, August Hoppe, reported as follows in June 1934:

'I had received information that certain members of the Bible Circle were meeting every Monday, ostensibly for "Bible Study." I went with two young men from Gevelsberg to the Evangelical Community House to see what went on. The lecture was given by that well-known, and too well-known, character, Kurt Gerstein of Hagen, the subject being, "The Position of Young Evangelical Christians in the State Today." The lecturer showed no lack of impudence. Not only did he criticize the measures adopted for the normalization of relations with the Churches, but he said that leaders like Rosenberg and Schirach were anti-Christian and should not be obeyed. He even went so far as to urge any members of the Hitler Youth who were present to leave that body and return to the Confessional organizations, and to try to persuade their friends to do the same. He said that the future caused him "grave concern," and he was insulting in his references to "the new paganism" . . .'

The *Wittekind* incident, in the Hagen theatre, occurred some months after this. Why was Gerstein still at liberty? There had been concentration camps in Germany from the beginning of the regime—why was he not in one? Did it suffice to be a Party member to be free to attack the Party? To whom had Gerstein sold his soul?

*Altroggenrahmede.*

Pastor Kurt Rehling, in November 1967, was living in a small house on a hillside about twelve miles from his parish of Hagen. I had no difficulty in finding him. The Protestant Church is a sturdy structure that preserves its living stones through every storm. The pastor's wife was dead and he lived alone, a red-faced, white-haired man, rather short of breath. 'It's my heart,' he said.

'I first met Gerstein in 1928. He was then twenty-three and I was a few years older. He came up to me and asked abruptly, without any preliminaries: "What is it that a pastor should not do?" I had no answer, and he said, "Preach for more than ten minutes." I was known in those days for the length of my sermons. But then he was kind enough to add that in my case I might perhaps be allowed to go on a little longer.'

Rehling had fought in the 1914 war, having gone straight into the Army when he left high school. He had been on the Chemin des Dames in 1917, and fifty years later he had gone back there on a pilgrimage. He had discovered something that surprised him. 'There was a sector that had been left untouched since the war. Not a blade of grass, nothing but a great expanse of chalk pitted with shell-holes. Looking over it from a height, I noticed something that we had not been able to see from our dug-outs: the huge crater was in the shape of a crescent moon.'

How many men had died there without seeing that crescent moon? And what sense is there in wars if they do not even allow a soldier to know the shape of the earth into which he is to dissolve?

'For a long time I had no very kindly feeling for the French. My brother was wounded in the leg in 1915, and while he was lying helpless a French soldier shot him in the chest at point-blank range. He was picked up later by our people in a counter-attack, and he lived just long enough to tell someone what had happened. I myself saw French soldiers finish off our wounded in 1917. To attack a defenceless man has always seemed to me a disgrace to the honour of any army. I have never heard of it being done by our army in that war, and certainly it would have been unthinkable in the regiment I served in. In my Sunday sermon after the "Night of the Broken Glass,"[1] in 1938, I reminded the congregation of those episodes and went on to say that our treatment of the Jews on this occasion was no better. As a former soldier in an army that had set great store by its honour, I could think of nothing more infamous than this mal-treatment of innocent persons unable to defend themselves. I had thought that although such things might happen in France they were impossible in Germany. Now I must apologize to the French and express my shame at the conduct of the Germans ... One can understand why even today there are countries—I am thinking particularly of the Dutch—who find it difficult to come to terms with us. One can only respect their attitude. At the same time you must not forget that I could have been arrested by the Gestapo for that sermon. It did not happen because, as they told me later, certain officials did not report the matter, knowing in their hearts that I was right. I was wrong in my opinion of the French, just as it would be wrong to blame the Gestapo for all the murders and persecutions that have taken place in Germany. It is not as simple as that.

'Here is another side of the picture. In 1934 I attended a big assembly of the Confessional Church in Hagen. The SS arrived in force and started to break up the meeting. The Chief of the Hagen Gestapo was a man called Heinrich Küthe. He was there, but in civilian clothes. He shouted to the SS: "Shut up! The

---

1 *Die Kristallnacht*: the night of 9–10 November 1938 when, following the assassination of a German diplomat in Paris, there was a savage persecution of the Jews throughout Germany.

Gestapo's in charge here." Whereupon an enormous SS trooper knocked him down with a chair leg. There was a retired army major standing just behind me, a fanatical opponent of the Nazis. He got the SS man by the throat and punched him in the face, after which he and I together shoved a table on top of him. Then we set about reviving Küthe. So far as I know, this is the only time the Confessional Church came to the rescue of the Gestapo.

'I had my reward later. I was charged on thirty-five occasions with offences against the Government, and every time the Gestapo contrived to cover my tracks or mislay the documents. Nor was my wife ever troubled, although she was working with me. So, you see, in the case of Gerstein you need not be too surprised that he got away with it.'

(The thought still does not please me. I would rather not have gone to Altroggenrahmede than be forced to admit that the Gestapo may not have been altogether what I had supposed—a great monolithic body operating like a machine according to a fixed programme, and indifferent to all other considerations. Was it really composed of men with human feelings, capable of doing worse than their fellows but also, it would seem, not incapable of doing better? The monolith dissolves into multi-coloured fragments . . . And if the Gestapo was not the Gestapo of our imagining, perhaps the SS was not either?)

*1934–35*. The regime disclosed its bloodstained countenance: slaughter of the SA leaders, assassination of Austrian Chancellor Dollfuss, concentration camps for thousands of political opponents.

Kurt Gerstein, who had just won his diploma as a mining engineer (the only thing he ever did that pleased his father), was now working without a mask but not without a voice. He had made the Protestant opposition his personal affair and had constituted himself its travelling representative.

Wherever he went he carried a briefcase stuffed with tracts and pamphlets, mostly written by himself and printed and distributed at his own expense. He posted them in all directions. He talked to the youngsters in youth camps about his struggle with the Nazis, but (it was a principle from which he never departed) without seeking to involve them, any more than he involved Elfriede Bensch, the pastor's daughter to whom he became engaged on 30 November 1935. (His mysterious comings and goings, meetings, telephone calls, were to invest their marriage with a melodramatic background like that of a spy-thriller. No woman could have endured it without disquiet. But whatever her anxieties—and certainly it was not the kind of life she had looked forward to—Elfriede Gerstein steadfastly bore it all, since this was the part she had to play in his life of hope and suffering.)

His activities took him across frontiers. In 1935 he went to Strasbourg to make personal contact with local Protestant leaders. His friend the chemist Robert Weiss noticed that he had difficulty in speaking, and Mme Weiss could scarcely understand a word he said. Gerstein pointed to his bruised jaw and told them what had happened in the theatre at Hagen. Later in that interview, referring to the growth of a totalitarian movement in France, he said: 'Please God you will never have to suffer what we are undergoing in Germany.'

\*

'Compartment reserved for travellers accompanied by mad dogs ... Compartment reserved for travellers suffering from contagious diseases ...' He had been given the task of organizing a congress of German miners at Saarbrücken, and these were two handmade window stickers which it amused him to send out with the invitations—a sardonic reference to the Party members who crowded all the trains. The joke was to cost him his liberty.

According to his brother Karl, officials in the Ministry of Mines noticed copies of these stickers on his desk. It was a sufficient pretext for the formal investigation of a man who was already regarded as a nuisance. On 24 September 1936 he was interrogated by the Gestapo in Saarbrücken. His office and domicile were searched and one thousand envelopes were found, addressed to leading officials, judges and lawyers. They contained illegal pamphlets relating to the Confessional Church. Another seven thousand envelopes, addressed to people of the same kind, were awaiting their contents.

Committed to prison in Saarbrücken, Gerstein believed that all was lost. He said to Karl: 'Tell Elfriede that I release her from our engagement.'

There was a Communist in the prison who was waiting to learn his fate. He and some fellow-Communists had been involved in a brawl with SS men, and the latter had threatened him with death if he did not testify in their favour. He was to swear that the Communists had attacked the Nazis, who had acted only in self-defence. The man gave way and did what was asked of him, but his perjury had not saved him. He was arrested on a trumped-up charge, and now, frozen with terror, he was waiting to be transferred . . .

Gerstein never lost sight of the possibility of his own collapse in similar circumstances. 'There is a streak of cowardice in each of us,' he was to say to Helmut Franz. 'One cannot easily master it. There is always the possibility of defeat.'

Elfriede Bensch notified all Gerstein's friends in the Confessional Church. Two separate rescue operations were promptly set in motion: that of the right-thinking Gerstein family, and that of the wrong-thinking Church—which, however, was not without influential friends.

Robert Weiss, Gerstein's Strasbourg friend, said in 1967: 'I heard of his arrest from Dr Hermann Ehlers, who was later to become President of the Bundestag, the West German Parliament. For the second year in succession Ehlers had brought a large party of young people to our country, "to breathe a little fresh air" as he said. He told me that in his opinion Gerstein had gone too far, particularly—Ehlers was himself a jurist—in sending out hundreds of pamphlets to magistrates and other people of importance. Not long after this Ehlers was himself arrested. When I heard the news I wrote to him in prison telling him that by the same post I was cancelling a large order for German pharmaceutical products, because I did not care to do business with Germans while two of my friends, Gerstein and himself, were in prison for their religious beliefs. Ehlers reminded me of this after the war, and he told me that my letter had got as far as Goebbels's office.'

After six weeks Gerstein was released. He was technically free—but expelled from the Party, dismissed from the Ministry of Mines, debarred from the public service, forbidden to seek professional employment in the private sector and banned from public speaking anywhere in the Reich.

He dreamed of starting a new life, as far away as possible from this hag-ridden country. He would go to Africa, to bring Christian teaching and modern drugs to the coloured peoples. The desire to heal the sick had always been present in him, as deeply rooted as his Christian faith.

He thought of Albert Schweitzer, installed in Lambaréné since the beginning of the century with his Bible, his organ and his medicine-chest. Hoping to get Schweitzer to follow in Hitler's wake, Goebbels had sent him an invitation ending with the Nazi formula, *Mit deutschem Gruss* (with a German greeting), which Schweitzer had politely declined, ending with the words, *Mit zentral-afrikanischem Gruss*. A wonderful man. Was this perhaps an example to be followed?

At the end of 1936 Gerstein went to study medicine at the Institute of Protestant Missionaries in Tübingen. For a short time he had wrestled with theology, but then had given it up. The prospects for theology in Germany were scarcely favourable, more especially for his particular brand. Medicine, he thought, would at least not bring him into conflict with authority. (In which he was wrong. Peace and tranquillity in any form were not for Kurt Gerstein.)

Despite his extravagances, he had not become a poor man. He could afford to live quietly. But if he was to continue his self-imposed task of opposition he must gain readmission to the Party, since this was the absolute prerequisite, without which all freedom of work and action was ruled out. How was it to be done except by paying the only price by which it could be bought—by lying?

Although in recent years Gerstein had made some attempt to disguise his struggle, he had never been untrue to himself. Now he would have to clothe himself in lies, parade a false face before the world, talk with the deepest accents of hypocrisy. He would have to apologize, say that he was a Nazi at heart, ready to die for his beloved Führer, if he was not to remain an outcast. His father and brothers, indeed the whole family, who had been incensed by his behaviour, were urging him to go on his knees and beg forgiveness of the Party. After much hesitation he gave way. At the time it was a heavy sacrifice, although later, when he had come to believe that he was acting under the direct orders of God, it was to cost him nothing.

In January 1937 he wrote to Elfriede: 'My letter of defence should go before the Party Tribunal today. In this matter my family has driven me almost to the point of lying and I am very unhappy about it.'

The sorry appeal, drafted finally by his brother Fritz, went to the Supreme Party Court in Munich: '. . . I am bound to resist the charge of having been lacking in fidelity to the National Socialist movement, and of joining those who seek to sabotage the work of the Führer. I feel deeply linked with the movement, and it is my most ardent desire to serve it, and to further the work of Adolf Hitler, with all my strength and by all the means in my power, even at the cost of my life. I may have made mistakes, but I cannot feel that they warrant the extreme penalty of my expulsion from the Party. Like any good German, I see in this a slur upon my character which I have not deserved . . .'

The reply was a long time coming. He had to wait some years for it, time to draw up his personal balance sheet. His attempt to influence events from within had failed. He had converted no one. He had compromised and humiliated himself, virtually for nothing. He was left in a state of emptiness and desolation, without any objective, any plan for living.

In 1937 Gerstein married Elfriede Bensch. The civil marriage took place in Hagen, and the religious ceremony was held in Bad Saarow, near Berlin. It was presided over by General Superintendent Otto Dibelius, of whom more will be heard later. As a leader of the Protestant Church, Dibelius had said in 1928: 'I have always had anti-Semitic leanings.' Later he became more or less attached to Martin Niemöller's Confessional Church.

Martin Niemöller had been arrested and sent to a concentration camp, and Hitler had every intention of keeping him there for the duration of the Third Reich, which was to last a thousand years. 'A man like Pastor Niemöller,' he said, 'cannot be allowed to remain at liberty.'

On 14 July 1938, Gerstein was again arrested by order of the Berlin Gestapo, charged, with seven other men, with plotting to commit high treason. This time he could truthfully deny the charge. He was innocent in fact, if not in feeling.

In the course of his studies and travels he had encountered some well-to-do gentlemen who professed to be opponents of the regime. They were in touch with a certain Reinhold Wulle, a former nationalist deputy and follower of General von Schleicher (liquidated in the purge of the SA in June 1934), who had hazy plans for the restoration of the monarchy. It was a strictly armchair conspiracy. The gentlemen met behind closed doors and over drinks and cigars amused themselves with scurrilous anecdotes about Hitler and the Party. Gerstein dismissed the whole thing in a sentence: 'You can't beat Hitler in a frockcoat.'

Information was given and the principal magistrate in Stuttgart sent a report of the proceedings to the People's Tribunal in Berlin: 'The suspicion that Wulle is involved in subversive activities aiming at the restoration of the Monarchy has been confirmed by the arrested men during their interrogation. In this connection the depositions of Gerstein and Mayer are of particular importance. It is clear that all the accused were in contact with Wulle, either directly or by letter, and that the latter, as an opponent of the Government, has been attempting with the aid of other influential persons to create a kind of shadow organization to pave the way for a Monarchist State in the event of a political upheaval. Where Gerstein is concerned, the charge is simply one of complicity; but the essential elements of the crime of premeditated high treason are present in the case of all the men. Wulle's attitude and behaviour have been described in detail by Gerstein and Mayer. In the course of their conversations he constantly referred to the Führer and other members of the Government in coarse and highly abusive terms.'

After which the report concludes on a surprisingly mild note: 'It seems that Wulle may be appropriately charged with misdemeanour under Clause 2 of the Law on the Spreading of False Reports.'

Imprisoned in Stuttgart, Gerstein fell into a state of despair, less because of the conditions of his imprisonment (he was being looked after, as we shall see) than for religious reasons. Because of a mock conspiracy in which he had played no active part he had fallen for an indefinite period into the hands of the enemy. For a man who believed that he had been especially charged by God to bear His banner aloft amid the tumults of the world, the irony could scarcely have been greater. His wife, when she visited him, found him huddled in his cell, pale and distraught, his mind a prey to the wildest thoughts, including that of ending a life which had become farcical.

'I reminded my own jail at Buechsenstrasse, Stuttgart; an unskilful hand had engraved in the metal of the bed: "Pray, Mother of God will help you." It was a great comfort to me in these hard days and my cell appeared to me as a small church. I salute with gratitude this unknown brother who sent me this encouragement in my deep affliction. God bless him.' (Gerstein, *Report*, see p. 298).

In October 1939 he composed the following prayer for his friend Helmut Franz:

*Beneath Your gaze, Almighty God, we do not seek to flee.*
*Neither do we deceive ourselves.*
*You do not let Yourself be mocked.*
*If You choose You can destroy us.*

*We should deserve it.*
*Lord, do not do it.*

In due course he was transferred, as an enemy of the State, to Welzheim in Swabia, where he was to have need of all his physical strength and willpower.

Welzheim was a concentration camp.

*Chapter 5*

# THE OUTCAST

'Do you sometimes feel a longing for true repose, far from the strain and turmoil of everyday? Do you want to restore your energies by breathing pure, scented air? Then come to Welzheim in the heart of the Swabian forest. You will find it wonderfully relaxing.' (Tourist hand-out.)

Welzheim is about forty miles east of Stuttgart, a town of 7,500 inhabitants very suitable for television documentaries: old houses, an ancient church, a museum, chestnuts and lime-trees. No one important has ever lived or died there (at least, the hand-outs do not mention him). The wall built by the Romans to keep out the invading Germanic tribes passed through what was then common land; traces of it are still to be seen in the countryside.

Welzheim jealously preserves its past, including the concentration camp, which is not at all in keeping with a town of this kind. It consists of one or two stone buildings with no open space except narrow courtyards: a very small camp for perhaps 100 inmates; a country annexe, so to speak, for overcrowded prisons. Nor has it changed its nature, even today. The caps of prison-warders are still to be seen. It is still a place of detention, even if the conditions are somewhat milder.

In 1938 working parties of slaves were marched daily through the town escorted by guards and dogs. 'Get a move on!' Impossible not to notice them in their thin, striped prison uniforms, and even less possible to distinguish one sort from another: Communists, socialists, Christians, Jehovah's Witnesses. They were all lumped together as *Häftlinge*, imprisoned men—enemies of the State—and therefore reduced to servitude and possible extinction; cattle to be driven, men to be abhorred.

Nevertheless it sometimes happened that a citizen of the town, passing close by one of these parties, would inadvertently let fall a packet of cigarettes or a hunk of bread. Not *given*, of course; just dropped by accident. Obviously one could not give anything to an enemy of the State without proclaiming oneself to be one; and the existence of the camp, and the rumours of what went on inside, were a sufficient reminder of what this entailed.

One of the prisoners was never to forget those hunks of bread let fall by the people of Welzheim. A time was to come when Kurt Gerstein was to be in a position to drop things accidentally for the benefit of other slaves (and still the process goes on, the free-masonry of the droppers of bread, as enduring as evil itself and perhaps in the end stronger). Meanwhile, a seemingly broken man, he was struggling to survive what he was to describe as 'the worst time in my life.'

Forsaken though he felt himself to be, a man was watching over him. His interrogation at the Gestapo headquarters in Stuttgart had been conducted by an investigating officer named Ernst Zerrer. Zerrer was a professional police officer who had served under the Weimar Republic but had made no bones about trans-ferring to the Nazis—a policeman is a policeman, no matter what government is in power. He was also a good Protestant, and his cross-examination of Gerstein caused him to become interested in the character of the prisoner. He read certain of Gerstein's moral discourses, and gave them to his young son to read. After this there was a decided change in the tone of the interrogation.

In April 1968 Kriminalsekretär Zerrer was living in retirement in the small town of Degerloch, where I went to interview him with my friend Herbert Weisselberg. At first he did not want to talk to us, saying that in any case he had told Frau Gerstein everything he knew. But Weisselberg persisted. As a youngster he had been a member of one of Gerstein's Bible Circles, and he is now superintendent of the Youth House erected near Berchum on the site of the old one. Zerrer could understand his being there, but he was not so sure about me. He eyed me with mis-trust. What secret power did I represent, what possible act of revenge?

He was a large, white-haired man, with a gentle, obstinate expression. With his hands behind his back, he stood at his garden gate stolidly defending his right to keep silent. But an instinct of courtesy—or was it curiosity, or misgiving?—kept him there chatting with us. He seemed torn between the desire to get away and the desire to confide in us. What finally emerged was neither one thing nor the other.

'It's true that I interrogated Gerstein when he was arrested with some other men in connection with the Wulle affair. He was different from the rest, more intelligent and very well educated. I soon realized that he was an implacable opponent of National Socialism . . . When it came to drafting the report of the interrogation I left the whole thing to him. He knew much better than I did what ought to be said. He dictated the questions and answers to my secretary . . .

'He was sent to Welzheim. It was a police prison, not a proper concentration camp. The real concentration camps, like Auschwitz and Buchenwald, were something different . . .

'I ran into Gerstein once during the war, in 1942, at the Stuttgart railway station. He told me that he was working at the SS Institute in Berlin, and that his work had to do with the concentration camps. He was wearing civilian clothes. I had my son with me, who'd been wounded and invalided out of the Army. Gerstein offered to buy him a bicycle, but I refused. It would have been no use to him.

'After the war I was put in an internment camp at Ludwigsburg. I don't know why. I'd done nothing wrong. They kept me there three years. I'm a Protestant, but the Catholics—they got out soon enough. At the time when I was working for the Gestapo in Berlin the present Chancellor[1] was in the Ministry for Foreign Affairs. As though Foreign Affairs didn't work with the Gestapo!' Ernst Zerrer shrugged his shoulders. 'Well, that's the way things are. It's only the small men who suffer.'

Gerstein to Günter Dickten: 'Do you know why I got out of Welzheim so soon? On the journey there I got talking to the

1 Kurt Kiesinger.

guards—you know how well I get on with simple people. Well, I quoted part of Mark Antony's speech in the Shakespeare play, "Friends, Romans, countrymen, lend me your ears," and I used it as a text to illustrate the tricks and subtleties of this world. By the time we got to Welzheim they were all on my side.'

Whatever the reason, whether it was due to Zerrer's influence, the goodwill of the guards or the weakness of the charge against him, he was out of Welzheim in about six weeks. But here, even more than elsewhere, time was not what mattered. The camp was another world, almost another dimension of life. Those who experienced it from inside, even for a month, were for ever set apart from other men. So it was with Gerstein. Although he saw more of that daily debasement than he actually suffered, he suffered from seeing it. Cold, hunger, vermin and the unbelievable brutality of the guards; constant beatings and the teeth of dogs. There were men who hanged themselves, who went mad or, worst of all, who went over to the side of their captors and beat their fellow-inmates to save their own skins.

*'Very likely these Martians will make pets of some of them; train them to do tricks—who knows—get sentimental over the pet boy who grew up and had to be killed. And some, maybe, they will train to hunt us.'*

*'No,' I cried, 'that's impossible! No human being—'*

*'What's the good of going on with such lies?' said the artillery-man. 'There's men who'd do it cheerful. What nonsense to pretend there isn't!'*

(H. G. Wells: *The War of the Worlds*.)

Once again he was free, after having taken a solemn oath before leaving the camp that he would divulge nothing whatever of what he had seen and heard.

He sank back into the melancholy and aimless existence of a man proscribed in his own country. He was out of work and almost at the end of his resources, having spent so much of his money on the Bible Circle holiday camps. (He continued to organize these illegally—at Borkum, Zingst and Berchum—right up to the war, despite the ban on them and the suspended sentence hanging over his own head.) All he could offer his young and glowing wife was a life of constant strain, haunted by the threat of a nocturnal visit from the police. They had not even the normal married consolation of sharing their sorrows: she must be allowed to know nothing, however much she might misjudge him.

*I thank you for having always misunderstood me, since it taught me to understand myself. I thank you for having been so profoundly unjust towards me, since this determined the course of my life.* (Kierkegaard.)

His experience in the camp completed his state of physical collapse. At the age of thirty-three Gerstein was an exhausted man who henceforth would always look older than his age. He slept very badly and was subject to fits of abstraction. (Later he was found to be suffering from hypoglycemia: his system used up calories abnormally fast, and he compensated for this by eating great quantities of sweets of all kinds.)

His father, who still hoped to see him reinstated, wrote to the Party Tribunal: 'My son has been released after six weeks' detention. Despite the favourable treatment he received, for which he has every reason to be grateful, his imprisonment has affected him both mentally and physically. His doctor has diagnosed a heart condition—of nervous origin, in his view—which might be cured by a course of thermal treatment.'

But who was to cure the world of Hitler, the cause of all the trouble? It was September 1938, the time of Munich, when the world was cast into doubt and disarray and the German opposition reduced to helplessness and despair.

In October 1938 Herr and Frau Gerstein set off on a Mediterranean cruise. It was their honeymoon, although Gerstein, knowing what he did, and wanting what he wanted, can hardly have been in a mood for honeymoons. Doubtless it was a honeymoon to Elfriede, travelling innocently at his side. We shall see very little of her in this book. She exists for us only in the company of Gerstein, and when she is with him we are not present.

An Italian liner took them to Venice and Trieste, up the Dalmatian coast and down to the isles of Greece. They went ashore, took photographs, bathed. Gerstein, whose favourite sport was swimming, amused himself by diving under the ship's hull. He even smiled occasionally, which was a marvel.

But then he would withdraw into his cabin for long periods during which he sat writing. One of his fellow-passengers was Otto Völckers, a Swiss architect travelling with his wife. In 1949 he wrote: 'Gerstein gave an impression of extreme reserve. After I had got to know him he told me that he had recently been released from a concentration camp, and that after being expelled from the Party he had been constantly spied on and persecuted. When we collected our mail at Fiume he learned that his house in Tübingen had been searched again, and he was wondering whether to go back to Germany or to take refuge in Switzerland.'

Otto Völckers teased him about the amount of writing he did. After all, they were on holiday! To which Gerstein replied in effect that the letters he was writing could not be posted in Germany. They would have cost him his life.

There was one particular letter which he did not send directly. He used an intermediary, his Strasbourg friend, the chemist Robert Weiss, who recalls having forwarded it and in due course passed the reply back to Gerstein by clandestine means. The letter was to his maternal uncle, Robert Pommer, who had emigrated to the United States as a young man and was now a prosperous grain merchant in St Louis, Missouri, where he had a nephew working with him. It is a letter of great importance because it was written in freedom, without any covering-up or ambiguity. Gerstein's only concession is to give Hitler credit for his positive achievements—roads, buildings, relieving unemployment—because these seemed to have impressed his uncle when he visited Germany.

The letter is quoted in full.

'Dear Uncle Robert and Cousin Robert,

'I must tell you of a situation that has become terribly serious for me. As Uncle Robert knows, during the past three years we have been the object of extremely unpleasant measures taken by the Gestapo. The reason for this lies in my religious convictions. Although I do not follow the strict line of dogma or orthodoxy, I am a convinced Christian. Since 1931 I have occupied a prominent position on the national committees for Protestant guidance and youth education. All our organizations, like all other Christian organizations, both Protestant and Catholic, have been dissolved. It was agreed, however, that we might continue to organize purely religious activities.

'In practice this right has long been trodden underfoot by the Nazi groups, and the Gestapo has forbidden us to exercise it. The totalitarian spirit of National Socialism sets out to gain possession of a man's whole being, body and soul, and to dominate him entirely. Despite speeches and writings which seem to proclaim the contrary, the view is taken in Germany today that not only the Protestant and Catholic forms of worship, but all Christian religion whatever, is useless and in the highest degree injurious, and that this applies to all serious forms of communion with God. The height of perfection for the boys and girls of Germany is held to be that by day and night they should think of no one but Adolf Hitler and of nothing but Germany. Any higher relationship, with God for example, is regarded as being in the highest degree obnoxious. At first we acquiesced as widely as possible in National Socialism on the political level; we "rendered unto Caesar that which was Caesar's." At the same time we pointed out, without making any distinction between Catholic and Protestant, that a people, and a younger generation, without God were a source of danger.

'We have gratefully acknowledged Hitler's material achievements, but we have been forced to realize that in religious matters National Socialism since 1933 has been leading the nation madly astray, and that its real purpose is not merely the total destruction of the Protestant and Catholic churches in Germany, but the elimination of all serious belief in God.

'Unlike what is going on in Russia, where the fight against God is conducted in the open, here it is veiled in the most shameful hypocrisy. Religious instruction in the primary and secondary schools, although it is still labelled Catholic or Protestant, is in fact simply designed to root out every belief in God, and to replace it by atheism and the materialist creed of blood and race. This has nothing in common with our early struggle for the acknowledgement of the Old Testament or our ancient professions of faith. Where I personally am concerned I hold very advanced views on those matters and I keep a very open mind; but this is a question of the destruction of virtually all religious aspirations. We have come a long way from our old rallying-cries and divisions: on one side the German Christians, and on the other side the militants of the Confessional Church or of Niemöller. It is a question of whether the German people and German youth are to continue to hear God spoken of in a manner that merits serious attention, or whether they are to believe in nothing but a bloodstained flag, and the sacred places and emblems of a cult—in blood, soil and race. Is Germany to believe that justice is a transcendent concept over which the human will has no power—"residing amid the stars," in Schiller's phrase—and that he who talks of justice does so in the name of an all-powerful Supreme Judge to whom he is responsible? Or are we to concede that "the law is whatever serves the people"—that is to say, a purely utilitarian affair? Is Justice to be the harlot of the State?

'Although there has been much to outrage our individual consciences we have all made every effort not to oppose National Socialism in purely political matters, since these are not our direct concern. We have sought only to defend the rights and responsibilities solemnly guaranteed to us by Herr Hitler and the Party, and which they still guarantee. And we have been scrupulous in distinguishing between the essential and the non-essential, the matter of principle and the minor detail. But we have been subjected to a campaign of lies directed against us by adversaries whose intention is perfectly clear. The situation in Germany is now such that the supreme values of Justice and Faith in God can only be maintained at the cost of struggle and suffering. The fight against violence can certainly not be said to be valueless, since injustice and lack of conscience would be even greater than they are if there were no fear of public opinion, in foreign countries as well as at home. Despite the restrictions placed on the press, enough information reaches us to enable us to tell fair-minded people—and these exist even among the Nazis—something of what is going on. Thus to some extent the national conscience is still awake and the worst may yet be avoided.

'I myself have had several serious run-ins with the Gestapo. Although I have done my best not to expose myself uselessly to attack, or to do so on ill-chosen grounds, the fact that I have played a prominent part in the spiritual education of the young and matters affecting the Protestant Church has had repercussions. My success as a publicist has caused the Gestapo to view me with extreme suspicion, and my books for the young, of which more than 250,000 copies have been circulated, have drawn upon me the personal enmity of Baldur von Schirach, the National Youth Leader. I was imprisoned for several weeks in the autumn of 1936. It was a very painful experience which I still cannot describe in detail. Anyone who has not been through it will be inclined to regard most of it as impossible; but I know that what is printed in the foreign press is on the whole not exaggerated.

'Although after this I was particularly cautious, and moreover could count on the goodwill of certain members of the Party, I was always in danger of being arrested again.

'This happened to me on 14 July 1938. After a few highly unpleasant days I was sent to a concentration camp, where I remained for six and a half weeks. It was the most dreadful period in my life. I find it impossible to describe the degradation, the ill-treatment, the hunger, the fact of being crowded into a very confined space with pimps and criminals. My fellow-inmates, all men who had been imprisoned elsewhere, had only one desire, which was to get back to an ordinary prison. Fleas, lice, rashes, semi-starvation, forced labour and indescribably harsh treatment. By great good fortune my case had come into the hands of a member of the Gestapo who was well disposed towards me and secured my release. More than once I was on the verge of hanging myself, or taking my life by some other means, simply because I had no idea whether I would ever be let out of the place, and if so, when.

'Since my release I have had no further trouble; but no one can foresee what the future has in store for Germany. One can only suppose that the success of Herr Hitler's policy abroad will so enhance the prestige of National Socialism at home that he will feel free to do whatever he likes. We are no longer in any doubt that the campaign against the Church, and against all religion, was not only conceived and planned by Hitler personally, but is directed by him. In view of the remorselessness with which National Socialism has pursued its aims, we see very hard times ahead.

'My expulsion from the Party led to my losing my post as a mining engineer, and since 1936 I have been studying medicine in Tübingen, where my wife and I now live. We were married in 1937. For the present I do not seem to be in any danger, but as one never knows what is going to happen I wanted to tell you and Cousin Robert what the situation is. I am being more cautious than ever, and hope to escape further persecution. A third arrest would undoubtedly be the end of me. I have friends in France and Switzerland who would give my wife and me shelter for a few days, but I should almost certainly be picked up if we returned to Germany.

'In case of extreme necessity, may I rely on your assistance in securing a home for my wife and me until I have found suitable employment as a qualified engineer? Please do not show this letter to anyone or make any reference to it in your letters to Germany: this could have serious consequences for me. My friend Dr Robert Weiss, pharmaceutical expert to the civil hospital in Strasbourg, may be trusted, and he will find the means of conveying your reply to me without loss of time. His address is 7 rue des Orphelines, Strasbourg. For the present I have no need of your help, and there is only one chance in four that I shall ever ask for it. But it would be a great comfort to me to know that I might count on it in the last resort.

'Dear Uncle Robert, your many visits to Germany have enabled you to see the undeniable successes of the Hitler regime in so many fields—roads, unemployment, building. But you cannot have seen the tragedies resulting from the loss of spiritual and religious freedom, and of justice. For a foreigner this is very difficult to understand.[1] I have heard that Cousin Robert has given some thought to these matters, which is why I am addressing this letter to him as well as to you, since he is your adviser in things of this sort.

'I send you greetings in profound gratitude for all the affection and kindness you have shown me.

'Your nephew, Kurt.'

This was the real Gerstein, the man who had not deviated but remained always constant in his thinking. What else he said and did was a matter of tactics. At the very time when he wrote that letter to America he was writing another in which, for the sake of gaining re-admission to the Party, he not only proclaimed his Nazi faith but went so far as to repudiate Niemöller. 'I warned him more than once, telling him that the lead he was giving did not suit our young people, who were ardent supporters of the Führer and National Socialism.'

It was the beginning of a vast misapprehension. Many people failed to understand him, then as now. Each of us is a riddle to someone.

*

The Gersteins got back to Tübingen after their holiday cruise in time to see the local synagogue go up in flames. This was the 'Night of the Broken Glass' already referred to, when the assassination by a Jew of a German diplomat in Paris was made the pretext for a nationwide pogrom—dozens of Jewish people killed, hundreds injured and 20,000 arrested, in addition to which 800 shops were looted and 200 synagogues burnt to the ground. This savage prelude to Auschwitz, although it must have torn

[1] 'The tourist business thrived and brought in vast sums of badly needed foreign currency . . . A foreigner, no matter how anti-Nazi, could come to Germany and study what he liked—with the exception of the concentration camps and, as in all countries, the military installations. And many did. And many returned who if they were not converted were at least more, tolerant of the "new Germany", and believed that they had seen, as they said, its "positive achievements".' (William L. Shirer, *The Rise and Fall of the Third Reich*.)

the blinkers off the nation's eyes, produced no counter-action. The whole country accepted it, and itself died in the process.

Kurt Gerstein resumed his medical studies; but things happened which caused him again to alter course, as though they were a warning that he had still to find his true vocation.

In 1937 a man collapsed with apoplexy in a public park in Würzburg. Gerstein went to his assistance, to be brushed aside, as a presumptuous student, by a qualified doctor who arrived a few minutes later. He went off muttering, 'But I'm a doctor too . . .'

Later he invented a new type of cystoscope, a device for the investigation of bladder disease, which he wanted to test on a human subject. He asked a junior student to undergo the test, and the boy agreed. The experiment, which was carried out under qualified supervision, went wrong. There was bleeding. When it was over Gerstein went anxiously into the room where the boy was resting. 'Do you still trust me?' The boy said that he did, and Gerstein, now radiant, held out his hand. 'Thank you. Now you have the right to call me *du*.'

He should have moderated his zeal; but what can the word 'moderation' mean to a man whose every thought is aflame, every project a matter of desperate urgency?

Following a further professional irregularity, a formal complaint was lodged against him. He was hauled up before the University Council and dishonourably expelled from the hospital. A letter he wrote to Günter Dickten tells us of this crisis:

'. . . I developed a passionate enthusiasm for medicine and I was so eager to practise it that I simply could not wait until I was able to do so freely in my own surgery or clinic. I practised on anyone who came along, the servant-girl who had burnt her arm or the old man who had an apoplectic seizure in the Schlossgarten in Würzburg. After that episode another man, a locksmith, came up to me in the street, and after thanking me in very moving terms for what I had done for the old man, he said, "If you lived in Würzburg I would choose you for my doctor." I told my wife about it. I would have liked the words to be written up in capital letters: To Help and Heal.

'Medicine was my vocation, if ever I had one, the true fulfil-
ment of my life; although I know—I know it now—that I should
have waited until I had passed my finals. I not only had this
longing to practise it but I undoubtedly possessed more than
average ability, as a healer particularly in the psychiatric and
physiological fields—an ability which I was the more impelled to
confirm by the fact that in those years I was not yet qualified to
use it. I would not want this to be confused with the attitude of
the second- or third-term student who takes it upon himself to
"treat" his landlady and personal friends (although admittedly
there is a connection) . . . There is another thing I would like to
say. It may be that our hospital experience made us too casual
and lacking in respect for the naked human body. When, for
example, it was a question of inflating the bladder by means of an
air-pump attached to the urethra, this was for many of us—including the girl-students who worked with us—a kind of romp
which was treated very light-heartedly. In one sense this was a
healthy release; but in another sense, it did not accord with my
view of the seriousness with which one should approach the
body of a defenceless stranger . . .'

Such was Gerstein's farewell to medicine.


On 10 June 1939 the Supreme Tribunal of the Party, sitting in
Munich, resolved that the sentence of expulsion passed on Party
member Kurt Gerstein, No. 2,136,174, should be commuted to
provisional membership.

The tireless efforts of Judge Gerstein, supported by Zerrer,
had at length borne fruit. It was not a complete rehabilitation.
Kurt was still excluded from State service. But at least the doors
of private industry were again open to him, at a time when the
Reich, on the threshold of war, needed all the qualified engineers
it could get.

The Judge, now aged seventy-one, approached former members of Teutonia, the student corps to which he had belonged.
Certain of these belonged to the powerful industrial group of
Wintershall in Merkers, and also subscribed handsomely to the
club known as the 'Friends of Heinrich Himmler.' At the same

time an approach was made to Hugo Stinnes, one of the industrial magnates without whose help Hitler would have remained a street-corner orator. Kurt Gerstein was already known to Stinnes. In the 'twenties he had published an article on political economy, and Stinnes had been so impressed by it, coming from a very young man, that he had written to him.

Shortly after the Tribunal's verdict was announced Gerstein received an offer from the Wintershall group, which operated a potash mine at Merkers, in Thuringia. Stinnes wrote to him: 'I was very glad to learn that that unpleasant episode was definitely closed. It seemed to me natural that I should come to your assistance, and I am happy to think that I have helped you to make a fresh start in life.' (July 1939.)

Kurt Gerstein had got back in deep water.

*September 1939*: war.

*October 1939*: birth of his first child, a son, Arnulf. 'People exist only when they can speak Latin.' (Kurt Gerstein.)

Although he was in a reserved occupation he volunteered for the Army. 'I cannot go on for ever living under suspicion in my native country.' He repeated his application in July 1940, but the matter remained unsettled.

The fact is that Gerstein had already found he could not stay with Wintershall. He was not allowed to forget his past. He was spied on, rebuked, bullied. The Nazi bosses had his dossier in their files and treated him accordingly: a man who had been imprisoned as an 'enemy of the State.'

Was he to run away or seek to redeem himself in battle? The Army did not seem very eager to welcome him as a volunteer. Should he apply for another job? But the Labour Office kept an eye on nearly all appointments, particularly in the case of political suspects. All Gerstein could achieve was his transfer to another Wintershall branch, at Merseburg, in the neighbourhood of Leipzig, while at the same time he was trying to secure, as soon as possible, a sinecure in the family firm of De Limon Flühme & Co, in Düsseldorf.

But none of this solved his problem. What was he *really* to do?

He was assiduous in attending Nazi gatherings, and he worked for the Hitler Youth—'on a fairly high level,' he wrote to a friend. He was invited by the local organization to write about youth problems. He responded with enthusiasm to appeals for the collection of scrap metal and himself delivered consignments in a hand-cart, for which he was awarded a 'certificate of good citizenship' by the Gauleiter of Weimar. When someone suggested that he was overdoing it he replied: 'If an effort is needed to help the nation, Kurt will not be the last.' He loudly proclaimed his respect for Hitler, and at the burial of a mine foreman in March 1940 he delivered a funeral oration in true Hitlerian style: 'We lose in him a faithful friend and comrade, and a faithful follower of our Führer.' He ended his letters with the ritual formula: '*Glückauf und Heil Hitler!*'

He coolly suggested to his protégé Horst Dickten, who was with him in Merkers, where he was preparing for his school-leaving examinations, that he should write a thesis on the subject 'We National Socialists are the Men of the Future.' When it was written (on parchment) Gerstein took possession of it and showed it to the Gauleiter. So greatly did it please that eminent person that he brought his influence to bear and Dickten passed *cum laude*. Gerstein's comment was: 'Exams are intended for fools.'

He was scarcely ever seen in Protestant circles, to the dismay of the militant element: another good man gone! In the course of that summer Pastor Kurt Rehling, who had just been demobilized, heard the news of his defection. But he refused to believe in it. He knew his man.

The Gerstein case was only a drop in the Protestant ocean of troubles in the year 1940. There was the war, which put a gag on all opposition, and there was something else—a thing so terrible that it could be talked of only in a whisper.

It had begun in 1939. In October the Führer had signed a secret decree (antedated to coincide with the outbreak of war and to cover the instances in which it had already been invoked) which ran as follows: 'Reichsleiter Buhler and Dr Brandt are hereby authorized, on their own responsibility, to extend the competence of certain selected doctors in order that the latter may be empowered to bring a merciful release to patients judged by human standards, and after thorough examination, to be incurable.'

The principle was one which Hitler had more than once publicly endorsed: the elimination of the weak. He was not the only one to think along such lines. In *Man, the Unknown*, published in 1935, Dr Alexis Carrel, Nobel Prize winner, had proposed that euthanasia be practised on criminals in establishments equipped with gas suitable for the purpose; and he had asked whether the same treatment should not be applied to lunatics guilty of criminal acts. A remnant of shame, or perhaps of prudence, had restrained him from suggesting that the 'treatment' might be extended to all those weaklings, whether of mind or of body, whose existence encumbered his concept of an orderly scientific world.

In the purely technical sense the operation presented no difficulty. The State of Nevada, USA, had installed the first gas chamber in 1924, a Chinese convicted of murder being the inaugural victim. A German review specializing in penal matters had devoted an article to the subject in 1932, and this had not been lost on Nazi criminologists.

According to the calculations of an expert, about a million Germans—certified lunatics and sick persons—came within the scope of the decree in the year 1939, which made it a large-scale operation, but one most fortunately facilitated by the war. Hitler himself kept an eye on its development. A special subsection of his Chancellery was created, presided over by Dr Philipp Buhler, a personal friend of the Führer, and his adjutant, Viktor Brack, for the general supervision of the 'Mercy Service'—'mercy,' in the Third Reich, being another name for 'death.'

Speeches, a mass of documentation and finally a film (the work of Viktor Brack) were devised to condition the public mind, although no direct reference was made to the operation. The task of execution was entrusted to a Stuttgart police commissioner,

Christian Wirth, who adapted a clinic at Grafeneck, in Württemberg, for the purpose. In the early stages the operation was confined to the certifiably insane, and Wirth and his assistants disposed of them with pistols, a clumsy method which was, however, soon superseded by the use of gas. Other establishments were set up at Hadamar, Sonnenstein, Irrsee, Bernburg and Hartheim, near Linz.

The operation was mounted in conditions of the utmost secrecy, all personnel being required to sign a written pledge. Its headquarters were in Berlin, 4 Tiergarten, and its official title was T 4. Questionnaires were sent out to every psychiatric ward and clinic in the Reich; a form had to be filled in for every patient. The documents were examined by 'experts' at the Ministry of the Interior who decided who should live and who should die. Special buses conveyed the condemned to the euthanasia centres, and later an urn containing their ashes was sent to their family.

'Observers least open to suspicion, clergy and certain German psychiatrists, gained the impression that these measures were no more than a prelude to a far greater process of organized extermination, which they would be called upon to witness after the total victory of the regime. It seemed indeed that the practice of scientific murder on a massive scale, for which the technique had been developed and perfected by analogous experiments in the concentration camps, was to be so vastly extended in the future as to acquire the status of a national institution.' (Dr François Bayle: *Croix gammée contre caducée*—Swastika versus Caduceus.)

*1946.* Trial of the doctors at Nuremberg.
The accused Karl Brandt: 'The Führer wanted euthanasia to be kept entirely secret, but this turned out to be impossible.'

In the fields round Grafeneck farm-horses reared up in terror when the smoke and smell of the crematoria reached their nostrils.

On 25 November 1940 a lady named Else von Loewis wrote

as follows to the wife of the presiding Party Judge in Munich:
'Dear Frau Busch,

'This is not a personal matter but the most terrible thing we
have so far had to bear. Until now nothing could shake my confidence in the victory of great Germany on its hard and dangerous
road, or my faith in the Führer; but what is now happening must
cause the ground to crumble beneath our feet.

'You doubtless knew of the measures affecting the mentally
incurable; but you may not be aware of the full extent of this
business, or the horror it is arousing in people's minds. Here in
Württemberg the scene of the tragedy is Grafeneck.

'It is not the thing itself which is terrible and dangerous. Indeed,
if a law were promulgated, on the lines of the sterilization law,
whereby persons no longer retaining a spark of human reason
were submitted to rigorous medical examination, I am convinced
that the initial indignation would rapidly die down, perhaps even
more quickly than in the case of the sterilization law. It is even
possible that in a few years we should be wondering why it was
not promulgated earlier.

'But a secret of this nature cannot be kept indefinitely, even
though those who disclose it incur the death penalty, as is apparently the case. And it is unrealistic to expect people to believe
in a mysterious epidemic of which their relatives have died. That
is a blunder that cannot be repaired.

'Have the persons in charge of these measures the least idea
of the amount of public confidence they have destroyed? Where
is it to end? Plenty of the sick people know perfectly well where
they are being taken when the grey SS bus arrives. The Württemberg farmers also know what it means when they see the bus go
past, as surely as they see the smoke rising from the crematorium.
And we all know that some of the mentally incurable are persons
of high intelligence, that some are only partly afflicted and that
some are only periodically affected and have long lucid intervals.
Is it not enough that they should be sterilized, and is it not horrible
to think of this sword of Damocles suspended over their heads
at Grafeneck?

'I feel as though I were living a bad dream. And what a theme this is for the Catholic Church! The people still cling to the hope that the Führer does not know what is going on. I feel that we shall pay dearly for this blow to public morale. Without faith in law and justice a nation must inevitably go astray. There must be some means of making the feelings of the German people known to their Führer. *Heil Hitler!*

'Yours truly, Else von Loewis.'

A Nazi district commissioner: 'It appears that the medical commissions have done their work too hurriedly and that mistakes have been made. We cannot prevent particular cases from becoming known. 1. A family was sent two urns. 2. A notice was sent stating that the cause of death was appendicitis, although the subject's appendix had been removed ten years previously. 3. Another notice referred to disease of the spinal cord; the subject had been seen by his parents a week previously and found to be in perfect physical condition. 4. A family received notice of the death of a woman who is still alive and in excellent health. The chief medical officer of Nuremberg reports that two charges of murder have been brought by the relatives of former patients. *Heil Hitler!* Kreisleiter Walz.'

Anonymous letter written on 9 July 1940 to the Minister of Justice: 'I have a son afflicted with schizophrenia who is in an establishment in Württemberg. I have been horrified to receive the following information from an absolutely reliable source. For some weeks past persons suffering from mental disorders have been removed from the establishments where they were being treated, ostensibly on the grounds of military evacuation. The directors of these establishments are ordered to preserve complete secrecy. Soon afterwards the family are informed that their relative has died of encephalitis, and that the ashes will be forwarded if desired. These are murders, exactly like those in the concentration camps, and they are carried out by order of the SS in Berlin. The establishments in question dare not inform the authorities. You should investigate the matter immediately. Ask to see lists of patients dated two months ago, check the number now remaining and then ask what has happened to the rest. For seven years this gang of murderers has been blackening the name of Germany. If my son has been killed I shall see to it that an account of these crimes appears in the foreign press. The S S may deny it, as they always do. I shall place the facts before the Public Prosecutor. I cannot sign my name or give the name of the establishment where my son is at present, otherwise my life, too, would be forfeit.'

This growing anxiety was acutely reflected in Church circles. Pastor Braun, vice-chairman of the Committee of Protestant Churches, addressed a memorandum to Hitler in person; by way of warning he was imprisoned for three months. Doctor Ernst Wilm brought the matter to the notice of the Confessional Church of Westphalia, and Doctor Wurm, Bishop of Württemberg, wrote to the Minister of the Interior.

Wurm was Gerstein's bishop; Tübingen came within his province. It was from him, during the summer of 1940, that Gerstein learned the details of the liquidation of the mentally afflicted. Other people also heard of it, but Gerstein had certain advantages over them. The circles in which he moved, his past and his character made him one of the best-informed persons in the Third Reich. He knew people on every social level, from Finance Minister Schacht and the magnate Stinnes to men and women in the most humble walks of life. Through the Confessional Church and his contacts with members of the old Army Intelligence, he was in touch with a very wide range of informers. If any man could get at the whole truth, it was he.

Towards August he left Merkers with Horst Dickten and went to Eisenach. According to Dickten, he wanted to volunteer for the Luftwaffe parachute corps. It was a fruitless errand because they were not accepting any more volunteers. In any case, he had injured a foot working in a mine, and this would automatically have disqualified him. The Luftwaffe was advising rejected volunteers to apply to the Waffen S S, which was organizing an air police force. Gerstein followed this advice. His application was noted and he was told that he would receive a reply in due course.

In October 1940 Robert Weiss, having been a refugee in France, where his father and brother still lived, had just returned to Alsace, which was no longer a part of France. The German regime was extremely rigorous. Everything French was abolished, including the Basque beret, General Kléber's coffin and the statue of Louis XIV. A man in civilian clothes knocked at the door, and it was Gerstein. It was the first visit Weiss had received from a representative of the Occupying Power; but Gerstein, with his troubled, compassionate face, did not look much like a conqueror.

'After so many years,' Weiss said in 1967, 'I cannot remember everything he said to me. If I had not known him so well I should have thought he was an *agent provocateur*. He told me about the way the inmates of lunatic asylums were being liquidated. I remember him saying: "It's quite horrifying. The poor devils are taken off like cattle to the slaughter-house, their eyes wide with terror, knowing perfectly well what's going to happen to them." And he talked about the casual way the murderers did the job: "Well, what shall we say this one died of—TB, pneumonia or heart failure?"

'Kurt's idea was that he could help people more effectively by working from inside—in the lion's mouth, so to speak. He even hinted, rather cautiously, that he might try to join the SS. And he said: "Germany must not win this war." But I got the impression that at the time he still was in a state of great uncertainty, not knowing what road to follow.'

## Chapter 6

# SS TROOPER

BERTA ... Nothing remained of her but a handful of ashes, conveyed in an urn to the Town Hall at Saarbrücken. It was preceded by a letter from the head of the clinic addressed to her mother, the widowed Frau Ebeling.

The customary formula:

'Dear Madam,

'We regret to have to inform you of the unexpected death of your daughter as a result of a cerebral thrombosis. She had been transferred to the clinic in accordance with measures adopted by the Commissioner at the Ministry of Defence.

'Her severe mental affliction caused her great suffering, and you must therefore accept her death as a merciful release.

'Owing to the danger of an epidemic in the clinic, the police authorities have ordered the immediate cremation of the body. The death certificate . . .' etc.

The morning of 22 February 1941 was mild for the time of year and a great many people were present at the ceremonial interment of the ashes. Everybody had known Berta's father, Julius Ebeling, the Protestant pastor. The long procession wound its way to the beautiful Saarbrücken cemetery, situated on what had formerly been the French frontier.

Poor Berta. To end in this way. She had been in good health and happy, until suddenly she fell ill and had to be hospitalized in her home town. Here she had been treated with particular care, for she was the daughter of Pastor Ebeling, and he was not forgotten. And then her mother had received an official notification that she had been transferred for administrative reasons to a clinic in Hadamar, a small town in Hesse, some two hundred miles distant. The new environment had not agreed with her—as seemed to happen, so rumour had it, in the case of a great many of the inmates of that clinic. She had died soon after her arrival. Well, perhaps after all it was a merciful release.

There were members of the Gerstein family in the funeral procession. Frau Karl Gerstein, who attended with her husband, was Berta's sister. That strange character, Kurt Gerstein, was also there, looking even more affected than the others, although he had never been on close terms with Berta. His long, bony face had an expression not so much of grief as of furious indignation.

After the ceremony the Gersteins walked back together into the town, and Kurt, in a state of intense agitation, suddenly burst out to his brother and sister-in-law: 'Do you realize what they did to Berta? Hadamar is a slaughter-house. The Nazis are clearing out all the mental hospitals in Germany by systematically exterminating the patients. Berta didn't die a natural death. She was murdered!'

*Hadamar, November 1967.* On one's left, as one walks up the main street, is the massive bulk of a castle with thick round towers. Just beyond it, invisible from lower down, is the psychiatric hospital, a dark, squat building which they have tried unsuccessfully to enliven by re-facing it.

The tiled entrance hall is bright and scrupulously clean, decorated with plants, and on the left as you enter there is a plaque. Its sculptured design shows a flame and a writhing human form, beneath which are the words, 'In memory.' But nothing is said about what we are to remember, and perhaps it is better that the truth should not be written on any wall. After an interlude the Hadamar Hospital has reverted to its normal functions, and nurses, patients and doctors pass the memorial plaque without asking questions.

They used to arrive in motor-coaches, grey vehicles with frosted windows. They were unloaded in the courtyard and taken in groups of twenty or thirty, sometimes more, into a room where they were undressed by nurses. Those who were over-agitated were given tranquillizing injections. Then they were taken into what was called the 'shower room' in the basement, lined with tiles and with a row of sprays which looked like showers but were not. What came out of them was carbon monoxide gas. There was a peephole through which Doctors Adolf Wahlmann and Bodo Gorgass could watch what went on.

The victims succumbed in from ten to fifteen minutes. The flow of gas was then cut off and the ventilating system switched on, after which attendants loaded the bodies on to trolleys and took them along to the crematorium. Since the whole installation was destroyed by the SS in 1942, we do not know exactly where this was, only that it was in the right-hand wing of the building: a photograph taken surreptitiously in 1941 shows smoke rising from this part. This smoke started to appear about half an hour after the arrival of the motor-coaches, as the people of Hadamar well knew. In conditions of low cloud there was a smell of burning flesh. The children watched what went on, and when they saw the coaches they cried: 'Another lot coming to be gassed!'

'Did the victims realize? Did they know what was going to happen to them?'

Doctor Philippi, a present member of the hospital staff, answered reflectively: 'Speaking as a psychiatrist, I would say that they certainly had an idea. Not the completely imbecile, but the rest, alas . . .'

Everyone connected with the place was sworn to silence. Men and women alike, they voluntarily undertook the work from fanaticism or cowardice; but mainly in that extraordinary spirit of submission to authority which is a German characteristic: it was enough that the Führer had ordered it. The SS set up a special, civilian section to camouflage the operation, and it was this bureaucratic machine that sent out the form-letters and the handfuls of ashes, taken at random from the heap. The office personnel were terrified by the need for secrecy. Who could trust his neighbour? A junior clerk who talked too much in a Hadamar wine-cellar on a night of heavy drinking—and how could one endure it without drinking?—was arrested and died in Oranienburg concentration camp, needless to say of 'heart failure.'

The executives, the ones who actually did the job, were less depressed. A party was held to celebrate the ten-thousandth murder, with the victim lying on a bier decked with flowers at the mouth of the crematorium furnace. Everyone had to attend, and they stood in a half-circle round the bier while one of their number delivered a mock valedictory oration and another, dressed in black, preached a mock sermon. After which the body was disposed of and bottles of beer were passed round.

'Berta was murdered!'

Karl Gerstein and his wife made no response. To them the idea was simply incredible, typical of the kind of lies the BBC was spreading to blacken the name of Germany and the Führer. They tried to reason with Kurt, but he would not be calmed.

'I intend to know what's going on,' he said, his voice rising in his agitation. 'I'm going to join the Waffen SS. That's the only way to find out.'

Leaving his brother and sister-in-law, he joined Pastor Wehr. He told him in some detail what his plan was, to try to get as far as the headquarters staff of the SS. The holy man, horrified, urgently enjoined him 'not to enter the camp of the powers of evil.'

During the next few days other friends in whom he confided said the same thing in much the same terms. All felt that it was the soul of Kurt Gerstein that was in danger, even more than his life—eternal salvation or perdition. Their apocalyptic warnings resounded in his ears.

Helmut Franz listened to him in dismay.

'According to Kurt, it was simply not possible for anyone in our day and age to live without taking the hard way and running risks. If a lot of his friends chose to consider him a renegade he would accept this for the sake of the purpose he had in mind, and even welcome it, however it might distress him, because it added to his camouflage. I thought him mad, as I had often done in the past, but at the same time I secretly admired him.'

Kurt Rehling was no less alarmed. Who would ever understand or accept his true reasons? To this Gerstein replied calmly that Rehling himself would vouch for him, since he knew what he really intended. 'Those people are so vicious that they must not and cannot win the war. They're so evil that they will bring down everyone who opposes them with themselves. The only course is to join them, to find out what their plans are and to modify them whenever possible. A person operating within the movement may be able to sidetrack orders or interpret them in his own way. That is why I have got to do what I've decided. I want to know who gives the orders and who carries them out: who sends people to the concentration camps, who maltreats them and who kills them. I want to know them all. And when the end comes I want to be one of those who will testify against them.'

*July 1967.* Berta's grave in the Saarbrücken cemetery lies amid ferns and flowering shrubs. The tombstone is inscribed with a verse from St Matthew: 'Come unto me, all ye that labour and are heavy laden, and I will give you rest.' In the same alleyway is another tombstone with the inscription, '*Meine Ehre heisst Treue* —My Honour is Loyalty.' This was the motto of the SS, and the grave is that of an SS officer who died in 1937. The two graves are only a few yards apart.

It may be that at the time when Gerstein volunteered for the Luftwaffe, a few months previously, he himself had not been altogether clear as to his motives. Had it been simply the desire to play an active part in the war? This was the view taken by his father, who never understood anything about him. The desire for reinstatement? The desire to escape his personal dilemma in the tumult of battle? Or a faint hope of adding to his knowledge of men and events? In any case, he had then been advised to try the Waffen SS, and this may well have seemed to him a portent, as though God Himself were pointing the way—the unknown God with whom he communed during his sleepless nights.

The events of recent years, from the beating-up in the theatre at Hagen to his confinement at Welzheim, had profoundly changed and hardened him. He wanted to be neither a hero nor a martyr; and he was no longer concerned with any meretricious concept of 'honour.' There could be no fair fighting in the world he lived in; no value, either, in a chivalrous martyrdom which would achieve nothing except perhaps a mention in official records. A man must be prepared to lie and cheat if need be. The task he had to perform called for nothing less than self-immolation, the total subjection of his true self.

Thoughts such as these must already have been in his mind, but it was the death of Berta—a relative, an innocent victim if ever there was one—that settled the matter. Gerstein now saw his way clearly. On 10 March 1941 he applied for admission to the Waffen SS, and on 15 March he was accepted and sent to Hamburg for a training course. The double S monogram, symbol of his alliance with the enemy, was to gleam on his collar for the rest of his life.

Extract from Gerstein's *Report* (see p. 281): (see p. 281)

'I wanted only one thing: to see to the bottom of this witch-pot and then tell the people what I would have seen there—even if my life was then threatened.

'I had not to scruple: I had been myself twice betrayed by SD agents, who had infiltrated into the most exclusive circles of the Protestant Church, and prayed close to me.

'I thought: "What you are able to do, I can do it better than you do," and I volunteered as SS. I was helped in doing so by the fact that my own sister in law, Berta Ebeling, had been murdered at Hadamar. I could be introduced by two Gestapo agents, who had been in charge of my case and was easily taken in the Waffen SS. Once a SS man had told me: "Idealist as much as you are, you should be a fanatic member of the Party." '

*April 1967*. In conversation with former Kriminalsekretär Ernst Zerrer:

'So, Herr Zerrer, you were one of Gerstein's sponsors with the SS?'

Zerrer, with a vigorous gesture: 'No, it wasn't I. How could I recommend a man with his record?' In a low but meaningful voice: 'They must have been very high up.'

'Schellenberg, for instance?'

'Someone like that.'

Walter Schellenberg, who died in 1952, was a leading member of the SS who became head of the Secret Service and Hitler's personal adviser on security matters. Born in Saarbrücken, where Gerstein spent much of his youth, he and Kurt were of the same generation. Judge Gerstein refers to him in a letter to his son:

'I talked to [Bartolo father-in-law of Kurt's brother Alfred] about your Wintershall affair. But I had no thought of pleading with him on your behalf, which in any case was unnecessary, since that matter is now in hand and will end in your favour. He told me a most interesting story. It was a member of his old student corps, Schellenberg of Saarbrücken, who lured the two British agents close to the Dutch frontier and had them arrested.[1] It seems to have been a very dangerous business for Schellenberg, who got a bullet through his hat while another singed his overcoat. He was sent for by the Führer, who awarded him the Iron Cross, First Class. Schellenberg is under an obligation to Bartolo, who came to his rescue when he was in financial difficulties and looked after him for nine months, during which he acted as Bartolo's assistant. He's now in the Gestapo. After the Dutch affair he spent two days at Bartolo's house.'

The date of this letter, 27 November—that is to say, only eighteen days after the Venlo incident, and at a time when the details were known only to the actual participants and to a few people on the highest level—is an indication of the close relations existing between the Gerstein clan and Schellenberg, a man who had found high favour with Hitler and whose influence was very great. It is certainly not unreasonable to suppose that it was exercised on behalf of Kurt Gerstein.

The remark, 'Idealist as much as you are, you should be a fanatic member of the Party,' may well have come from Schellen-

1 This was the famous 'Venlo incident.' In November 1939 two British Army Intelligence officers, Captain S. Payne Best and Major R. H. Stevens, were tricked by a pretended anti-Hitler conspiracy and kidnapped on Dutch territory. A Dutch officer escorting them was killed. The British officers spent the war in a POW camp.

berg. A Doctor of Law, he belonged to the group of intellectuals enrolled in the Security Service, of which one of the leading spirits was Otto Ohlendorf, that terrifying professor of economics who ended up as the leader of a butcher-commando on the eastern front. The whole Nazi system was based on the principle of not letting talent go to waste but making full use of all that was available. In this respect the SS took even greater risks than the Party itself. As an élite corps, modelled on the Jesuits, it sought to attract only the 'cream.' An SS chief who succeeded in bringing in a man of Gerstein's obvious potentialities had as much reason to congratulate himself as a gangster who has suborned his chief rival's top hatchet-man, or—perhaps this is a more apt comparison—a missionary who has converted the most obdurate of heretics.

SS Stormtrooper Kurt Gerstein went for training to the school of the 'Germania' division, in Hamburg–Langenhorn. He had done no military service. His instructor was Sergeant Robert Weigelt, a professional soldier from Hesse whose every thought and aspiration was conditioned by his devotion to the Army.

At the sight of Gerstein, as he said later, Weigelt shook his head, feeling instinctively that this was far from the ideal soldier, and more probably the opposite. He took him to draw his kit and found that to clothe him tidily was impossible—'unless Gerstein was doing it on purpose.' Nothing fitted him. His cap sat awkwardly on his head, his belt sagged, his uniform hung in folds on his tall, lean frame. All this might have been borne if the man had been capable of marching correctly, but he was not. He threw the whole squad out. Weigelt, giving him solo training in the barrack yard, was bound to admit that he did his best. The strange but undeniable fact is that volunteer Kurt Gerstein was incapable of keeping step. 'I was always out of line,' as he himself said.

This was something that in the ordinary course of events should have been reported, but Weigelt could not bring himself to do so. He had in a sense become Gerstein's captive, as he was shortly to become his hostage. The secret lay in Gerstein's aptitude for coming to terms with simple people, his friendliness, his complete absence of 'side' and his interest and sympathy for other men's problems. Weigelt's heart was melted. He did not report the matter, and he arranged for Gerstein to visit the sick-bay on the day his group was inspected, so that his inability to do the goosestep was never discovered.

The group was composed of university graduates, doctors, engineers. Among them was an Austrian named Kaltenbrunner, a personal friend of Hitler who was destined to succeed Heydrich as head of the entire German police force.

At the end of a month the group was transferred to Arnhem, in Holland, for further instruction. When they de-trained one of the party was found to be missing, namely Gerstein. After marching the rest to the barracks Sergeant Weigelt kept watch by the guard-house. Eventually Gerstein appeared, riding a bicycle! He had, it seemed, taken advantage of the momentary confusion at the station to slip away on a visit to some friend or other. As the furious sergeant strode up to him he murmured: 'Don't bawl me out here. I've brought you some *Schnapps* and cigarettes. Let's go inside.'

This was the beginning of the conspiratorial relationship between Gerstein and Weigelt, one which grew steadily deeper without the sergeant's ever realizing the appalling risks he ran.

He was interviewed by the author of this book in Kassel, in April 1968. His wife had advised him not to consent to the meeting, but still he came, a lean, bespectacled man with a bony chin.

'I was made to work in a Donetz coal-mine,' he said. 'Some-body gave me away, and I was grilled by the NKVD, the Russian secret police, and sent to Siberia—all because I was an SS man, doing my duty as a German. I escaped three times, and the last time I nearly got to India, but they caught me every time and brought me back. I wasn't released till '49. And the state I was in—well, look at this.' We were talking in the Swiss tavern at the Kassel railway station, amid the smell of cooking, the clatter of dishes and the popping of corks, with the voice of an unhappy street-singer trying to compete with the noise. Weigelt pulled up his trouser and rolled down his sock to disclose a scarred and withered leg. 'And mark you, I was a regular soldier,' he went on, as though to forestall any charge that he might have been something else. 'Kurt . . . Yes, I remember him all right. I was always putting him on the sick-list. There was nothing of the soldier about him, and I knew that wasn't what he was there for. He was what you might call an ultra-Christian. I don't know much about what he did, but he was a fighter in his own way.'

*Arnhem, April 1941.* The industrialist J. H. Ubbink, of Doesburg, got a telephone call from Kurt Gerstein, whose acquaintance he had made in Protestant Church circles. Gerstein said that he was in Arnhem and would like to come and see him, but—

'But what?'

'I'm in uniform—SS.'

This made it a matter for thought. Holland was an occupied country. Ubbink risked compromising himself with his own people if he were visited by a German in uniform, particularly the most hated uniform of all. Nevertheless he said:

'All right—seeing that it's you.'

When Gerstein arrived he said immediately, pointing to the uniform:

'This doesn't mean a thing. The man inside it hasn't changed.'

He went on to tell Ubbink exactly what he was doing, and why. They knelt together in prayer, and then he asked his host to summon a gathering of his family and friends, whom he addressed as follows:

'We Germans have got to lose this war. Better a hundred Versailles Treaties than that the present gang of criminals should remain in power. What does it profit a nation to gain the whole world if it lose its own soul?'

The underground work of Kurt Gerstein, mining engineer, had begun.

Ubbink lent him a copy of Hermann Rauschning's *Hitler Speaks*, that account of conversations with Hitler, in the days when he was still fighting for power, which reveals all the hatreds and obsessions fermenting in his mind. The book was banned in

Germany. Gerstein said of it, 'It is only too true,' and he asked to
be allowed to keep the copy to show to his friends of the Confessional Church when he returned to Germany from Holland.

His method of smuggling it in shows his ingenuity in such
matters. He carried the book in an envelope addressed to Himmler,
together with a letter saying that he had picked it up in a compartment on a Dutch train, and suggesting that the question of
how it came to be in circulation should be investigated. If the
book was found in his possession he had his answer ready. His
method of passing it on to Pastor Rehling, when he got back to
Hagen, was equally circumspect. He thrust it into the letter-box
at the Presbytery, rang the bell and hurriedly departed. Rehling
thought for a long time that it had been planted on him by the
Gestapo.

\*

Sergeant Weigelt went on talking while he sipped his drink in
the Swiss tavern.

'At Arnhem he was never there when he was wanted. I've got
a photo of the group, and he's the only one who's missing. One
evening he vanished just before lights-out. I had to cover up for
him. When he got back he said he'd been visiting an Embassy or
something of the kind. You never knew what he'd be doing next.
And yet I trusted him. It was I who got him through the test
at the end of his training period.'

Herbert Weisselberg, who was with us, produced a document.
It was Gerstein's examination report, studded with the words
'Good' and 'Very good,' except in the case of 'Gymnastics,'
which Weigelt, having no choice but to be candid, described as
'awkward.' But his general summing-up amounted to a panegyric:
'Loyal, submissive and good-humoured, Gerstein has all the
necessary qualities for the duties that await him. He shows both
ability and stamina, expresses himself admirably, is disciplined
and resolute.'

Weigelt looked it over, nodding, and we chose this moment to
produce the order for Gerstein's arrest issued by the Gestapo in
1938. The effect was sensational. After reading the first lines

Weigelt started, glanced apprehensively at us, wiped his spectacles, went on reading and finally leaned forward with his arms on the table and his head bowed in an attitude of total dismay.

'You mean to say he'd been arrested! A man sent to me for training. I can't believe it.'

He sat there thinking it over, only now realizing the risks he had run twenty-seven years earlier, when unwittingly he had covered up for a man under surveillance by the Gestapo.

'Well, of course, the SS was different. I suppose that was what I was there for, to make things look proper and legal where the head office was concerned.'

His manner towards us changed. Assuming that we, too, had been in one way or another connected with the SS, he inquired after former comrades. Could we put him in touch with X, and did we know what had happened to Y? Of the men he mentioned, one had been hanged, another had gone abroad, a third had changed his name, and a fourth had simply vanished. As for Kurt—

'You say he's dead, but I can't believe it. He's too clever for that. For Kurt to be dead, just like that—it doesn't make sense.'

It was dark by the time we left the tavern. He got his old car out of the car-park and, putting his hands on my shoulders, breathed alcoholically into my face.

'We're pals, aren't we? . . . The SS weren't as black as they're painted.'

*Letter from Kurt to Elfriede Gerstein, 26 April 1941*: 'It's a queer sort of life I have to live . . . I'm often reminded of Welzheim, where a lot of things were hideously like what they are here . . . Yet I'm not sorry to be here. It has broadened my outlook and clarified my thinking. I often think of Nietzsche's phrase, which I used to quote to you: "Live dangerously." We shall be leaving here soon, perhaps for Oranienburg, a name that fills me with profoundly mixed feelings.'

The excellent reports on Gerstein, added to his impressive university record, brought him to the notice of SS headquarters, which is perhaps what he was counting on. A senior officer[1] sent for him in Arnhem and told him that he was to be posted to the Waffen SS Institute of Hygiene in Berlin. Serious problems of sanitation had arisen in the concentration camps with which his combination of engineering and medical knowledge rendered him peculiarly fitted to deal. His duties were to come under the general heading of 'Decontamination'—which, as the event was to show, was a word with many meanings.

'Even today,' he was to write later in his *Report* (see p. 282), 'I believe that a chance, strangely resembling the providence, put me in a position to look at where I did want to see through. Among hundreds possible jobs I was offered right the post which made the most close to the field I was the most interested in. This seemed as more incredible than, in the past, I had been several times interned by the Gestapo and SD for anti-nazi activity. My chiefs knew this through the denunciation of the Party. Truly, the SD and their chief the RSHA did sleep in this case and took the very wrong man.'

1 Probably General Karl Genzken, head of the Waffen SS Health Service.

## Chapter 7

# THE INSTITUTE OF HYGIENE

THE town of Oranienburg, eighteen miles north of Berlin, was the nerve-centre of the SS. Gerstein was sent there to attend a course at the 'School of Decontamination.' He was tattooed with the letters AB, blood-group IV. His SS number was 417,460.

*

The news that 'Vati' had joined the SS caused a sensation among the Protestants of Westphalia.

Dr J. Gerckens (1964): 'I was in the Catholic library in Hagen. An officer in SS uniform entered, and I could scarcely believe my eyes when I recognized Gerstein. He came up to me, took my hand and said simply: "Don't worry, I haven't changed." And I believed him.'

Pastor Niemöller, when the news reached him in his concentration camp, exclaimed: 'But—but he isn't even a Nazi!' Nevertheless the fact was undeniable, and Gerstein himself informed people who did not know of it. He wrote to the eighteen-year-old Herbert Eickhoff to ask what the younger generation thought of him. What they thought can be conveyed in a very few words: 'What on earth does he look like?' They did not doubt that Vati himself was the same man. They were simply amused at the thought of him in SS uniform.

Ernst Weisenfeld, a former member of the Protestant Youth, now living in Paris, had the following to say in 1967: 'I called him by phone in October or November 1941, when I happened to be in Berlin. We arranged to meet near the Tiergarten. He arrived on the dot, as I had been sure he would, and at the sight of him I burst out laughing. So did he, and we both knew why. It was that SS uniform. His cap was too wide for his face.

Altogether he was a comical figure. We walked through the Tiergarten, talking. He was still pretty new to the SS and he hadn't yet made up his mind about it. I remember him saying: "You know, there are some extraordinary characters in it," by which he seemed to mean diabolical characters who needed to be carefully studied, and also misguided idealists whose attitude to life was totally different from his own. It horrified him to find men whom he detested in charge of the machine, possessors of such immense power and exercising it with such cold-blooded passion. But it also fascinated him.'

Gerstein had his own passion, as much a part of his being as his physical need of sweet foods. It was his insatiable curiosity, his passionate desire to know. If he was Christian in his love of his fellow-men, he was Faust the experimenter as well.

The SS, or the 'Blackshirts' . . . The poet Heine, writing i the first half of the previous century, had sensed its coming. 'There is being born in Germany a black cult which in a positive delirium of the imagination is propounding a creed of *Deutschheit, Volkstum und Ureichelfrasstum*[1] and conceiving fantastic methods of putting it into practice. Its votaries are ideologists who have read everything and enlist all their encyclopaedic knowledge in the service of this barbarous stupidity. They are scholars, critics, historians. They can determine with absolute exactitude the degree of racial affiliation which, under their new order, will cause you to be eliminated. All that remains in dispute is the method of extermination.' (Lucca manuscript, 1829.)

The letters SS stand for *Schutzstaffel*, meaning, roughly, a defence force. The functions of this body were as ill defined as its name. Created out of nothing, it came by degrees to incorporate everything. From being simply a bodyguard in the early days of the Nazi movement, it became, after the suppression of Röhm's Brownshirts in 1934, the Praetorian Guard of the regime, into which were gradually absorbed the Intelligence Services, the management of the concentration camps and the police. It was the most distinguished of all the bodies incorporated within the

[1] Germanness, race-consciousness and (roughly) primitive acorn-devouring.

98

Reich, an élite corps to which it was an honour to belong, and as time went on it became filled with 'idealists' in search of a crusade. At the beginning of the war it gave birth to the Waffen SS, a para-military force that came under the strategic command of the Army but in all other respects was administered by the SS. By the end of the war some 900,000 men, partly volunteers and partly 'ethnically German' conscripts, had been enlisted in the Waffen SS, which gained a remarkable reputation for both soldierly virtues and ferocious savagery. The burning of the French village of Oradour-sur-Glane, and the massacre of the entire population, carried out by the 'Das Reich' division under General Lammerding, is but one episode in its record of barbarous achievements.

By systematic looting—in particular, the confiscation of Jewish property—and by the exploitation of slave-labour, the SS constituted itself a capitalist power within the Reich, doing business with other capitalist powers, such as Krupp, Siemens and I.G. Farben. The range of its activities was constantly being extended. Commercial undertakings of one sort and another were set up in the twenty larger concentration camps and their 160 affiliated labour camps. The SS was prepared to manufacture and sell anything from stone-masonry to mineral water. It had its own values, its own modes of thought, its literature, art, style of furniture and courts of justice; also its own humour, which, with no play on words intended, could be nothing but 'black.' It had its own quirks of language, borrowed from Himmler, who borrowed from Hitler, who borrowed from nothing but his own provincial, middle-class origins. It had its singers and its men of learning. A large number of scientific or pseudo-scientific cults and establishments sprang up in the shadow of the death's-head cap which was its symbol: the *Ahnenerbe* (Ancestral Heritage), *Lebensborn* (Well of Life), Institutes of Health and Hygiene and so on. In short, the SS was a galaxy in a constant state of expansion.

Nor was there any limit to its thirst for power. Had the Third Reich won the war, the SS by its own logic would have been impelled within a short time to eliminate the one obstacle still standing in its path, the Führer. The tragical farce of National Socialism would then have achieved its apogee with one of the stupidest men of the century, Heinrich Himmler, at the head of a world-empire.

Himmler, the supreme head of the SS, was the child of nullity and the father of nothing, thrust by the accident of circumstance into a position that conferred upon him a strange lustre to which he made no contribution of his own. A schoolmaster and the son of a schoolmaster, he was a man who solemnly passed on book-learning enriched by nothing but his own pedantry. He modelled the SS on the Society of Jesus. He set up scientific foundations while at the same time evoking the mythology of the past: Valhalla, runic tablets, legends of the Holy Roman Empire. He was quite incapable of thinking of himself as a new man in a new world released from the trappings of history. Indeed, he believed himself to be the reincarnation of Henry the Fowler, the German monarch who was the contemporary of Charlemagne, and in his castle at Quedlinburg, near Paderborn, he presided over gatherings of devotees who comported themselves in the manner of the Middle Ages as conceived by a writer of Gothic romances.

Except for his romantic imagination and his enormous industry he was a man of second-rate qualities, both good and bad. He was not particularly cruel, and indeed he was generally amiable in his private dealings. He was fond of his family, and being (like Hitler) a former Catholic he had twinges of conscience when he was unfaithful to his wife. Unlike the majority of SS leaders, he was reputed to be honest, and this bourgeois virtue was at the root of his popularity with the SS as a whole. But above all he was *der treue Heinrich*, the faithful follower of Hitler, and for him this was the beginning and the end of life.

From the day when he carried a banner in the abortive Munich *putsch* of 1923, Himmler had ceased to have a life of his own. He became Hitler's puppet, responding to every pull on the strings, not merely submissive but as rapturously acquiescent as an adoring mistress. Every order was meticulously carried out, and if Himmler had anything of his own to propose a word from Hitler sufficed to alter or dismiss it. Professor Gebhardt, his personal physician, described him as 'the typical second-in-command, who takes upon himself the odium of unpleasant duties, precisely as, while Mahomet smiled, the Khalif executed.' At the end of the war Schellenberg and a few others hinted to Himmler that the time had come for him to play his own hand and dispose of Hitler in order to save Germany. Despite the temptation, and indeed the necessity, his decision was so long delayed that when it came it could hardly be called a betrayal. The truth is that if Himmler had rebelled his rebellion would have been that of a faithful follower. He would have preserved the ashes of the 'greatest brain of all time' in a golden urn and done homage to it in the crypt at Quedlinburg, as he did to the Fowler.

Once his place in the scheme of things was determined, Himmler never departed from it, in small matters or in large. Larger matters being Hitler's province, it is in matters of detail that we discern Himmler's sinister, ubiquitous hand. He it was who marked the photographs of his SS men and their fiancées with green pencil to indicate the features that did not seem to him wholly Aryan. It was he who sent mystical missions to the East and who at the height of the war ordered the removal of the tombstone of a forgotten Hohenstaufen emperor who had died in Italy to a safer place. He was much concerned with matters of diet. Gebhardt tells us: 'The SS was the only body that had porridge for breakfast, accompanied by mineral water. Some of his experiments were terrible. All the divisions at the front were suddenly forbidden to drink anything but water . . . He wore out his personal staff. He insisted on the use of live ammunition during SS manoeuvres even in peacetime, with the result that there were fatal casualties on every field day.' And Gebhardt concludes: 'Himmler was never interesting.'

The empire built up by this meticulous lunatic was of such labyrinthine complexity that it can be depicted only in diagrammatic form. Enough to say that it consisted of a dozen major departments, with innumerable sub-divisions, of which only three need be mentioned here: the RSHA (Reichs Sicherheits Haupt Amt), which was responsible for the internal security of the Reich, including counter-espionage and the Gestapo; the WVHA ([SS] Wirtschafts und Verwaltungs Haupt Amt), which dealt with matters of finance and administration and ran the concentration camps; and the SSFHA (SS Führungs Haupt Amt), which was the head office of the SS and directly responsible for the Waffen SS. The Waffen SS Institute of Hygiene thus came directly under the SSFHA, but it also came indirectly under the WVHA and under General Ernst Grawitz, the head of the SS and police health services.

The Institute of Hygiene, which occupied a large building in the Knesebeckstrasse, in the Charlottenburg district of Berlin, worked at high pressure and to a rigid timetable. Like everything bearing the imprint of the SS, it was constantly being expanded, so that eventually it employed 25 full-time scientists with 200 assistants. Its numerous research departments included chemistry, parasitology, bacteriology, meteorology and a department of 'water hygiene' presided over by a Doctor Krantz.

It was to the last of these that Kurt Gerstein was appointed, in June 1941.

*Bonn, April 1968.* Dr Fritz Krantz, aged sixty-seven, former Hauptsturmführer (captain), seemed somewhat taken aback by my visit.

'How did you find me?'

The answer to this was, in the first place, that he is mentioned in Gerstein's *Report*; secondly, that another ex-Waffen SS officer had told me that he believed he was running some kind of 'natural history' business in the region of Bonn; and thirdly, that he was in the Bonn telephone directory.

He listened in silence, on the defensive like so many former members of the SS, not openly hostile but decidedly reserved. He was living in a small detached house in a neglected garden, a gloomy place with dilapidated shutters, which might have been uninhabited, rather like something in an English detective story. Nevertheless it was full of 'trophies' of one kind and another: rock samples, cases of specimens, albums, stuffed animals. Doctor Krantz came of a line of mineralogists going back to 1850.

'I joined the SS out of idealism. In those days we were all proud of being in the SS. We admired Hitler, who often visited these parts. The proprietor of the Hotel Dreesen, at Bad Godesberg, was a friend of his, and he had a permanent suite there. He mixed with people like any other hotel guest, except that one couldn't smoke when he was present. He was particularly nice to children, and that made him very popular ... And by the time I'd seen the other side of the SS I couldn't get out. I wasn't a hero. We were proud of being in the SS—and suddenly we found that we were criminals!'

Doctor Krantz had never got over it. His solace was to dig up stories of atrocities committed by the other side which might in some sort extenuate his own dubious past. As for Gerstein:

'His revolver belt sagged and his cap was always crooked. He really was a disgrace to the Service. I was always saying to him: "Do for God's sake try and smarten yourself up." I first met him in 1941, the day he joined the Institute. He came into my room and gave the Hitler salute, quite correctly. I was engaged in hydrological research, and he was to be my assistant. We took samples of water for chemical and bacteriological testing and reported on them. It entailed a good deal of travelling. I remember one time we went to a police prison north of Berlin where the prisoners went out to work. They didn't seem unhappy; they spent the day in the open air and were better treated than in many places. We took our samples and the governor invited us to lunch. There was a splendid haunch of venison, and Gerstein had two helpings. As we were leaving something rather interesting happened. We passed some prisoners and Gerstein dropped a pack of cigarettes. It looked to me as though he had done it on purpose. When we were starting on our analysis, back in Berlin, he suddenly said: "I dropped my cigarettes. I hope they haven't got anyone into trouble." Anyway, they didn't get *him* into trouble.

'There was a phrase that was constantly on his lips: "Man must be honourable, helpful and good." I liked him very much as a person. His scientific and general knowledge was enormously useful to him. He was a qualified engineer, a mining engineer, what's more, and also a doctor. An exceptionally capable man. The Chief took a great fancy to him.'

The Chief was Joachim Mrugowsky, aged thirty-six, the head of the Institute, a lecturer at Berlin University and a long-standing member of the Nazi Party, which accounted for his rapid promotion. He was a tall, thin man with tight lips, ears that stood out and hard, penetrating eyes in which there glowed a light of almost savage energy. In his zeal he was another Himmler, and like Himmler he was always on the look-out for ideas and always ready to carry them to extremes. Also like Himmler, he had bees in his bonnet. He set up a special section in the Institute for the purpose of proving by statistics that epidemics were 'absolutely cyclical' in their nature. On one occasion he sent Gerstein and Krantz into Poland to interview a scientist who claimed to have invented a water-divining machine. ('We thought it unreliable,' said Krantz.)

Mrugowsky was respected by all his staff. He was a fair-minded man, disposed to favour the more industrious but sympathetic to those in poor health, skilful at mixing leniency with severity. Though his name was Polish, he refused to change it. 'If I found that one of my ancestors had changed his German name to Polish, I'd certainly go back to the German,' he said. 'As it is, I'm sticking to what I've got.' They liked him for this. In general, he was a demon for work, remaining in his office until late at night, dictating notes, drafting reports, forwarding endless proposals to the Reichsführer SS, that is to say, Himmler.

'He made the mistake,' said Krantz gloomily, 'of tackling all kinds of things that were not his business.'

A somewhat different picture is offered by François Bayle, the French naval doctor and neuro-psychiatrist who examined Joachim Mrugowsky at Nuremberg.

'The subject is virulent, capable of a malice that is generally concealed, of a permanently vicious temperament in which latent animosity is deeply embedded. He is deceptively calm in appearance, so that one might not suspect that his placid manner conceals a high degree of pugnacity, or that he is capable of being carried away with fury. His real character is excitable, vindictive, tenacious, touchy and excessively recalcitrant; unsociable and strongly individualistic. His terminal rages render him coldly malicious and dangerous, and it is in this way that he exteriorizes his enormous accumulation of venom.'

If Mrugowsky modelled himself on Himmler, Kurt Gerstein, when he joined the Institute, modelled himself on Mrugowsky, at least where the intensity and range of his work were concerned. He had an initial handicap to overcome. Whereas the majority of the scientific staff were, like Mrugowsky, army officers on the active or the reserve list, he himself was a civilian plunged into this hierarchy without having proved himself. Nor was he a true scientist in the eyes of his colleagues; a mere mining engineer could not be classed with a chemist or biologist. Although he was probably the only member of the SS capable of reciting long passages from the *Iliad* or the *Odyssey*, he was received with a faintly suspicious hostility by men very conscious of their own unique merits. One of them, Sturmbannführer (Major) Dr Erwin Ding, an ambitious person anxious to curry favour with the Chief, saw in him a possible rival and was not slow to proclaim the fact.

Gerstein had joined the Institute at precisely the right time.

The Russian campaign, launched in June 1941, was creating an appalling problem, that of typhus. By the end of that year 150,000 cases had been reported, 10,000 in the German Army. The growing epidemic was a matter of the utmost concern, a 'front-line priority,' and one that came directly within Mrugowsky's jurisdiction. It was becoming a nightmare to him, for he could not this time resort to the drastic measures he had used at Buchenwald concentration camp on a previous occasion. 'In the spring of 1939 [according to Doctor Ding], we had an outbreak of typhoid fever with which Professor Mrugowsky, as chief sanitary expert of the SS, was called upon to deal. He ordered that the most serious cases, those with no hope of recovery, were to be killed off with soporifics to conserve our scanty medical supplies.'

Mrugowsky, in short, was at his wits' end and the man who could help him out would earn his undying gratitude. It was an assignment that exactly suited Gerstein.

The problem was one of decontamination, basically of water supplies, but also of garments, cooking utensils and everything else. Gerstein, aided by two of his former pupils, Armin Peters and Horst Dickten, proceeded to show what he could do. They devised, first, a de-lousing apparatus for uniforms, blankets and underclothes, using high-pressure steam, which destroyed not only the lice but also their excrement, and secondly a mobile water-filter unit. Both were approved by the Army and proved highly successful. They were mass-produced at factories in Munich and Celle and rushed off to the front. Mrugowsky was in raptures.

But this was only the beginning. The team of Gerstein and Armin Peters was later to produce a floating pump for use against mosquitoes, a new type of hospital bed and special de-lousing vehicles. Gerstein was summoned as a sanitation expert to Bremen and Hamburg after the heavy RAF raids on those towns. The range of his activities was enormously extended. He ceased to be merely a back-room boy and was made responsible for manufacture and supply. He spent his life on trains, travelling the length and breadth of Germany and occupied Europe—Brussels, Riga, Helsinki, Asnières and Puteaux in France, where his decontamination trucks were fitted out—signing contracts, inspecting the product, speeding up delivery. The result was an unquestionable improvement in sanitary conditions at the front; and Mrugowsky, who got the credit, came to regard him as a positive genius of sanitation. He was promoted Untersturmführer (sub-lieutenant) SS, skipping the non-commissioned grades.

Mrugowsky's secretary, Frau Virk, was instructed never to question Lieutenant Gerstein's requirements. Special authorizations, safe-conducts, reserved compartments, official cars—he was to have whatever he asked for. A special relationship grew up between Mrugowsky and his blue-eyed boy, not one of genuine friendship but something that looked like it. Each had his own motives: Mrugowsky to establish a personal link with this most valuable assistant, Gerstein to make his chief so dependent on him that he would be able to ' draw his claws'—*entschärfen* was the word he used.

With all the prestige of the SS behind him, he made full use of it. *Frechheit siegt*, said the Nazis. 'Sheer cheek pays off.' He cultivated the SS manner, the harsh, arrogant voice, and could be brutal when he had to. He also got his personal friends into the Institute, men he could rely on. These are their respective testimonies:

Robert Weigelt: 'Before leaving Arnhem for Berlin, he said to me: "Robert, I need you. One of these days you're going to join me." At the time I didn't think anything of it, but then I was suddenly transferred to Berlin and he was on the platform to meet me—an officer! He laughed and said: "Well, I promised, didn't I?" (Sergeant Weigelt, the professional soldier, was invaluable in bringing a show of military order into the Gerstein outfit—the heel-click, the soldierly salute, the correctly faked document, the neatly covered tracks.)

Horst Dickten: 'As a result of a wound I was partly paralysed in the right side and unfit for front-line service. He fetched me out of the Sprottau hospital in 1941 and took me straight to the Institute in Berlin, where we worked together.'

Günter Dickten: 'My unit had been brought back from Russia to re-form at the Glau-Treppin artillery school. Kurt Gerstein turned up one day in a car and called on my commanding officer. He produced a letter from SS Doctor Grawitz according to which SS Stormtrooper Günter Dickten was to be instantly seconded to Berlin for medical studies. Anyone familiar with German Army routine will know that this was contrary to all regulations. An order of that sort had to go through the proper channels. But my battery commander was so completely taken in that he let me go, and Gerstein took me away with him. He had got hold of an official stamp and got some underling to forge a signature. If it had ever come out he would have been court-martialled.'

Armin Peters. Gerstein ran into him in Berlin and at once proposed that he should join him. Peters, who was a Luftwaffe meteorologist, refused. Gerstein said nothing, but shortly afterwards Peters was sent on leave with instructions to place himself at the disposal of the Institute of Hygiene. He had to obey, and he was installed in an office of his own in Rangsdorf, Berlin— needless to say, under 'Vati's' supervision.

The last and humblest member of Gerstein's team was an eighteen-year-old Alsatian, Fredrich Geissert.

*October 1967.* Geissert, now in his forties, is a small, plump man, vivacious but not very happy. He has an unimportant job in the small Rhineland town where he lives, but his real interest is in palaeontology. He attends scientific congresses and writes papers for learned societies. The cellar of his house is filled with the fossils of plants and animals that he and his family have collected in the region.

'I was at Oranienburg,' he said, 'training to be a car and truck driver. The first time I saw Gerstein I didn't know who he was. We were on parade, all my company, and an officer walked across the parade-ground and we all noticed him. I don't know why. He didn't do anything. But we all thought, "That's an extraordinary type." He was tall and he looked older than his age. He didn't look at all like a soldier—an obvious civilian in uniform.

'I'd been studying to be a pharmacist in civilian life, and two months later I was posted to the Institute of Hygiene. They asked me what sort of job I'd like, and I said I didn't want anything there, I wanted to go to the front. They suggested I might look after guinea-pigs or rats, but I wasn't keen. Then the officer we'd seen in Oranienburg came in.

' "How would you like to work for me?" he asked.

'I accepted at once.

'He had me in for a private interview, which was pretty unusual in the German Army. All the same, a few days later I again said I'd like to go to the front. He surprised me very much by asking:

' "Have you had any leave since you joined?"

'I said no.

' "Then you'd better go home and think it over. We'll talk about it when you get back."

'Well, the end of it was, I went to work in Gerstein's outfit. I was with him for about a year, acting as liaison, mainly, between him and his numerous contacts in Berlin. But because I spoke French he sent me once to Paris, to the Pasteur Institute, in connection with anti-typhus vaccine.

'I've forgotten almost everything about the people I met at that time, even their names. He's the one man I remember. He had an extraordinary personality. When I argued about his orders, as I often did, he said: "Geissert, you're a bad soldier," and then added, "not that I blame you."

'He was pretty excitable. He carried his head high, coughed a lot, breathed loudly. As a rule he was nice to everyone, but he could be tough when necessary. There was a young botanist, the nephew of an SS general, who made jokes about him, the way he walked and dressed. Gerstein had him on the carpet and gave him a dressing-down, and the young man came out completely crushed. He was carrying a book by Michurin which Gerstein had lent him as a peace-offering. It was an astonishing thing to have done, even dangerous—Michurin was a Russian scientist.

'Gerstein made no bones about saying things that other people didn't dare say—sly digs at the high-ups: "How the hell do they expect to win the war if they go on like this?" That kind of thing. He was always doing it. And he would leave important papers lying about on his desk. One time I saw a sheaf of lists of people in concentration camps, a great pile of them, there must have been tens of thousands of names. It started me wondering if he'd done it on purpose, because otherwise I didn't see how it could have happened, knowing how secret those things were. It's only quite recently that I've found out who he really was ... Well, anyway, I know now that when Gerstein took me in he saved me from getting involved in all that filth, the camps and the exterminations and so on. I'll always be grateful.'

Not once as he told his story had Fritz Geissert mentioned the SS. He simply said 'the Army' or 'the military.' But we both knew that he meant the Waffen SS and finally he took the plunge.

'You're wondering why, as an Alsatian, I should have volunteered to join them. Well, you see, I was seventeen and German was my native language. I wasn't the only one. After the start of the war against Russia they set up a recruiting centre in the market-place: bands, flags, speeches—the lot. It got me, that's all. I felt it was my duty to join. Later I discovered what it was all about. I paid, all right. I threw away the best years of my youth, and even now, twenty-five years later, I still feel the moral and physical effects.'

Gerstein's conquest of the Institute was almost complete. The scientists who had been disposed to look down on him were, with one exception, won over by his capacity for work and the success he achieved. The exception was Major Ding, who alone resisted his growing influence. To Ding, Gerstein was a sinister figure, a dangerous man, by no means as useful as he seemed. He opposed his promotion to officer rank, and even when he himself had been appointed head of the typhus experimental station at Buchenwald concentration camp (which was to make him famous) he continued to refer to Gerstein as 'the enemy.' A discerning man.

But otherwise Gerstein gave his colleagues no cause for resentment or jealousy. He sought to harm no one; on the contrary, he was noted for his open-handedness. Extravagant generosity had always been a part of his nature, and it was one that now served to turn away malice. He bought for the pleasure of giving; but in doing so he got back.

As had happened in his youth-camp days, he would appear at the Institute loaded with gifts: French books, bottles of liqueur, stockings and scent for the typists, shoes, even fur coats. A lot of his spare time abroad was spent going round the shops: antiques in Brussels, pictures in Paris, amber in Riga. He bought in batches and presently in car-loads. He loaded a whole Christmas tree with the proceeds of his foraging. This insidious lavishness penetrated to the highest quarters. According to Dickten, it was through him that General Grawitz, head of the SS Health Service and Mrugowsky's superior, acquired from Speer's

Ministry certain premises next door to the Institute that he had long had his eye on. Nor did Mrugowsky, a man with a fondness for the good things of life, fail to benefit. His farm in the country owed much to the invaluable Gerstein, who now and then constituted himself inspector of his geese and chickens.

The man of extravagant gifts was also a man of memorable sayings. He could always find words to turn away an indiscreet question or prevent its being asked. He was known as a man of wise counsel, and his office became an SS confessional where occasionally enormous truths were disclosed which he affected to treat as commonplaces. 'Better ask Gerstein,' was a phrase which became a keynote in his official career.

So, what did it matter if the Lieutenant was something of an eccentric, as he undeniably was? The way he dressed, for example; and his habit of raising his uniform cap to ladies, instead of saluting in a correct, soldierly manner. The frantic busy-ness which no one understood and which he himself had coolly summed up in the words: 'One needs to do so many things that no one can ever be sure what one is up to.' And again, his frequent absences. 'For God's sake, Kurt,' telegraphed the worried Weigelt, 'be sure you're here for the general meeting.'

Weigelt: 'He was always doing silly things.'

Doctor Krantz: 'I never ceased to wonder how a man like that came to be in the SS.'

Geissert: 'We used to say, "Gerstein's a queer fish." '

Many sayings and incidents have been recalled which throw a light on the character of the man. On the subject of air raids, for example, he said: 'We ought to be delighted that our towns are being flattened. It gives us a chance to rebuild them in a sensible way.'

He came back from Paris with a life-sized papier mâché male figure which he installed in his office, draped in a smock with a vase of flowers in front of it. When one of the cleaners asked what it was, he said that it was a friend of his who had been killed at the front. The lady's expostulations were repeated throughout the building. 'Really! It's one thing to honour a dead friend, but to embalm him—!'

He carried a clothes-brush in his revolver-holster. 'The hardware's too heavy,' he said to Dickten. And Geissert, during one of his absences, came upon his service pistol, a Walter 7.65 automatic, in a drawer of his desk.

The Institute overlooked all this and much more. 'It must be said,' Gerstein was to write later, 'that it was a broad-minded establishment.'

This fact still causes Doctor Krantz to marvel, after twenty-five years.

'We had large photographs of Himmler, Hitler and Goebbels, and we turned them face to the wall and pasted art reproductions on the back. It would have been unthinkable anywhere else. And we discussed events very frankly. We were all comrades and friends, and Mrugowsky was a good chief. It was a most pleasant atmosphere.'

But there is much that Doctor Krantz has since forgotten: the secrecy that pervaded the entire building, the teams working on research projects that could never be mentioned. The Institute had its branch offices in Poland, occupied Russia, even in Germany, one of them being designated 'Department of Typhus and Virus Research, Weimar–Buchenwald.'

All Germany was a land of secrets. The Führer's rigorous decree that no service and no officer was to be informed of any secret matter except for reasons of duty, that no one was to be told too much, or too soon, and so on, was no different in essence from the service regulations laid down in all the warring countries. But in the Third Reich secrecy was raised to the level of religion, a moral imperative. Nowhere was this more the case than in the Waffen SS Institute of Hygiene, where the jolly camaraderie recalled by Doctor Krantz was a brittle cover over a pit of darkness. It was the place of questions not to be asked, conversations broken off, 'freedom' that was free to change the subject.

Every member of the staff swore a personal oath of secrecy to Mrugowsky; but still the ears heard and the eyes saw. Everybody knew more than he should. Sometimes the need to talk—about things that went on in Buchenwald or Mauthausen, for instance, or behind the lines of the German Army in Russia—must have been overwhelming. But to whom? Not to the affable professor of neurochemistry or the beaming specialist in virus diseases, either of whom might also be a security agent. How unburden one's soul in a world where secrecy was God?

## Chapter 8

# 'NEVER LET ANYONE FATHOM
# YOU AT A GLANCE'

AFTER living for a time in the apartment of his father-in-law, Pastor Bensch, Gerstein found an apartment at 47 Bülowstrasse. His wife and son were still in Tübingen, where he visited them from time to time, always keeping his life in separate compartments. All his habitations were provisional; he had no real home.

Bülowstrasse was in the Schöneberg quarter of Berlin, a street of large apartment-houses, built during the reign of Wilhelm II but now gone seedy, some of which had once housed officers of the Berlin Regiment. Those dashing occupants had been replaced at No. 47 by less distinguished citizens, including a dentist and a sign painter. Frau Frieda Hoeflich ran a hairdressing salon and Fräulein Klonek a lending library. The house had belonged to Jews who had been swept away in the purge, and its rents were now collected by the Gestapo—ninety marks a month from Untersturmführer Gerstein. Strategically it was well placed, since it afforded a view of the intersection, and it was admirable in another respect: its walls were so solid that voices did not penetrate them. Finally, it was handy for the Institute and near the small drinking place on Potsdamerstrasse where from time to time Gerstein met emissaries from the Confessional Church.

The old-fashioned apartment, on the first floor left, consisted of five rooms with windows overlooking Goebenstrasse and Bülowstrasse. It came to resemble a junk-shop as Gerstein filled it, higgledy-piggledy, with the things he picked up on his travels: furniture, pictures, bottles, antiques, bric-à-brac of all kinds. The disorder might appear unintended, but in fact it was a part of the Gerstein system: 'Never let anyone fathom you at a glance, or at least make sure they get you wrong!'

In this dingy place Gerstein lavishly entertained old friends, former members of the Protestant movement on leave from the front, occasionally his wife, when she came up from Tübingen, and, very rarely, his brothers and his father. There were also new friends such as Frau Nebelthau. 'He gave my husband and me wonderful meals in that dreadful apartment on Bülowstrasse. The table was always loaded with things that made my mouth water: chocolate, butter, cheese, sausage, white bread, real coffee —things that were no longer easily obtainable. I loved going there, mainly, I must admit, because I was always so hungry. The radio, when we arrived, was always tuned in to London, which was risking the death penalty in those days. The first four notes of Beethoven's Fifth Symphony and then the news in German, and Gerstein would sit there listening with his SS officer's tunic unbuttoned.'

Horst Dickten also had a room in the flat, and the third bedroom was occupied by Leokadia.

Leokadia Hinz was a silent, uncommunicative woman in her late fifties, with strong features suggesting a Slavic origin. Little was known of her background. She had spent her life in the service of others, for a long time a Jewish family who adopted her, and when that came to an end she had become a cleaning woman at the Institute.

This was where Gerstein had found her, on her knees polishing the floor. With his knack of coming to terms with people on their knees he had quickly summed her up, sensing not only her ingrained loyalty but also the deep reserve of affection for which she had no outlet. When he suggested that she should come to work for him as his housekeeper the proposal was as carefully considered as his choice of personal assistants in the Institute.

For him it meant the assurance of a devoted watchdog at his door, the utterly discreet and incorruptible guardian of his life and secrets. For Leokadia Hinz it became a reason for living, a substitute for the husband, home and children she had never had. From the moment she joined the establishment of the Herr Doktor she had no other life, and wanted none. She grasped instinctively what was expected of her. No needless word ever passed her lips, no undesired visitor ever crossed the threshold of the apartment. She had no dealings with the other occupants of the house, who, when they passed the grey, withdrawn figure on the stairs or in the hall, could only say: 'That's the woman who looks after the SS officer on the first floor.' It was all they ever knew of her—or of him.

The affection that grew up between master and servant was so deeply hidden beneath conventional appearances that the visitors for whom she cooked those elaborate meals were never conscious of it. 'Hinz!' Gerstein would bellow, and from her kitchen she would come running. '*Bitt' schön, Herr Doktor.*' 'Hinz,' he would sometimes growl, 'you're a fool,' and she would answer submissively, '*Ich weiss es, Herr Doktor. Ich bin ja dumm* (I know it, Herr Doktor, I know I'm stupid.)' It was her safeguard in the desperate world in which her master lived, and a comedy that no doubt pleased them both.

Like Regina, the servant-girl in Münster who had vouchsafed the little boy, Kurt Gerstein, his first glimpse of true faith, Leokadia was profoundly religious. Indeed, it was as though he had rediscovered Regina; as though in the last years of his life, as at the beginning, he had been driven to seek in the humblest of beings the understanding he could never find among his own kind.

Gerstein's Berlin has ceased to exist, not because it was destroyed by air raids but because it belongs to the past. To the eye of memory the cities that remain intact are those that have vanished. We must dismiss our wartime picture of Hitler's Berlin, the bombarded barracks of a town with a million arms raised in the Nazi salute. Berlin in the years 1941–42 was still at peace, still comfortable and in no way worried about the future. No one believed that fleets of bombing planes would presently sweep through the dense curtain of anti-aircraft guns which, it was claimed, rendered the city unassailable. The war was something happening far away to the east, with which Berlin was only remotely concerned. It suited the authorities to sustain the populace in this wonderfully untroubled frame of mind.

Life flowed past like a film that no one expects to burst into flames, although there are occasional flickers which perturb the projectionist. Cafés and restaurants were crowded, and although there were a great many uniforms these did not have the drab starkness of the front line but were largely smothered in gold braid. Traffic in the streets was much diminished by the shortage of petrol, but the first-class compartments on the overhead railway were still scented. Berlin still had something of the ponderous, overblown appearance bequeathed to it by the Prussian monarchs and their architects; the same luxury stores with their gilded fronts and obsequious doormen were still in business under the wrought-iron lampstands of the Kurfürsten-damm, the Leipzigerstrasse and the Friedrichstrasse, and unlike the great stores of Paris they still had plenty to offer. The looting of Europe helped to preserve Berlin in its illusions. Although food-rationing was in force, it did not prevent anyone who could afford it from having a fine meal at Kempinski's, or from eating *Sachertorte* under the lime trees at Kranzler's; and the forty-odd brands of cigarette offered by the pre-war tobacconists were still on sale.

The people of Berlin were well dressed and often elegant, disposed to look the other way when they passed the under-dog in the streets, tattered and half-starved working parties from the labour camps, or prisoner-of-war parties clad in threadbare uniforms dating from the 1914 war. Women tended to wear trousers and turbans in the winter months. But everywhere there was uniform: the uniform of the Party, of the Todt organiza-tion, of the corps of Nazi drivers, of the Hitler Youth and the League of German Maidens, of railwaymen, firemen and so on. The saluting was endless. Berlin was a city of aching arms. A time was to come when soldiers would be less and less disposed to salute Party members.

There were districts such as Steglitz and Lichterfelde (where Hitler's personal bodyguard was quartered) where the SS was much in evidence, but this meant little to the Berliners in those days. The SS trooper was a man like any other, strolling through the streets, visiting cafés, theatres and music-halls, humming the latest song hit, discoursing on the crimes of Britain and the

Bolsheviks. Its very familiarity had robbed the runic S S of its earlier, sinister implications. The uniform simply covered a soldier. And at the same time the big yellow star of David, which set the Jews apart, was becoming increasingly rare: one saw just an occasional, haggard couple, generally elderly, seated on a public bench staring blankly into space. No one quite knew why this was. They seemed to be simply fading away. *Es geht alles vorüber, es geht alles vorbei*—Everything passes, everything ends, as they sang on the radio.

But the café Bei Wälterchen, near the Janowitz bridge, was doing a roaring trade. Some fifteen hundred men and women visited it daily in search of an escape from solitude. The tables round its large dance floors, beneath lofty ceilings hung with crimson draperies, were attended by waiters who also ran a postal service, conveying messages from table to table. The bulky proprietor, 'Wälterchen,' richly deserved his title of *der Seelentröster*, the comforter of souls.

There was bathing in the Wannsee in summer, lovemaking in the Grunewald in spring—brief, feverish embraces which perhaps expressed what the city dared not say.

When he had been a student in Berlin, Gerstein had occasionally amused himself by strolling in pyjamas along the Kurfürstendamm and pretending to be English. But his present role was one of absolute conformity, invisibility, a figure lost in the crowd like a million others. In the year 1941 he felt that he had come to terms with himself. He had, after all, not been born in vain. The years of tribulation lay behind him, the moral dilemma, the sense of wasted life. Everything was now going well. His furious industry at the Institute had broken down the barriers, affording him not only liberty but the means of action. He was now moving steadily forward on his predestined course.

Moreover, it seemed to him that he would soon find allies among the German people themselves.

At six o'clock on a Sunday morning Günter Dickten was dragged out of bed.

'Get up at once,' said Gerstein. 'We're going out.'

'What for?'

'Hurry up. You've got to come.'

'But where are we going?'

'You'll see.'

They travelled by train and bus to Westphalia, and in due course were outside the Cathedral of St Hedwig, a Catholic church. Dickten exclaimed in astonishment:

'But this isn't our church! What are we doing here?'

'You'll see.'

The cathedral was exceptionally full, and there was a perceptible tension in the air. From the pulpit a priest read a pastoral letter from the Bishop of Münster, Monsignor Klemens von Galen. This was the text:

'Men and women of Germany! Article 211 of the German Penal Code, which still has the force of law, states: "Premeditated murder shall be punishable by death." Article 139 stipulates: "Whosoever has knowledge of any criminal intention against the life of another person and omits to inform the authorities or the person threatened is himself liable to punishment . . . ." When I learned that patients in the Marienthal Hospital, near Münster, were in danger of being removed elsewhere and put to death I at once brought the matter to the notice of the High Court in Münster, and the Chief of Police, by registered letter dated 28 July. I wrote as follows: "I am informed that during the present week—the date mentioned is 31 July—a large number of persons considered to be 'unproductive citizens,' at present patients in the provincial hospital of Marienthal, near Münster, are to be transferred to the hospital at Eichenberg and there deliberately put to death, following the precedent of similar proceedings in other hospitals. Since this is contrary both to Divine Law and to ordinary morality, and since moreover it is an act of mass homicide and subject to the death penalty under Article 211 of the Penal Code, I am bringing the matter to your notice, as it is my duty to do under Article 139 of the Code, with the request that you take the necessary steps to protect the persons who are thus threatened and to deal with the services which are planning their removal and eventual murder. I further request that you will inform me of the steps you have taken."

'So far as I am aware no action has been taken, either by the police or by the Court . . . We must therefore assume that sooner or later these defenceless invalids will be executed.

'Why? Not because they are guilty of any crime punishable by death, or because their behaviour towards their guardians or nurses has been so aggressive as to justify the latter in resorting to force in self-defence. There is no extreme reason of this kind, such as justifies the killing of an armed enemy in time of war. Nothing of the sort applies here. These unhappy invalids are to die because a commission has decreed it, because they are judged to be "unproductive citizens," of no further value to the State. It has been decided that, since they no longer produce, they are to be treated like machinery that no longer functions, or an old horse, or a cow that has ceased to give milk. I need not pursue the analogy, which is sufficiently obvious. When the machine, or the horse or cow, no longer serves the purpose for which it was intended we may legitimately destroy it. But here we are dealing with our own kind, men and women who are our brothers and sisters. Certainly they are unhappy people, unproductive invalids, but is that to say that they have forfeited the right to live? Is our own right to life, yours and mine, to be measured according to our productive capacity, as reckoned by others? It will go hard with us, in the weakness of our old age, if the right to destroy our unproductive neighbours has been accepted as a principle. It will go hard with those who have sacrificed their health and strength to the necessities of production, and with the gallant soldiers who return wounded and broken from the front.

'Here is an instance of what happens these days. One of the patients in the Marienthal Psychiatric Hospital was a farmer, about fifty-five years old, who came from a neighbouring village of which I could give you the name. He had suffered from mental disorder for some years, but he was not gravely ill; his family were allowed to visit him whenever they pleased. A fortnight ago he was visited by his wife and one of their sons, who was on leave from the front. The son was very devoted to his father, and their parting was a sad one, since he could not be sure that he would ever see his father again. He might be killed in the service of his country. Now it seems that they will not meet again on this earth for a different reason. The father is on the "unproductive list."

'Another relative who called to see the father during the present week was informed that he had been transferred elsewhere by order of the Ministry of War. They could not say at the hospital where he had been taken but expected news of him in a few days. And what will the news be? Will it be the same as in other cases— that the man is dead and has been cremated, and that his ashes will be sent to his family on payment of costs? The soldier risking his life for his fellow-countrymen will not see his father again because his fellow-countrymen have murdered him! This is a true story! I can give you the names of the family and the place where they live . . .

'If we agree that unproductive members of society are to be destroyed, even if we limit this to those who are without means of support or defence, if we accept the principle, then it means that all people incapable of useful work may be destroyed, including ourselves, when we grow old and infirm. The principle may be extended to include not only the mentally afflicted but all persons suffering from chronic or incurable diseases, tuberculosis, for example, as well as men wounded in war. None of us will be safe. An arbitrarily constituted committee may draw up lists of "unproductive persons" which will include anyone whom they consider unworthy to go on living. There will be no police to protect the victims, no court of appeal. Who will then be able to trust his doctor? He may report us to be "unproductive" and receive an order to destroy us. How can we fail to perceive the state of moral anarchy which such a principle must create if it is accepted and applied—the mistrust of every man for his fellow, spreading among families and even into the home? Woe to mankind, woe to the German people, if we thus transgress God's commandment, delivered amid thunder and lightning from

Mount Sinai and implanted in the heart and conscience of man,
"Thou shalt not kill!" '

Gerstein and young Dickten left the cathedral.
Gerstein: 'Well, now you know the kind of criminal State
we're living in.'
'What does the word 'euthanasia' mean, Kurt?'
'It comes from the Greek. You ought to know.'

The pastoral letter, and the means of dealing with its author,
were discussed in the highest circles. Goebbels, Minister of
Propaganda, wanted the Bishop to be publicly hanged. Hitler was
not averse to the idea but decided against it. Public opinion was
already aroused. Militant bodies were forming in Westphalia, and
there was a danger that Catholic morale in the Army would be
seriously affected. The man who never retreated decided this time
upon a policy of prudence. 'We'll settle with the Bishop after the
war,' he said.

In the meantime an order went out that the euthanasia programme was to be discontinued, and by the end of the year the
extermination of the mentally afflicted had ceased. According to
the judges at Nuremberg, some 70,000 persons had been put to
death; but German and Allied experts put the figure at not less
than 200,000.

The records were sent to Berlin and destroyed. In one or two
camouflaged establishments extermination on a small scale, by
poison or starvation, still went on: abnormal children were got
rid of, children of Jewish–Christian unions, Poles suffering from
tuberculosis and so on. The equipment—gas chambers and
furnaces—was dismantled and sent to the eastern front, together
with the invaluable personnel who were conditioned to the business of mass extermination. The Führer had already foreseen
another use for them, based, no doubt, on the presentiment that
no Pope or other cleric would speak out, as Bishop Klemens
Augustus, Count Galen, had done, in defence of the victims he
now had in mind. But that lay in the future.

The halt of the euthanasia programme confirmed Gerstein's belief in what he himself was doing: to penetrate to the heart of the cyclone, to find out what was happening and tell the people. It was the force of public opinion (expressed in the voice of the Bishop), which had withstood that evil.

In August he wrote to Elfriede in Tübingen (she was shortly to bear his daughter, Adelheid):

'. . . I meant to come, but alas the Chief keeps asking for my report (a colleague has just rung me up about it). I'm going to have to do a lot more travelling, mostly to the east and north (Bremen, Hamburg). At present I'm working on the construction of a large number of decontamination trucks, a most interesting job but a difficult one . . . For some months now my personal inclinations have been in harmony with my work, which is largely technical in its nature (engineering). I'm in a position where I can be extremely useful and prevent a great many things from happening. It's a very pleasant sensation.'

Prevent a great many things . . . In a letter subject to censorship he could not be more explicit. Nor could Horst Dickten, when, travelling with Gerstein in September 1941, he sent his mother a postcard with the following enigmatic message:

'1) Things are happening differently

'2) from what one thinks.

'One of these days you will learn the inner meaning of those highly charged words. Affectionate greetings. H.D.'

On this occasion, so Dickten said in 1968, it was a question of his eventual transfer to the Wehrmacht in Norway, to facilitate Gerstein's contacts with the Scandinavian Resistance movement. This never came off because the SS would not let him go. The incident throws a little light on what was happening at that time, but for every such gleam there are a thousand obscurities.

Gerstein had control of considerable sums of money. Where did they come from? His private means and the subsidies he received from the Confessional Church cannot have been sufficient, even if one adds to these the under-the-counter commissions he may have received from the firms with which he was doing official business. We know almost nothing about his contacts. He came and went across Europe, mysteriously informed of what was going on, and of the necessity to be at a given place at a given time.

Robert Weiss (1967): 'He suddenly descended on me in Strasbourg in January 1943. He had somehow learned that I was in trouble . . . As he was leaving he said very loudly from the doorway, *"Ohren steif halten"*—"Don't weaken!"' '

The precautions he took were extraordinary. The people in his immediate circle were forbidden to take notes or to keep any kind of appointment book or diary. Once when Horst Dickten was about to take a snapshot of Leokadia Hinz he stopped him in a fury—'Don't you know that photographs are the most dangerous of all documents?'—and confiscated the camera. One searches in vain for Gerstein in group photographs of the schools at Hamburg, Arnhem, Oranienburg, or at the Institute: he is the one who is always missing.

He taught his disciples to preserve absolute silence, sometimes quoting Polonius: 'Give thy thoughts no tongue, nor any unproportion'd thought his act.' Instead, life must be filled with action designed to cover the perilous truth. A man must make himself impenetrable by his very multiplicity. He must be all things at once: sage and fool, moderate Nazi and Nazi moderate, Christian and atheist, man of good counsel and man of disorder. So effective was Gerstein's camouflage that his very imprudences did him no harm but merely added to the weird and complex picture he presented to the world. It was secrecy that spoke from his mouth, secrecy so smothered in a spate of words that while he seemed to be saying everything he said nothing.

Some of his journeys were like a two-faced mirror. He travelled enormously on Institute business; this was what one might term the right side of the mirror. But turn it round and another scene, no less real, is reflected: a dimly lighted room half lost in darkness, but a whole room, quite different. He was often in France, visiting the Creusot works near Paris, and he was in close touch with firms such as Souza and Lucanes, sub-contractors to German concerns engaged in manufacturing equipment for his decontamination trucks.

*July 1968.* The speaker is Franz Bäuerle, employed by the firm of Goedecker, which had commercial dealings with Gerstein during the war.

'I met him frequently in Paris. He was a very vigorous man, very alert and approachable. He was also very accommodating. He provided my secretary, who was half-Jewish, with false papers and got her transferred to Paris. He had official stamps and everything that was needed for forging documents. He helped some of the workers in the Souza firm in Pantin to avoid being sent to forced labour in Germany.'

A mission in Paris.

Gerstein, having worked hard for several days, had completed his assignment. Sergeant Weigelt proposed that they should go out on the town (Paris is always Paris).

Gerstein: 'Sorry, I'm not free.'

Weigelt: 'But you've done everything.'

'No, I've still got something to do.'

'Well, I'll go with you.'

'Thanks, but this isn't your affair.'

Gerstein went off, and Weigelt, perturbed and curious—perhaps more curious than perturbed—followed him at a distance through the streets of the Left Bank until they came to the Bon Marché. Gerstein turned abruptly into the big department store. 'He seemed to know that place like the back of his hand,' said Weigelt. 'Within a minute I'd lost him.'

Another evening they went to the Moulin Rouge, Gerstein having obtained tickets for a 'general's box.' Shortly after the curtain went up he murmured to Weigelt, 'I'm not interested,' and disappeared. Obviously, he could have said so before they went there, if he had not wanted to immobilize Weigelt. He returned just as the show was ending, and when Weigelt asked where he had been he said, 'Oh, here and there.'

They had rooms in the Hotel Ambassador, on the Boulevard Haussmann. One night Gerstein mislaid his key, and Weigelt climbed across from the balcony and got into his room that way.

'There were things scattered on the bed,' said Weigelt. 'Well—the sort of things that could have got him shot.'

'You didn't see anything,' said Gerstein.

(Nor can we see anything, because Weigelt, talking at Kassel in 1968, would not say what the things were that had been scattered on Gerstein's bed. Concerning another detail that he unwittingly let fall in the course of our conversation he asked us to say nothing. *Geheimhaltungspflicht*—the duty of silence.)

Horst Dickten said of Gerstein: 'He took enormous trouble to conceal his contacts in Paris.'

Gerstein never stopped buying. He bought everything conceivable, and by the truck load. What had it to do with his work at the Institute? Some of his former colleagues still shudder when they think of it.

Friedrich Geissert (1967): 'We were always teasing him about it in the Institute. He bought the most improbable and useless things. He bought truckloads of disused oxygen containers and huge quantities of sweet drinks. I think he took a malicious pleasure in sending railroad cars on useless errands all over Germany, because he often made fun of the slogan "The wheels must turn for victory," which was posted in all the stations and trains. He sent men all over Europe for no apparent reason, unless it was to get them out of his immediate neighbourhood for the time being. In my opinion he was doing what he could to sabotage the regime, wholesale and retail.'

That is one way of looking at it. But there were others.

Armin Peters (1948): 'I frequently bought large quantities of food and tobacco at Cracow in Poland and sent them by rail to Berlin, to be delivered to his apartment. He put the stuff in tins which he put in packing-cases labelled "prussic acid," or in mess-chests, and sent them on to Oranienburg, Dachau and other camps. Because of the security clearance he had from the RSHA he was able to go anywhere. At the Gestapo prison in the Grosse Hamburger Strasse, Berlin, where I installed a de-lousing unit, I saw prisoners greet him—surreptitiously, but with obvious gratitude—and I saw him slip them tinned food and packets of cigarettes . . . Large numbers of letters intended for prisoners in the concentration camps were delivered at my address in Rangs-dorf and I passed them on to Gerstein . . . I also received large sums of money which I disposed of according to his instructions. I had his full authority.'

Horst Dickten (1968): 'I only know what he told me. He said that he was in touch with Resistance groups in France and that thanks to these he had been able to have a metal die cut bearing the words "Waffen S S supplies." He used it on all the trucks and packing-cases. Everything went out of Germany, but he was the only one who knew where it was going . . . He had two objects in mind. First, to suborn important people with the princely gifts he made them. It was a triumph every time he got another high-ranking soldier or civil servant in his power—and I may say that there were plenty of them. And this first operation paved the way for the second, which was far more important: helping people in the concentration camps. I know something about that because I had a share in it. We sent stuff to certain camps, such as Oranienburg, which Gerstein knew particularly well. He was never directly involved. This was understood between us, for obvious reasons. The goods—mainly food and medical supplies —were either sent in through the aircraft factory at Oranienburg or else smuggled into the camp at night with the help of guards whom we had bribed. It was extremely risky, but there was only one time when my life was in serious danger. That was on a night when a prisoner escaped and there was a general alarm just as I was delivering a consignment. Luckily, we weren't spotted.'

Walter Eckhardt, a former fellow-student of Gerstein's, later a senior civil servant (1945): 'He sent a great deal of food to the concentration camps. It was thanks to me that he was able to do so. He bribed the S S guards with thousands of gallons of spirits and great quantities of tobacco, with which, as supervisor of the Ost Monopol, I supplied him.'

A restaurant bill was found among Gerstein's posthumous papers. Since he never did anything unintentionally, he must have left it there for a purpose, presumably to provide a clue for anyone seeking later to piece together his life. But a clue to what?

The Restaurant Louis XIV is on the Boulevard Saint-Denis, a good restaurant of the de Gaulle era, with an admirable cuisine and a cellar of vintage wines. The present proprietor, Jean-Germain Descombes, was shown a photograph of Gerstein in May 1967. He said:

'Yes, that's him. He looked older to us than he does here, but it's him all right. I often saw him. I was twenty then, working under my father. We've changed the place a lot since then. In those days —in the 'forties, that is—it was a brasserie with billiard tables, seven of them, and dining tables in between. We had a band—an accordion, violin, piano, double-bass and percussion. It brought in a lot of customers. They sometimes played international song hits, and it amused us when the Germans applauded. This gentleman came here very often, sometimes to lunch, sometimes to dinner, but always alone. He was tall but rather thin, with his hair cropped short. We reckoned he was about forty-five. He always wore civilian clothes. After a time we got to know him fairly well. He said he was a chemist and that he had a factory in Germany. From the way he talked and acted—it's a long time ago, you understand—one got the impression that he didn't much like whatever it was he was doing. Of course in those days everyone was careful; people didn't talk freely, the way they do now. I remember him because he was anti-Nazi. Anyway, we didn't get a great many Germans in here. And then, a lot later, he turned up one day in SS uniform. It gave my father and me a shock. He saw this, and he said he couldn't help himself because he was under surveillance. One felt that he was a worried and harassed man . . . What's he doing now?'

(I learned later from an officer in the special services that the Louis XIV had been used, without its knowledge, by secret agents of all colours, before, during and after the war. As Horst Dickten's postcard says, things happen differently from what one thinks.)

*December 1941.* One of Gerstein's elder brothers, Alfred, died of wounds. He was the second member of the family to be killed in war, and the old Judge, heartbroken but stoical as ever, rose to the occasion with a Greek inscription for his tombstone: 'Those whom the gods love die young.' The funeral, which Kurt Gerstein attended in uniform, was at Hamm, in Westphalia. Cemeteries seemed always to be filled with signs and portents for Gerstein. Among those present on this occasion was Councillor Keimer, a Nazi jurist who had played a prominent part in Gerstein's arraignment before the Party Tribunal in Munich. It was a most unfortunate coincidence, and for Gerstein it could have had very serious consequences. The outraged Councillor reported the matter. A declared enemy of the State, a man who had been expelled from the Party, had contrived to insinuate himself into the ranks of the SS! The report got as far as Himmler, and was referred back to Mrugowsky.

Doctor Krantz, in 1968: 'I didn't know he had been expelled from the Party. Someone told me that he'd been in a concentration camp, but that's all I ever heard. He was very solidly protected by Mrugowsky.'

The head of the Institute was not the man to be worried by trifles of that sort. For him Kurt Gerstein was the genius who, by combating the typhus epidemic, had taken a great weight off his mind and saved his reputation. Compared with this achievement, what else mattered?

Gerstein said to Günter Dickten:

'The Reichsführer has decreed that as a punishment I'm to be temporarily barred from wearing uniform.'

'Which makes you the only member of the SS who goes round in civilian clothes.'

'Yes, and I'm proud of it.'

The knight errant had come unscathed through the first ordeal of his arduous quest. He had lost—and that only for a little while —nothing but his shield.

## Chapter 9

# THE 'FINAL SOLUTION'

*January 1942.* SS Colonel Mrugowsky was still showering favours on his protégé. Gerstein was made a departmental head, the department being that of 'technical hygiene' which he had himself built up within the Institute and which was concerned with all methods of decontamination and disinfection, including the use of gas. He had become the great white chief of water purification.

His higher status meant a wider range of activities, also a widening of his field of vision. But if in one sense he had more liberty, in another sense—everything in that world having two faces—he was more shackled. By allowing his chief to protect and promote him, he bound himself to him the more closely. Mrugowsky could never allow himself to be compromised by a subordinate for whom he had made himself personally responsible. The link between the two men, an endless mingling of gratitude, mistrust and fear, was one that only death could break. In that world of shadows a helping hand could lead only into still deeper darkness.

Since November 1941, Mrugowsky, as Doctor Krantz said, had been busying himself with more and more matters that did not concern him. There had been a policy meeting at the Institute, and the following are extracts from the journal of Doctor Ding—that same Doctor Ding who was Gerstein's sworn enemy:

'Year 1941–42. Typhus and Virus Department of the Waffen SS Institute of Hygiene.

'29.11.41. Conference attended by Professor Handloser, Inspector General of the Army Health Service, Gruppenführer Doctor Conti, Secretary of State for Public Health, Professor Reiter, Director of the Robert Koch Institute, Professor Gildemeister and Colonel Mrugowsky, at the Waffen SS Institute of Hygiene, Berlin.

'The conference agreed upon the necessity of testing the efficacy of the typhus serum derived from yolk of egg, and the resistance of the human body to this serum. Since experiments on animals are not sufficiently reliable, experiments on humans must be carried out . . .

'2.1.42. It has been decided that the testing of typhus vaccines shall be carried out at the concentration camp at Buchenwald. Major Doctor Ding is placed in charge of the tests.

'19.4.42. Final report on the first series of tests of the typhus vaccine. Block 46 has been made available for typhus experiments.

'Five deaths: three test subjects, one vaccinated with normal Behring serum, one with strong Behring serum.'

Many more were to die from among the 729 inmates of Buchenwald artificially infected with virulent typhus and placed by the Institute of Hygiene at the disposal of Doctor Ding.

Kurt Gerstein was bound to be informed of what was happening. He was the specialist in technical matters related to the anti-typhus campaign, and, as we know, he had sent Friedrich Geissert to the Pasteur Institute in Paris 'in connection with anti-typhus vaccine.'

But while he was preoccupied with matters of equipment and supply, others were going to the heart of the matter, searching for an absolute specific in icy disregard of the number of human guinea-pigs they slaughtered in the process. Scharführer Holländer, in the Institute, supplied Gerstein with regular reports on the Buchenwald tests. Moreover, he learned more and more from highly placed medical acquaintances about other things that were taking place in that world so closely connected with his own: experiments of all kinds on human beings, army researches, the large-scale massacre of Jews and political commissars on the eastern front. And still his innocence in these matters remained great.

Doctor Krantz (1968): 'One day when we were having a drink together at the Institute two men came in, doctors I think. They said to Gerstein, who had already made a name for himself as an engineer and expert in decontamination: "We need two trucks capable of pumping exhaust gas into a closed chamber. Can you suggest a suitable method?" Gerstein roughed out a design on the spot. "You need only fit the trucks with an auxiliary engine," he said. "For instance, a Sachs Diesel would do excellently for pumping out exhaust gas." After which the two men departed.'

Did Gerstein ever hear of them again? From the beginning of the Russian campaign a team of specialists, working in great secrecy, had been trying to find a rapid and effective means of liquidating entire populations without the use of machine guns, which was demoralizing for the execution squads and anyway too noisy. At Mogilev, in White Russia, the method had been tried of pumping exhaust gases from a vehicle into a sealed chamber. It had not worked. The victims had had to be finished off with bombs under the eyes of a special commission come to witness the experiment. A later method was a truck with a sealed back, packed tight with people, the exhaust gases being introduced through a pipe. This had not been very successful, either. The frantic victims tended to push to the back of the truck, tipping it up. Modifications were called for and more experts had to be consulted.

If Doctor Krantz is to be believed, one of these was Kurt Gerstein. All unwittingly he was being drawn into the dark centre of revelation.

On a morning early in 1942 Horst Dickten found his chief in a state of stupefaction. Gerstein handed him a report having to do with Jews said to have been *gassed*.

We do not know exactly what this document was, but probably it was similar in substance to the following letter, addressed on 25 October 1941 by the German Minister for Occupied Territories in the East to the Commissioner for those territories:

'Subject: Solution of the Jewish Problem.

'Reference: Your report of 4 October 1941 on the solution of the Jewish problem. Further to my letter of 18 October I have to inform you that Herr Brack, a high-ranking official in the Führer's Chancellery, has declared himself ready to assist in the installation of the necessary buildings and gas appliances. At present we do not have a sufficient number of these appliances and

more will have to be manufactured. Brack considers that it will
be easier to manufacture them on the spot, rather than within the
Reich. The best course will be to send suitable personnel to Riga,
in particular his chemist, Doctor Kallmeyer, who will do every-
thing that is necessary. Brack points out that the method employed
is not without risk and that safety precautions will therefore have
to be taken. You are requested to approach Doctor Brack at the
Führer's Chancellery through your senior police and SS officer.
You will ask him to send Doctor Kallmeyer and other personnel.
I may add that Sturmbannführer Eichmann, who is in charge of
Jewish matters at the Central Office of Security, agrees with this.
Lieutenant-Colonel Eichmann wishes you to know that camps for
Jews are to be set up at Riga and Minsk, and that even Jews from
the former Reich may be transferred to them. At present Jews
evacuated from the former Reich are being sent to Litzmann-
stadt [Lodz] and other camps, from which they will be transferred
farther east, to labour camps if they are fit to work.

'In the light of the present situation we need have no misgivings
about using the Brack method for the liquidation of Jews un-
fitted for work. Under this system incidents such as those which
occurred at the shooting of Jews at Vilna (which took place in
public, according to the report I have in front of me) will no
longer be tolerated or indeed possible. On the other hand, Jews
fit for work will be sent east and incorporated in the labour
forces. It goes without saying that men and women will be
separated.

'I request you to keep me informed of all other measures taken.'

We who read know what all this meant, what it implied. We
have heard the hideous tale so many times that perhaps it has
almost ceased to outrage us. But what did it mean to Kurt
Gerstein when, in the coldly official phraseology of a document
similar to the one we have quoted, he came upon the words 'the
gassing of Jews'? In the case of the euthanasia programme there
had been at least a pretence of justification, on scientific or social
grounds, or simply as a drastic war-measure. But here there was
none: no suggestion that these Jews were insane, or criminals,

or in any respect enemies of the State. They were to be exterminated simply because they were Jews. We may judge of his horror, if in fact he had had no idea of what was going on.

On 20 January 1942 a number of official cars converged upon the Wannsee, the lake where in spring and summer the people of Berlin went to bathe and sunbathe, to picnic and make love. But the business of that winter's day was somewhat different. The black cars drove in through the gates of No. 56–58, Am Grossen Wannsee, a stately colonnaded official residence standing in a garden embellished with urns and statuary and fountains. Fourteen dignitaries descended amid the click of soldierly heels and the presenting of arms, and there was a solemn exchange of ceremonial greetings: Herr Staatssekretär . . . Herr Gauleiter . . . Herr Obergruppenführer . . .

A conference was to be held, summoned by a tall man with a narrow face, Obergruppenführer Reinhard Heydrich, Chief of the Security Police and Himmler's right-hand man. This 20th of January was Heydrich's big day. Having been invested by Reichsmarschall Goering with summary powers 'for the organization of the final solution of the Jewish problem in Europe,' he had become absolute master of the destinies of a population reckoned by the chief SS statistician at 11,000,000 souls, a figure that included a few millions at that time out of Germany's reach. His absolute mastery resolved itself into a single task: to exterminate every Jew he could lay hands on.

The Führer had decided, Himmler had provided the means, Goering had cleared the way: it was for Heydrich to carry out the policy.

He had had photostats of his letter of appointment sent out with the invitations to the conference, so that all might know that he, Reinhard Heydrich, was the Führer's chosen instrument for the purpose he had most dearly at heart. The object of the conference was to determine 'matters of principle.' The invitations had been drafted, and the necessary documentation compiled, by an obscure Obersturmbannführer (Lieutenant-Colonel) named Adolf Eichmann, the Gestapo specialist in Jewish affairs.

'It was the first time I had attended a conference on this high level. It was conducted in a most civilized way, with great affability on all sides, excellent manners, the whole thing extremely pleasant. There was not much to discuss, and it did not take very long. We were served with drinks by army orderlies, and —well, that is what the Wannsee Conference was like . . .' (Eichmann.)

Indeed, nothing could have passed off more smoothly. In that high circle of initiates nothing needed to be spelt out. The minutes of the meeting consisted of three short paragraphs in which the word 'corpse' nowhere occurs.

'In accordance with the final solution of the problem, the Jews are to be transferred to the East under sufficient escort and there assigned to the labour service. Able-bodied Jews will be formed into working parties, men and women being separated, and sent out into the country to build roads. It goes without saying that many will be eliminated naturally as a result of their physical disabilities.

'Those remaining, who must be considered the most robust, are to be treated accordingly. The experience of history teaches us that this natural élite, if set at liberty, would carry within itself the seeds of a Jewish revival.

'By the effective achievement of the final solution, Europe will be swept clean from east to west . . .'

The top brass, the Secretaries and Under-Secretaries, then took their leave amid a slamming of car doors and a final exchange of courtesies: 'See you again soon, my dear fellow. Do remember me to your wife.'

Only three men remained in the conference room: Heydrich, its promoter, and his two henchmen, Eichmann and Müller, of the Gestapo. They stood round the fire excitedly talking. For the first time Eichmann saw Heydrich laughing, drinking and smoking. Beyond the trees gleamed the shining surface of the lake. They were well content, those admirable men, our brothers, warmed with the gratifying consciousness of having done a good day's work. And why not? How can we call them monsters? Monsters do not play violin sonatas, like Heydrich, or rejoice in the family circle, like Müller, or give flowers to their wife on her wedding anniversary, as Eichmann did ...

That mansion by the Wannsee, when I visited it in April 1967, had been converted into a recreation centre for the poor children of Berlin. The Municipal Council had vigorously opposed the suggestion that it should be made into a 'Museum of the Final Solution.' Nothing macabre must be allowed near the Wannsee!

Since seeing the document on gassed Jews, Gerstein had known no rest. He could not doubt its truth. Indiscriminate massacres of Jews, including children, had already taken place behind the German lines on the eastern front, carried out by special formations (*Einsatzgruppen*) of the Waffen SS and police. In any case, why should Hitler recoil from the killing of Jews when he put sick Aryans to death? But a single document could not tell the whole story; it simply showed that there was a story.

One night Gerstein and Dickten carried out a private investigation in the neighbourhood of the Tiergarten Synagogue, now used as an assembly centre. Jews of all ages and both sexes were kept there for a night and a day under police guard, and on the next night sent on to an unknown destination. They were brought in and taken away under cover of darkness, moving silently on unshod feet. Gerstein slipped in among them and tried to find out where they were being taken. There was no reply. No one knew. Somewhere in Berlin there was an official seated in his office with the files in front of him. He must know. Without leaving his desk he was directing the silent columns and their guards towards some place where doubtless the grass was so tall that there was no need of shoes, the air so pure that there was no need to breathe it, and men as good as dead already.

Later Gerstein learned that Jewish girls were being sent to the Institute in Riga. A lot went on at Riga. The Institute sometimes called for human subjects on which to feed typhus-infected fleas ... Perhaps these girls would be a means of discovering a fragment of the truth. Gerstein sent Horst Dickten to Riga. It was an absurd idea. How could the unhappy creatures, haunted by the fear of death, be expected to talk to a man in SS uniform? The trip was a failure, as was the attempt to penetrate the traffic in women destined for the brothels in the concentration camps.

In Berlin, or out of Berlin, the barrier of secrecy seemed impenetrable.

Some other means had to be found, more effective than these hazardous and unsystematic probes. There had to be a methodical plan, operated through more and more highly placed contacts. Gerstein already had contacts which could be cultivated, and where these did not exist he could make them. It was a game he was good at. The nerve-centre of the concentration camps was the SS Office of Economy and Administration (WVHA), presided over by SS General Oswald Pohl, its premises at Unter den Eichen, in Lichterfelde. The Institute of Hygiene was financed from this source. It was here that Gerstein, distributing bribes wholesale, went in search of allies and informants. It was here that he found them, so that he came to have a thorough knowledge of the concentration camps, completed by personal visits. But this too was disappointing. Although much was to be learned from camps such as Buchenwald, Sachsenhausen and Dachau, these were not extermination camps. Individuals were killed or died of exhaustion; there were beatings and shootings, men flung to their death in the quarries; but this was not the Final Solution. If there were people who knew about it they held their tongues and looked strangely at the questioner. 'We were in the heart of Hell,' said Horst Dickten. 'Any curiosity was suspect.' Like a mirage, like a mythical continent, the Final Solution seemed to recede as one drew nearer to it.

Horst Dickten recalls a very powerful radio receiver, stolen from Oranienburg and brought to Bülowstrasse, which Gerstein and he rigged up in a sort of tent on a thick carpet in the hope of picking up clues—anything that might help them—from English, Swedish or Swiss broadcasts. It was a sign of despair, almost of madness.

Gerstein had only one thought in mind: to get the Jews out of the country before they were all exterminated. But how, and where were they to go? One was up against a solid barrier of impossibility. The war blocked all escape routes. The Jews were caught in a net in which there was scarcely a tear.

Scraps of information constantly reached him. There were slaughter houses in Poland where the victims were killed in circumstances of unbelievable inhumanity, not even accorded the privilege of a quick death. Their sufferings were said to be appalling.

*What have you done to your brother?*

Gerstein was at the end of his tether, unable to endure those faceless cries for help which he was almost the only one to hear in the world he lived in. And there was nothing to be done—nothing, unless it were some act of madness. If he openly protested he would be shot. If he fled, God would condemn him as a deserter. If he proposed the evacuation of the Jews he would be told, 'Go ahead,' and would be forced to admit his powerlessness. He could do nothing to affect the *lives* of the Jews; the only field in which he might venture a tentative move was in the matter of their death—that is to say, the manner of their death. Writing in his official capacity as a technician, he might suggest that the useless suffering inflicted on the victims was degrading to the 'Nazi ideal.' The argument might cause authority to review the matter, to consider other methods of extermination, to call for suggestions, which at least would gain time.

Incomplete though Gerstein's knowledge was, it was enough to make him a changed man. In the spring of 1942 he went to see his friend Helmut Franz, who was recovering from wounds in hospital at Neustrelitz.

'He appeared at my bedside in SS uniform looking like a ghost. His mood of black pessimism was horrifying. At that time the worst was still ahead of him, but what he had already seen and heard in the SS had been enough to transform him into a desperate and helpless man. His nerves were worn to shreds by his constant fear of exposure. The satanic power of the Nazis seemed to him so immense that he was now inclined to believe in their ultimate victory, and this added to his profound despair ... He was a bundle of nerves, hatred and misery compared with which I seemed calm and collected.'

The heartrending account depicts not so much a man in a state of collapse as a man wholly disoriented, deprived of all reason for living. Gerstein had taken the measure of the SS empire; he had intimate knowledge of its power, its objectives, its chances of success. What, then, was he doing in it? His presence in that 'camp of the powers of darkness' was meaningless if he was to be nothing but a privileged witness of its triumph. He was like a spy who, having discovered in the enemy's safe the proof of his invincibility, realizes the uselessness of the risks he runs.

One thing alone could save him: a thorough and complete knowledge of the secret. This alone could justify him in what he was doing, because if the secret was what he believed it to be, then it was of a nature so black and far-reaching that God Himself was committed. God could no longer remain aloof; He must descend into the arena and do battle with the SS. And so they would not be victorious, and despair would have an end: for Gerstein would be where God was, where he had always wished to be.

If Hell were not to prevail, the SS Lieutenant who was God's servant must be put in possession of the secret.

On Monday, 8 June 1943, a man in civilian clothes walked into Kurt Gerstein's office at the Institute.

He was the emissary of the Final Solution.

## Chapter 10

# DECONTAMINATION

'LIEUTENANT GERSTEIN, you are required to procure 260 kilos[1] (572 pounds) of prussic acid within the shortest possible time.'

The visitor had formally introduced himself. He was Major Günther of the Central Security Office (RSHA). Gerstein had not met him before; but Rolf Günther, like his colleagues in Section IV B 4 of the Gestapo, was a man who preferred to remain unknown. His boss was Adolf Eichmann, Heydrich's assistant on the Final Solution.

He went on to say that this was a top-secret matter. Gerstein would be informed of the method of transport and where the consignment was to be delivered. He would be required to accompany it and to make arrangements for its use in place of the gas at present being used.

Having again emphasized the need for extreme secrecy, Major Günther withdrew. Gerstein had not refused to carry out the order.

His personal statement contains a few words of explanation:

'I could understand more or less what was the nature of this mission; yet I accepted it ... without any scruples, for anybody else would have carried it out for the purposes of the SD.' (Gerstein's *Report*, see p. 288.)

This was written when he was awaiting trial. It is an explanation for the jurists, not the revelation of a state of mind. He said to Horst Dickten: 'I've got to go ... The whole thing reeks of death.'

The matter then under discussion in the corridors of the Final Solution was the best means of speeding up the process. Asphyxiation by gas had been decided upon; but what kind of gas? Section IV B 4 of the RSHA had been studying the problem—although

1 One of Gerstein's accounts makes it 100 kilos.

Eichmann, when he was under cross-examination in Israel, protested frantically against the use of the word 'gas,' repeating it six times in as many lines: 'I never had anything to do with gas. The first time I even heard gas mentioned was in Hungary in 1944. Günther had got hold of some sort of gas, and I said to him, "What do you want gas, for? Gas is nothing to do with us." I repeat, we never, never had anything to do with gas.'

But at the stage which the discussions in Eichmann's department had reached, in that year of 1942, further clarification was called for. A specialist was needed, and this brought the matter within the sphere of the S S. Only the Institute of Hygiene was likely to be able to produce an expert with the necessary qualifications.

The problem was officially described as one of decontamination or disinfection.

The German word used was *Entwesung*, a word fabricated out of the prefix *ent-* (un-) and *Wesen* (essence, or being). *Entwesung*, the process of robbing living organisms of their being; decontamination when applied to lice or fleas, disinfection when applied to germs—both matters with which Gerstein was already concerned. Goebbels had made a pronouncement on the subject: 'Of course you can say that the flea is a living creature—but what kind of creature?' How easy to rise in the scale from the flea to the sub-human! A German thinker named Lagarde, speaking of the Jews in the reign of Wilhelm II, had been no less forthright: 'We don't argue with bacilli or with thread-worms; we don't try to re-educate them; we render them harmless as speedily as possible.' Any tiresome or worthless creature—a germ, a Jew, a louse, a madman, a Negro, a Pole, a Russian—might be subject to the process of *Entwesung*. It could even be applied, as it was in the eventual cataclysm, to the genius who had first thought of it.

Thus it came about that the executants of the Final Solution, as obedient to the laws of language as they were to the decrees of Nuremberg, finding themselves confronted with a problem termed 'decontamination,' turned quite naturally to the S S's leading decontamination expert, Kurt Gerstein.

The man who had crept as it were surreptitiously into the S S had, by outstanding competence, attracted the notice of his superiors. He had sought to distinguish himself, and he had done so.

Now he might well tremble. Written confirmation reached him two days after Günther's visit. 'You are ordered to procure 260 kilos of potassium cyanide and to convey it to a destination of which you will be informed by the driver of the vehicle allocated for the purpose.'

The game that was beginning was, for a man like Gerstein, the most hazardous of all, imperilling not only his life (what did that matter?) but his immortal soul. The player must believe not only in himself and his luck, but in the grace of God.

It seems to have been at about that time, or perhaps a little later, that Pastor Mochalsky encountered Gerstein wearing civilian clothes and carrying a suitcase, like a man on the run.

*Frankfurt-am-Main, January 1967.* Pastor Herbert Mochalsky sat opposite me, a round-faced man with hair only beginning to turn grey, his dark suit enlivened by a red tie. His name occurs in Gerstein's *Report*. I had had no difficulty in finding him. He now leads a very tranquil life, marred only, perhaps, by a shadow of regret when he recalls his meeting with Gerstein.

'I was a little over thirty. I had been appointed to the Church of St Anne in Dahlem, the former parish of Pastor Niemöller, who had been in a concentration camp for several years. I was doing my best to replace him. We were under close surveillance by the Gestapo, partly because of Niemöller, of course, but also because we were still holding services on the lines of the Confessional Church. In any case, I was known to the authorities. I had been arrested several times and driven out of Silesia, my native province. We held a daily service. The total congregation was about fifty, all of whom attended from time to time, so that I knew them all by sight. A newcomer was bound to be noticed.

'My sermon on that particular day was on the Fifth Commandment—"Thou Shalt Not Kill." While I was preaching I saw that there was a stranger present. I thought he was probably a member of the Gestapo, and that my sermon was going to get me into trouble. After the service he came into the vestry, where I was taking off my surplice. He was carrying a suitcase.

'He seemed to be in a state of terrible agitation. He said: "I saw lights in the church as I was passing and so I came in. I listened to your sermon on the Fifth Commandment. It's a matter that touches me very nearly. Providence must have guided my footsteps. Something terrible has happened to me." Then he got a sheet of paper with a red border out of his pocket, and when he said that he was a member of the SS I was badly frightened. Anyone who had had dealings with the Gestapo knew what that red border was likely to mean. I thought he had come to arrest me. But he thrust the paper under my nose and said, "I want you to read it. It's an order to me to procure a consignment of prussic acid. Do you realize what for?" I was too amazed to say anything. That an SS man should be showing me a document headed "Top Secret"!

' "It's very secret indeed," he said, and I still said nothing. I thought it was a trap. But he went on: "This consignment is intended to kill thousands of people—you know what I mean, the sort of people who are labelled sub-human." Then he said: "Herr Pastor, what am I to do? If I carry out the order I shall be an accomplice in mass extermination. I'm thinking of committing suicide."

'He told me that he had joined the SS because he wanted to discover the murderers of some near relative—his sister or sister-in-law, I think. "My uniform's in there," he said, pointing to the suitcase. "I want to commit suicide, but if I do two other men will die. Every member of the SS is vouched for by two others. If I kill myself they'll both be shot."

'Again he asked, "What am I to do?" I don't remember what I said to him. Finally he went away with his suitcase.'

What counsel had he hoped for? From the pulpit Mochalsky had pronounced the words 'Thou shalt not kill.' What more could he say? Gerstein had to make do with that. Neither the pastor nor the Church—not even his own Church of Resistance —was equipped to resolve a problem of conscience without parallel in the Scriptures.

With his suitcase containing the dreadful burden of which he now longed to rid himself, Gerstein was an outcast thrust into the solitude of the heretic, for now at last he realized the terms on which his battle must be fought. It was not in daylight that he could combat the powers of evil, but only in their own labyrinthine darkness, where he, the Christian and pacifist, must of necessity have a share in the very abominations he sought to combat. Could he obey this order and still call himself a Christian? On the other hand, apart from the danger to himself and those close to him, would he be any more a Christian if he refused to do so? Would he not rather be taking refuge in the timid ranks of those professing Christians who, in the shelter of neutrality, awaited the outcome of the battle—the triumph or the death of God?

The firm of Degesch of Frankfurt, the German company specializing in decontamination, directly or indirectly controlled the whole supply of hydrocyanic acid (HCN), popularly called prussic acid because its discoverer, the Swedish chemist Scheele, had first isolated it from the dyestuff known as 'Prussian blue.' Scheele himself had been killed by the acid, whose extreme toxicity made it an invaluable weapon against vermin and parasites of all kinds. It had been experimented with for that purpose in the 1914 war, but accidents had been so numerous that the French Government had forbidden its use for the decontamination of inhabited premises. (People had died while sleeping on mattresses impregnated with the fumes in rooms where prussic acid had been used to destroy bedbugs.)

But there was a variant known as Zyklon B, in which the acid was fixed in an inert porous base which released the fumes slowly on contact with the air. Zyklon B, manufactured by Degesch and its subsidiaries, was what Gerstein had been ordered to procure.

Why, then, was the matter so secret? There was no apparent

reason. The SS administration of the camps at Lublin, in Poland, was at this time openly ordering very large quantities of Zyklon B (900 kilos, for example, on 25 July 1942, without counting amounts purchased on the spot at about the same time by a special envoy, Oberscharführer Perschon) from the firm of Testa in Hamburg, a Degesch subsidiary. The secret lay in the use to be made of the acid: whether it was to be used for normal decontamination purposes or for something else—to get rid of lice, or to get rid of men? There were a number of channels, cunningly interwoven by Eichmann's department, through which Gerstein's contribution could flow.

Early in August the potash plant in Kolin, near Prague, was in a position to deliver the amount he had ordered. 'If I obey I become an accomplice,' he had said.

A service car and a truck set out in company from Berlin for Prague. The passengers in the car were Gerstein and a certain Doctor Wilhelm Pfannenstiel, Professor of Hygiene at Marburg University and Lieutenant-Colonel SS, who was also travelling east in connection with matters of sanitation. Kolin was about forty miles from Prague, a small, ancient town overshadowed by the chimneys of the potash plant, the only one in the Protectorate of Bohemia which produced potassium cyanide.

While the containers of acid were being loaded on to the truck Gerstein questioned workmen and members of the plant staff about how the stuff should be handled and how dangerous it was. 'The staff of the factory of prussic acid ... understood through my voluntarily awkward technical questions that the acid was made to kill human beings.' (Gerstein's *Report*—p. 283.) One can imagine the kind of question. 'Is it really as lethal as all that? How many people do you think the contents of a single container would kill?' While they were in the neighbourhood of Kolin pickets kept a close watch on the truck.

The Zyklon B party went on into Poland, and Gerstein chatted with Professor Pfannenstiel, who was very much at his ease, very professorial and urbane. He was the father of a large family, a well-to-do Nazi living in a dreamland of his own. His affable conversation afforded a counterpoint to Gerstein's furious and sombre thoughts. While the car travelled through the Polish countryside Gerstein was racking his brains. Something had to be done—now.

Friedrich Geissert (1967): 'A man in the Institute said to me in 1942: "That boss of yours, Gerstein, he's an extraordinary bird. Amazing sense of smell. It seems he can smell even the tiniest leakage of prussic acid." He'd been one of Gerstein's escort in Poland. Gerstein had suddenly ordered the truck to stop, sniffed and said that one of the containers was leaking. He said they'd have to ditch the load at once, a matter of life and death.'
For a start they 'ditched' one container.
Pfannenstiel did not question this proceeding; and Pfannenstiel was a professor and an expert in sanitation. If he saw nothing wrong, it meant that Gerstein's standing and credibility were sound. It was a decisive test. Gerstein now knew that no one suspected the game he was playing. He could declare any consignment defective and order its immediate destruction. His word would be enough.

The Zyklon B party reached Lublin on 17 August 1942. Gruppenführer Odilo Globocnik, SS Police Chief for the district and Brigade Commander, was anxiously awaiting them. There were important matters to be decided.
Globocnik, whom his friends called Globus, had been born at Trieste in 1904, and after first being a naturalized Austrian had later acquired German nationality. A Nazi from the beginning, he had been Gauleiter of Vienna and boasted of his friendship with Himmler.
Globus's first words were to impress upon them that everything they were about to see was under the ban of the strictest secrecy. 'A State secret, and not merely one of the most important but, we may honestly say, the most important of all. Any man who breathes a word of what he sees here is committing suicide. We shot two men only yesterday for gabbing. The Führer and Reichsführer Himmler were here the day before. They ordered me not to issue passes to people needing to visit our installations for service

reasons; I have to escort them in person to ensure absolute security.'

Pfannenstiel, who had listened to this in rapture, asked: 'And what did the Führer think of it all?'

'He said: "Faster. Faster. Hurry it up and finish the job." '[1]

The SS had humorously given the operation the code-name 'Catholic Action' because it had been conceived in a place having Catholic associations. But the name was now changed to 'Operation Reinhard' in memory of its presiding genius, Reinhard Heydrich, who had been killed by the Resistance in Prague ('His death equalled the loss of a battle,' Hitler said).

The head office was in the Julius Schreck barracks at Lublin. The premises were remarkably small and occupied by only a handful of men under the command of SS Captain Höfle, Globocnik's special aide for Operation Reinhard. It was here that the special messengers came from the Führer's Chancellery, here that the monstrous statistics of corpses and possessions were compiled, here that the solemn oath of secrecy was signed:

'SS Hauptsturmführer Höfle, head of the Operation Reinhard section under the SS Chief of Police for the district of Lublin, has informed me in detail of my duties in connection with the following:

'1. the absolute ban on disclosure of any information, verbally or in writing, to any person outside the Operation Reinhard section, concerning the transfer of Jewish populations or the incidents that may ensue;

'2. the "State secret" rating of this operation in accordance with Instruction V on the safeguarding of secret documents;

'3. the special instructions affecting the administrative services of the SS Chief of Police of the Lublin district, particular emphasis being laid on the fact that these are to be considered "service orders" within the framework of "obligations and prohibitions" as laid down in Article 92 of the Penal Code of the Reich;

1 *Schneller, schneller die ganze Aktion durchführen!* It may be noted that although Himmler's presence at Belzec has been confirmed, that of Hitler remains questionable. No reference to it has been found in any document.

'4. the absolute prohibition of photography in all camps concerned with Operation Reinhard;

'5. the interpretation of Articles 88 and 93 of the Penal Code as issued on 24 April 1934, and of the texts dated 3 May 1917 and 12 February 1920, concerning entry and the violation of secrecy by non-authorized persons;

'6. Articles 139 (obligation to report) and 353 (violation of professional secrecy) of the Penal Code of the Reich.

'I have taken note of these instructions and of the texts referred to, and I am fully aware of the obligations they impose on me. I undertake to execute them faithfully to the best of my conscience and ability. I am aware that I shall remain pledged to secrecy even after I have left the Service.

'Signed . . .'

(Article 139—'Whosoever has knowledge of criminal intentions and fails to inform the authorities or the person threatened shall be punished'—was the line invoked by the Bishop of Münster in his protest against euthanasia. One may wonder why it is cited here—whether this relic of ancient laws was deliberately inserted as a trap to catch the signatory if the Final Solution were to be cancelled.)

In addition to the oppressive atmosphere of secrecy a kind of excitement prevailed among the persons concerned, a mingled pride and apprehension such as any new undertaking may give rise to. Even the most dull-witted of the participants in Operation Reinhard could not fail to know that what he was doing was without precedent: the conveyor-belt destruction of human life. The artisan of death had never before existed in history. There had been executioners and murderers, but never craftsmen trained in a school of mass extermination.

These were what was to be found in Lublin and other places: pioneers of mass death, trained in the camps and euthanasia clinics. Specialists from Hardheim Castle, men who had watched and photographed through peepholes, noting the efficacy of different methods of liquidation as applied to human guinea-pigs, had been assembled at Travnik for this greater task. There were connoisseurs of suffocation, experts in agony, scholars of the death-throe. Should any shadow of misgiving afflict them, they could remind themselves that Adolf Hitler was personally interested in what they were doing. They saw his emissaries coming and going between Berlin and Lublin. They could take a pride in their business. And Operation Reinhard was treated as a front-line service, with promotion and decorations to be won safely out of range of gunfire, to say nothing of revelry and comfortable living.

Globus, that well-pleased factory manager, proudly listed his establishments in the Lublin area: Belzec, Sobibor, Treblinka, Maidanek, frontier names sounding of snow and wind.

'I'm most anxious to see them,' said Professor Pfannenstiel.

'You shall,' said Globus. 'You shall.'

A car took Globus, Gerstein and Pfannenstiel to Belzec, some ninety miles to the south-west, along the main road which by way of Krasnystaw, Zamosc and Tomaszow Lubelski reached the former Soviet demarcation line. Beyond lay Rava-Russkaya and Lvov. The monotony of the Polish plain gave way to woods of birch through which the gleam of marshes could be seen. A lonely countryside with few human beings: an occasional old woman in a red shawl, gazing at them with astonished eyes, a countryman driving farmhorses whose shoes struck sparks from the cobbles.

> In the hamlet of Pitschepoï
> Where all the roofs are thatched
> The rain rains and the snow snows . . .

The village consisted of a few solidly built houses, the rest being of wood, low hovels with a front yard. Hens clucked along the village street, and a soaring church-tower proclaimed the glory of God.

Then came the encampment with its assembly of huts. 'Belzec. Special Establishment of the Waffen SS.'

'Gentlemen,' said Globus, 'this is Sergeant-Major Oberhauser,

who will show you round the camp in the absence of his commanding officer, Police Captain Wirth.'

Oberhauser, a former member of the euthanasia organization,
was somewhat embarrassed. In a matter of such formidable
secrecy it is preferable that the responsibility for divulging it,
even to initiates, should be borne by someone else. Gerstein
afterwards recalled the evident reluctance with which he took
Pfannenstiel and himself on their conducted tour.

Outside the village, some four hundred yards from the railway
station, a wooded slope ran east and west, its summit marking the
boundary of the camp. A special siding of the Lublin–Lvov railway ran to the edge of the slope, in which there were a few huts,
one of which served as railway station: a charmingly rustic
building enclosed in a brick wall heavily lined with barbed wire.

The camp was an irregular quadrilateral, with sides between
250 and 300 yards long. At the exact centre was a look-out tower
equipped with a searchlight and a machine gun. Only a man on the
tower, or someone in an aircraft, could see the entire layout of the
installations.

Clumps of trees separated the different sectors, and hedges of
young conifers along the railway line and the road prevented the
village people from looking in. (No outsider entered the plant:
the suppliers of raw material dropped their loads at the gate and
got away fast.) Gaps between the trees were blocked with leafy
branches tied laterally. Verdure concealed the rites of Belzec.

About a hundred yards from the station was a very large shed
labelled 'Cloakroom' in which there was a collecting-office
bearing the sign 'Objects of value.' Beyond this was a 'hairdressing salon' with a hundred seats. An alleyway 150 yards
long, densely fenced with barbed wire on either side, led beneath
the searchlight and machine gun of the watch-tower to the 'Inhalation and Bath Rooms.'

Pfannenstiel and Gerstein were led by their guide towards a
squat building solidly bedded in concrete. Over the door was the
inscription, 'Heckenholt Foundation.' One entered by way of a
flight of steps with iron rails, to find oneself in a dimly lit
corridor with three rooms on either side about 20 feet square and

a little over 6 feet high. Like garages, Gerstein thought. There were a great many flowers, geraniums, outside the Foundation, and on its tar-paper roof gleamed a large, six-pointed star—the star of David.

Baths, Foundation, flowers, star, these struck the keynote of Belzec—beauty, comfort, charity. Gerstein, knowing the truth, yet felt a wild hope leap in his heart that perhaps it had all been a nightmare; perhaps nothing had happened or ever would, and Belzec might continue to bask in peace under the summer sun.

But why were there no birds?

And why such myriads of flies?

## Chapter 11

# BELZEC

A VOICE aroused them at seven in the morning announcing that the first consignment had arrived.

Christian Wirth, Captain of Police, former liquidator of the insane at Grafeneck and now in charge of Operation Reinhard at Belzec, Treblinka and Sobibor, appeared on the scene, a jovial figure in immaculate uniform and gleaming boots, riding-crop in hand—the Virgil who was to lead Gerstein into a Hell Dante had never dreamed of.

The train had come from Lvov, the locomotive puffing in the rear of forty-five goods trucks while they were being shunted on to the siding.

Stefan Kirsz, railway guard domiciled in Belzec, Roman Catholic, under no charge and having no political affiliations, deposed on 15 October 1945 as follows:

'The convoys which I personally conducted from Rava-Russkaya to Belzec were divided into sections of twenty trucks each and driven along the siding to the camp. The trucks went first, with the locomotive pushing behind. Standing by the locomotive shed there was always a party of about a dozen Jews, laughing and singing marching songs. This happened every time a train arrived at the camp.'

Mecislas Kudyba, aged thirty-seven, a smith, also domiciled in Belzec, deposed on 14 October 1945: 'There were up to three convoys a day, each of forty to sixty goods trucks. The Jews, always very quiet, stared out through the barred windows.'

With a grinding of wheels and the thud of buffers the trucks were brought to a stop within the outer wall of the camp. Railwaymen and the men of the police guard immediately left the train. They were forbidden to cross the railway track. This was a privilege reserved only for those who, administratively speaking, were already dead.

White faces showed behind the windows, for the most part women and children, all Galician Jews, picked up in their villages under the watchful eyes of Christians. (The Poles, except for an honourable minority, witnessed the elimination of the Jews with a serenity approaching the sublime.)

The faces behind the windows . . . they were nothing but eyes, wide and staring, searching for the reality behind what they could see. There were no cries, no complaints, no sound except perhaps the wail of an infant or the voice of a sick person asking for water. The trucks moved on a little way.

'I must confess that, after eighteen years, not even we who were there can describe that feeling of terror. Today as I stand before you that feeling has vanished, and I do not think it can be conveyed to any other person . . . The circumstances of that time cannot be re-created in a court of law. I do not think that anyone can understand it. I can no longer do so myself, although I experienced it in the flesh.' (Doctor Besky at the Eichmann trial, 1961.)

Two hundred Ukrainian and Baltic auxiliary troops—they were known as the 'Blacks' or the 'Askaris'—lined the platform armed with leather whips. At the word of command they strode forward and flung open the barred doors. 'Out! Out! Everybody out!'

The whips cracked across shoulders, across faces. The trucks seemed to be bursting apart amid a creaking of metal and a wincing of flesh. They came out in bunches, and the air was filled with flying objects as bundles and old valises tied with string were flung out after them. Within two minutes the trucks were empty—everyone out except those already dead.

A loudspeaker at maximum volume bellowed orders. 'You are to take a bath. Everyone without exception is to undress entirely. Spectacles and false teeth are to be removed. Clothes to be piled in a heap. Objects of value to be handed in at the office.'

Chaim Hirszmann, of Janow Lubelski, aged thirty-four,

master plumber, Jewish religion (19 March 1946): 'Then we were told to strip because we were going to have a bath. I knew at once what this meant. When we'd undressed we had to get into two files, men on one side, women and children on the other. There was an S S trooper pointing to death on one side and forced labour on the other. He waved me into the death group. I still didn't know what was going to happen, but I reckoned it would come to the same thing in the end, whichever group you were in. Just as I was moving that way the S S man came up to me and said, "You've got the look of a soldier, you might be some use to us," and pushed me over to the labour side. We were allowed to put our clothes on again. I and a few others were given the job of seeing the people into the bath. I was allotted to the women.'

'We have learned with satisfaction that the Germans have decided to park the Jews in Poland.' (Jean Pialy, writing in the French satirical weekly, *Gringoire*, during the war. His article was entitled: 'Towards a Happy Solution of the Jewish Problem.')

Five minutes. There were now 5,000 pallid bodies lined up on the platform (1,500 corpses remained in the trucks). The children were seeing the nakedness of their parents—the dark triangle of pubic hair—as a first step in the course of worldly knowledge which they were to complete before the sun was at the zenith. (In the world of Belzec they were wrinkled at 7:10, old at 8 o'clock and by 9 o'clock had entered their last sleep.)

One of the auxiliaries had given a child of three the job of distributing pieces of string to tie shoes and boots together. The infant bustled to and fro, a tiny cog in the machine.

'Even a little boy,' reflected Gerstein, standing rooted to the ground in horror, a creature of eyes and ears. 'Even that one!'

'Only Aryan blood runs in our veins; you must preserve our

racial purity.' Judge Gerstein's admonition to his descendants, inscribed in the family album.

Stefan Kirsz: 'Then they moved in a naked column towards the hut on the second alleyway.'

Urged on by bellowed orders, the women and girls scurried into the 'hairdressing salon.' They came out with their heads shaved, running like plucked fowls. (The hair was stuffed into sacks. The SS man in charge murmured to Gerstein: 'It goes to make a special contraption for use in submarines.')

Written by Gerstein in French: 'Then the march began. Barbed wire on either side and two dozen Ukrainians behind them, armed with rifles. An extraordinarily beautiful girl led the way. I stood outside the death chamber with Captain Wirth and some of the police. They were all stark naked, men, women, girls, children, babes in arms, people with only one leg, all naked . . .'
Over their heads the star of David glittered in the early-morning sun.

Stanislas Kozak, aged fifty-one, locksmith domiciled in Belzec, Roman Catholic, under no charge and having no political affiliations (14 October 1945): 'During the 1942 harvest I managed to get a look inside the camp from a hilltop, using a telescope. I saw the Blacks driving naked Jews into the gas chamber with whips—it was in a small copse in the middle of the camp. The Jews were made to run along a path through the copse, and I heard cries and groans and rifle-shots.'

Those who could not walk, and those who looked as though they might give trouble, were singled out and thrust to one side, under the emblem of the Red Cross. They were disposed of with bullets.

Gerstein noted a large, plump SS man who addressed the advancing column in a fatherly tone:

'Don't worry, you aren't going to be hurt. All you have to do is take a deep breath. It strengthens the lungs—a precaution against disease.'

They murmured among themselves, repeating what he had said. Some asked: 'But what's going to happen? What are you going to do with us?'

'Well, of course, the men will have to work, building roads and houses. But not the women. If they want to they can do the housework and the cooking.'

A ray of hope for a few of them, Gerstein thought.

As though the smell were not in their nostrils, and the myriad flies buzzing around them! . . . But they had to hurry. They must not linger on the threshold of that doorway to Hell. And the star of David still shone invitingly on the roof of the 'Heckenholt Foundation.'

The first reached the flight of steps, thrust on by the pressure of those behind. They walked up without a sound, and saw the open doors of the chambers on either side of the corridor.

And then, from those throats dried with thirst and terror, there arose the notes of the Kaddish, the prayer for all men, believers and unbelievers alike, the immemorial prayer for orphans, the song of praise and thanksgiving rising from a submissive earth to an eternally victorious Heaven—*Yisgaddal v'yiskaddash sh'meh rabbo* . . .

'Extolled and hallowed be the name of God throughout the world which He has created according to His will. And may He speedily establish His Kingdom of righteousness on earth. Amen.

'Praised be His glorious name unto all eternity.

'Praised and glorified be the name of the Holy One, though He be above all the praises which we can utter. Our guide is He in life and our redeemer through all eternity.

'Our help cometh from Him, the creator of heaven and earth.

'The departed whom we now remember have entered into the peace of life eternal. They still live on earth in the acts of goodness they performed and in the hearts of those who cherish their memory. May the beauty of their life abide among us as a loving benediction.

'Amen.

'May the Father of peace send peace to all who mourn, and comfort all the bereaved among us.

'Amen.'

Some asked for water 'for their death.'[1] Before crossing the threshold a woman of forty 'with flaming eyes' turned and cursed the three observers, Pfannenstiel, Gerstein and Wirth. Wirth lashed her with his riding-crop and she went on with the others. Just before going up the steps a little girl burst into tears because she had lost her coral necklace. A little boy picked it up and gave it to her, smiling. A moment later they were thrust into the corridor.

'What have we done, O God, what have we done? It is beyond belief. How can the world survive so much suffering, so much crime? The Bible says: "Angels, these are your deeds and these are your rewards." But today we see innocent children, true angels, massacred simply because they are purer than the angels; and the world does not change, the world goes on living as though these things did not concern it.' (Rabbi Kelmisch.)

The last thing those people saw as they went to their death was Gerstein, standing near the doorway. What did they read in his face? Horror? Pity? Was he so very different from the wise-cracking Wirth, or from Pfannenstiel, drawn there by curiosity like the flies by the stench?

'The Ministry of the Interior is in possession of reports concerning my constant struggle against the scandalous activities of the Galician Jews and their action centres, Fromms Act and Prim Eros, which distributed . . . millions of free samples among the

1 There is no Jewish ritual of water, but the bodies of the dead have to be carefully washed before being wrapped in the garments of death.

youngest adolescents.' (Gerstein's letter of application for re-admission to the Party, 28 November 1936.)

'Some people were applying to me: "Oh sir, do help us, do help us . . ." Many others were praying. I could not help them. I started praying with them and, hidden, I shouted toward their God and toward mine. I allowed myself to do so as there was a great noise all around me. I should have willingly entered these death rooms, I should have liked to die there with them . . . I had not yet the right to fall into the temptation of dying with these people . . . I must now proclaim what I saw there, and charge the murders.' (Gerstein: *Report*—see p. 287)

Wirth called out in the corridor: 'Stuff them in tight!'

The Blacks thrust in the naked bodies until they were packed together like a solid mass of flesh.

'Seven to eight hundred to each chamber,' said Wirth. Gerstein did sums in his head. Seven to eight hundred human beings in an area of 270 square feet. It wasn't possible. 'Yes, it is,' said Wirth. Gerstein thought again. Most of them were children, many very small. Wirth was right. It could be done.

It was done. SS men and Blacks with their shoulders against the metal doors compressed the yielding human mass. The bars were slammed down. The lights went out, and from within the chambers came a prolonged wail.

The rest of the consignment were still outside waiting their turn. And more trucks were now being shunted on to the siding, the second consignment of the day.

Someone said: 'They have to wait naked in any weather, even in winter.' For the first time Gerstein, forgetting himself, allowed a few words to escape him: 'But they'll die of cold!' He was stared at in amazement. An SS man said bluffly: 'Well, that's what they're here for, isn't it?'

A man's name was shouted. 'Heckenholt!' He was the man in charge of the Diesel engine supplying exhaust gas to the chambers.

Gerstein now perceived the origin of the inscription, 'Heckenholt Foundation.'

But what was Sergeant-Major Heckenholt playing at?

The Diesel wouldn't start. SS men rushed to and fro while the auxiliaries cursed. Those about to die stayed quiet enough; it was the living who now panicked.

Wirth was in a towering rage. For the engine to break down in front of visitors—men who might report the whole thing to Globocnik, even to Himmler himself!

Gerstein kept an eye on his watch. Minutes passed—half-hours—hours. The packed bodies stood waiting in the chambers, held upright by the pressure of naked flesh, gasping mouths turned upward to the ceiling, the younger children dead already in their mothers' arms.

The sound that came from them was not a cry but an unvarying plaint, a long, low sob. Professor Wilhelm Pfannenstiel pressed his ear to one of the doors, and Gerstein heard him exclaim: 'It's like in a synagogue!'[1]

And still the Diesel would not start. Wirth, his fury beyond bounds, lashed Heckenholt's Ukrainian assistant a number of times across the face with his riding-crop. The mills of God were grinding slowly for the martyred Galicians.

And finally they got it going—after two hours and forty-nine minutes by Gerstein's watch. Death must have been welcome in those chambers. The lights went on again and the guests were invited to watch through peepholes while the exhaust-fumes did their work. Wirth, anxious to be friendly, asked Gerstein what he thought of it. Did he think it was better to let people die in darkness or in light? He might have been asking him if he preferred tea or coffee, white wine or red.

At the end of thirty-two minutes it was over. The Diesel was switched off and the discharge doors at the far end of the building were noisily opened. The three observers, Wirth, Pfannenstiel and Gerstein, moved down the corridor to witness the last stage

1 After the war Pfannenstiel denied uttering those words, and said that if he did speak them they had not the cynical meaning attributed to them by Gerstein. Were they, perhaps, a scientific observation?

of the operation. They looked in at the open doors of the chamber; or rather they looked at the mass of upright bodies still packed inside, awaiting the right to fall down.

'The deads, like marble statue, stood closely one to another. They had no room to fall down or even to be bent. Even dead, members of one family could be easily recognized: they were still clutched to each other by their stiffened hands and it was difficult to separate them when emptying the room for a next "turn".' (Gerstein: *Report*—see p. 288.)

Bodies still with their arms round each other were sent rolling in the dust of the yard at the far end of the shed. Children's bodies were tossed through the air. The crowded space resounded with the cracking of whips over the backs of the frantic slaves pressed into the service of death, and the voices crying: '*Schnell! Schnell!*— Hurry up!' They were behind schedule. The next consignment was waiting. And with the slamming of the doors at one end of the building the entrance doors were opened and the next consignment flowed in up the steps as though on a conveyor-belt. They had seen nothing of what went on inside. The trees were there, guardians of a momentary secret, everything betrayed but nothing shown.

In the yard, workers moving like automata were obscenely searching the bodies for anything of value, rings, ear-rings, other objects possibly concealed. Makeshift dentists were drawing gold teeth. Wirth, voluble and beaming, his good humour restored, strode here and there, stepping over bodies or thrusting them aside with his foot. He produced a large metal box and showed it to Gerstein, rattling the contents.

'Have a look at this, Lieutenant. Nothing but gold teeth, and only two days' bag—yesterday and the day before.'

Among the consignment two days earlier had been Rudolf Reder, a soap-manufacturer from Lvov; some of the teeth in the box Wirth was rattling had belonged to his fellow-travellers. But Reder was still alive. He was a short distance away, at the eastern edge of the camp, bowed over the spade with which he was working. When those capable of work were being singled out he had said that he was a mechanic, and therefore had been spared despite his age (he was sixty-one) and put to grave-digging. He was to be one of the two survivors of Belzec.[1] At the inquiry he said:

'When the pit was dug the corpses were flung in anyhow until they were piled up three or four feet above ground-level. The next day there would be a great pool of blood soaked into the sandy soil around the pit. Quicklime was scattered over the bodies and later they were covered with sand.'

From Gerstein's *Report* (p. 289): 'The naked corpses were thrown into nearby ditches of 100m. by 12m. and 20m. After somme days, the corpses swoll, then, a few days later, sank down, and so they could be covered of a new lay of corpses; then about 10cm. of sand were spread on them, and only a few heads or limbs emerged from that.'

Reder: 'The camp maintenance parties totalled 500 men, of whom 30 or 40 died every day. They were under Jewish foremen. At midday every day those no longer capable of work were herded over to the pits and shot, to be replaced by men from the next convoy who were told their lives would be spared. It made no difference if they said they preferred to die with their families. They left their hut at four in the morning and drew tea and a hunk of bread from one of the kitchen windows. Then they paraded in the yard and sang songs to order.

'Sergeant Feix, a tall, blond, good-looking man, walked round to make sure every one was singing. He was particularly fond of a Polish song from the Carpathians: "Man of the mountains, have you no regrets?" '

The camp orchestra, which performed near the locomotive shed, was conducted by Wassermann of Cracow. In principle the instrumentalists did not change, although at a pinch they could be replaced by new arrivals. Wassermann knew perfectly well that

1 The other, Chaim Hirszmann, whose testimony has already been quoted, was murdered on the evening of the day he testified (19 March 1946) by members of the Nationalist Struggle Group, a Ukrainian, anti-Semitic body. Reder, who went blind, fled to Canada after the war and was still living there a few years ago.

he would end up in a charnel pit with the rest of them. However, the orchestra went on, and every day had its music.

Still in the best of humours, Captain Wirth presented the Jewish foremen to his guests. This one was a former floorwalker in a big Berlin store. And this little man had been a captain in the Royal and Imperial Army of Austria. 'What's more, he had the Iron Cross, First Class,' said Wirth. 'And he can play the violin.'

The ex-captain and violinist touched his forelock while the slaves in the yard continued to drag away the bodies with long-handled hooks.

'The Jews aren't always easy,' said Wirth. 'There are tiresome incidents. One woman managed to hide a razor and slashed several of the Jewish workers with it when she was on her way into the gas chamber.' What annoyed Wirth was that she had nevertheless been thrust into the chamber, instead of being subjected to exemplary punishment before she was allowed to die. 'Of course when a Jew gets hurt we treat him,' he went on. 'Just to give them the idea that their lives are safe. The poor fools believe it.'

(A day was coming when the fools would rise, in Sobibor, Treblinka, Warsaw and a hundred other places now forgotten. Wirth was to know about this before his own death.)

'But you simply can't imagine,' said Wirth, 'the amount of gold and jewels we pick up. Come and have a look.'

He displayed his treasures, among which Gerstein noted two shining twenty-dollar gold pieces. Wirth, too, had spotted them and he could not resist: he stuffed them hastily in his pocket.

Deposition of Konrad Morgen, former SS judge, at Nuremberg, 7 August 1946:

'I thought at first that what Wirth said was pure fantasy, but then, at Lublin, I saw one of the depots where the belongings of his victims, or a part of them, were stored. The size of the hoard —there was a huge pile of watches—was enough in itself to show that appalling things were happening. There were a great many precious objects, and I have never in my life seen so much money, particularly foreign money, currency from all over the world. On top of all this there was gold melted down into ingots, great bars.'

Sergeant-Major Oberhauser told Gerstein of a recent happening that had greatly surprised him. He had discovered in one of the neighbouring villages an old Jewish acquaintance, a man he had played with when they were boys. The Jew, who had been a non-commissioned officer in the Army, was a fine fellow; he had even saved his life.

'I'm going to take him and his wife into my labour contingent,' said the Sergeant-Major.

'And then?' asked Gerstein. 'What will happen to him in the end?'

'What will happen?' Oberhauser was astonished. 'Well, of course, the same as the others. There's no other way. But I may have them shot.'

And Wirth also had a little tale to tell. 'One morning they found a small child, still alive and cheerful, in a chamber that hadn't been cleared out the night before.' As to what happened in this case—why bother to ask?

'In order to encourage his subordinates in their zeal for massacre Zeki Bey would lean down from his horse, pick up a small child by the arm and fling it from him after whirling it once or twice in the air. The children were killed when they hit the ground and Zeki Bey would cry to his followers: "Don't imagine I've killed an innocent. Even the newborn of this race are guilty because they harbour within themselves the germs of revenge. If you wish to be assured of the future you must not spare even the youngest." And the men did not spare them.' (A. Andonian, in *Official documents concerning the Armenian massacres, 1915*.)

'Lieutenant,' Globocnik had said in Lublin, 'you have two tasks to perform. First, to examine the best means of decontaminating the huge quantities of garments, shoes and so forth which come out of our places. Secondly, and this is more important, to devise some better method of carrying out the operation. At present we're using the exhaust-gases from an old Russian Diesel engine, but that has got to be changed. It's much too slow. The Führer wants things to be speeded up. Prussic acid may be the answer.'

A problem of the industrial era: rationalization of corpse production. There were two schools of thought: that of Wirth, using exhaust-gases, and that of Rudolf Höss, the commanding officer of Auschwitz, who in recent months had discovered the possibilities of prussic acid. The exhaust-gas school had the advantage of long experience acquired in the euthanasia clinics, but easy handling and rapid action were on the side of Zyklon B.

Opinion was divided. Eichmann and Günther supported Höss, but Wirth, sticking to his own method, was not without allies. His attitude towards Höss, his former subordinate, was that of any industrialist who fears that a rival may be getting ahead of him; while Höss, for his part, was loud in his scorn for Wirth's crude, outdated methods.

In this strange contest, unparalleled in human history, Kurt Gerstein was required to act as arbitrator.

Captain Wirth could not have been more affable. Gerstein might be no more than a junior lieutenant, but he came from Berlin; he had the ear of the high-ups and clearly his views were of importance. It was the greatest pity the Diesel had failed to start, since this might cause him to condemn the whole system. An order to change over to prussic acid would amount to an official slap in the face for Wirth, besides causing other complications.

'You know, Lieutenant, I really don't think we ought to suggest to Berlin that our method should be changed. Its efficiency has been proved. The trouble with the Diesel was quite exceptional.'

Gerstein seemed to agree. Wirth had no reason to suspect that in this matter their wishes coincided, and that the last thing Gerstein wanted to do was to deliver the consignment of Zyklon B he had brought with him.

He had prepared the ground already with Pfannenstiel when he had declared that one of the containers was leaking. It was simple for him now to tell Wirth that the whole load was suspect and therefore unusable, and that it must be got rid of as soon as possible.

'If I am correctly informed,' said Professor Pfannenstiel in 1950, 'all the containers were buried.'

Robert Weigelt told me in 1967: 'They were jettisoned half way between the camp and Lublin. Kurt said they might be dangerous.'

Nevertheless a second trainload of human material was delivered to the Heckenholt Foundation on the day of Gerstein's visit. About 12,000 people died that day in Belzec.

*18 April 1967*. A sickly spring was peering through the trees. I walked from one mound of ashes to another through Little Poland, and came to the landscape that is still called Belzec. The tops of the pine trees trembled under the rain.

A head wearing a forage-cap peered cautiously round the door of a cottage. Visitors! The owner of the head made ready to receive us. His name was Dominik Wojtek and he was the custodian in charge. In charge of what? There was nothing there but empty space—no more barbed wire, no more huts or concrete. Nothing but a patch of deserted woodland on the Soviet frontier, where the trees had multiplied during the years. The yellow star of Belzec had blown up in the end.

Dominik Wojtek told us about it in Polish, which the driver of my car, who came from Cracow, translated as best he could into Low German: 'Trains ... Flies ... Germans and Poles drunk in the cafés ... The Belzec Jews bolted into the woods; only one was caught and killed by the Blacks ... The camp was liquidated ... They worked for days and days destroying every trace ... And the smell, *panie*, the smell! ...'

We walked in silence up the slope to where the camp had been. A block of white stone marked the site of the Heckenholt Foundation, and in front of it were two metal figures, emaciated bodies in postures of despair: 'Help us! Help us!'

Farther on, at the eastern boundary of the camp where the charnel pits were dug, the earth was pitted and furrowed. The place was a miniature Klondyke, the scene of a latter-day gold-rush.

'From about the middle of the northern boundary of the camp and along the eastern boundary'—so runs the report of the Polish Commission of Inquiry, dated 10 October 1945—'over an area of about 100 square yards, the ground has been ploughed up. According to information supplied by the officials of the Belzec militia who helped us, this was the work of the local population searching for gold and jewels left behind by the liquidated Jews. Human bones were found scattered throughout this area.'

(Who can blame them, the wretched peasantry, creeping out with their spades and lanterns, braving the miasma of death, the distant howl of wolves, even the risk of future haunting, though the priest might grant them absolution? It was their only chance of growing rich.)

That rectangle of earth saw the end of Polish Jewry, after a thousand years. They ended in that shallow trough, the pious inhabitants of the mediaeval ghettos, sages and doctors, men of learning, wearers of curl-papers and of the tallith, fearless preachers, labourers who sang, beggars and madmen greeted by the name of Elijah. The chariot of Israel and its riders.

Reb Alter Shapiro was studying the passage in 'Questions and Answers' relating to the wife of the prophet Elijah.

'We know that Elijah vanished from the sight of men, but we do not know whether he is still alive. This being so, is his wife free to marry again or should she be regarded as deserted without the right of re-marriage?'

Reb Isaac Schneersohn: 'Uncle, the wife of the prophet Elijah would now be two thousand years old. What man would be so mad as to want to marry a Jewess that age? And why should I vex my head with the question?'

Reb Alter Shapiro: 'To the greater glory of the Law. To study, that is what matters.' (Memoirs of Isaac Schneersohn.)

The custodian picked something off the ground and placed it in my hand. It was part of a skull. I tried to give it back to him, but he had already moved on. I walked after him still carrying the fragment, which filled my thoughts more than it did my hand. He called to me through the curtain of rain, and I put it in my overcoat pocket.

Wojtek and the driver from Cracow showed me a row of small blue flowers exactly marking the edge of the pit, and then Wojtek pointed to himself. Did he mean that he had planted them? Yes, he did, and he flung his arms wide in a gesture of enthusiasm. Did I understand? He plunged his finger into the damp earth and brought up a fragment of ashen matter which crumbled under his thumb while he tried to explain to me the extraordinary fertility of that earth that was not earth. I nodded without conviction, and he turned in despair to the man from Cracow, who said loudly: '*Herr Redaktor! Herr Redaktor!*' I did not understand him either. What was I to understand, with that fragment in my pocket?

We went to the Memorial, our heads bowed, almost running under the rain. Wojtek opened a small door disclosing a dark store-room where everything dug up from the earth was deposited. There was a gleaming pile of bones. I wanted to add my own sample, but the door was promptly closed.

'All over the area of the camp, but more especially in the sector used as a cemetery, there are traces of conifer plantations. According to the head keeper of Rivers and Forests, Tadeusz Dunajowicz, they were planted by the Germans after the camp had been finally destroyed.'

The Nazis planted trees to cover their tracks. Six million trees were planted in the gardens and on the slopes of Israel as a reminder to the world.

At Treblinka, eighty miles north-east of Warsaw, Gerstein saw similar things. This was a larger establishment with eight gas chambers. It was intended to deal with the entire population of the Warsaw ghetto, 500,000 people. Captain Wirth had no doubt that it was adequate for the task. Personnel and equipment were both excellent; there had been no failures. The piles of empty baggage, garments, boots and shoes, in the yard were like the Pyramids.

Delighted to think that the visitors were departing without having criticized his methods, Wirth gave a party in honour of Pfannenstiel and Gerstein. It was held in the officers' mess of the Treblinka garrison, a Gothic banquet on Himmler lines, with venison and unlimited supplies of everything. Wine flowed by the caskful, to drown fear, if there was any, misgivings for the future, even a twinge of remorse. Twentieth-century man may do anything, but still he is a man and carries within him the age-old conscience of humanity. This must be stifled, and so the State thunders its message of Duty, the Noble Task, the Historic Mission, while at the same time it keeps up the supply of drink and sees to it that the faithful servant is rewarded.

Mecislas Kudyba (14 October 1945): 'The commander of the Belzec camp was a man named Wirth. I was told by the Blacks that he was awarded a special decoration and promoted major for having exterminated a million Jews.'

Globocnik to the Central Security Office, 13 April 1943: 'Promotions recommended for meritorious service in the special commando of Operation Reinhard ... The Reichsführer after visiting Sobibor camp gave his formal approval for the promotion of officers and men who have proved outstanding. The attached list covers the three camps.

'Police Captain Christian Wirth (S S No. 345,464), the officer in charge, is promoted Major as of 30 January 1943. I recommend that he should be promoted simultaneously to the rank of S S Sturmbannführer.

'I recommend that Police Lieutenant Franz Stängl (S S No. 296,569) should be promoted to the rank of Captain and S S Untersturmführer. Stängl is the senior officer of his rank and the best.

'The following promotions are also recommended:

'Waffen S S Hauptscharführer Josef Oberhauser to the rank of S S Untersturmführer.

'Waffen S S Oberscharführer Lorenz Heckenholt to the grade of S S Hauptscharführer.

'Waffen SS Oberscharführer Kurt Franz to the rank of SS Untersturmführer.'

Professor Pfannenstiel subsequently denies having been at Treblinka, but according to Gerstein he raised his glass to that table of killers and talked of the importance of their task, the 'humanity' of their methods and their 'fine' work. He is also reported to have said: 'Seeing those Jewish bodies, those lamentable faces, one realizes even more the greatness of your work.'

After the war the wretched professor, juggling with words like a man with loaded dice, sought to show himself in a different light.

'I certainly talked to the men serving in Belzec. I may say that they were not entirely villainous, because they were all obviously unhappy about the duties they had to perform. They told me that they would give anything to be transferred elsewhere ... I may have said in the course of these conversations that they must stick it a little longer and I would try to get them relieved ... I think I also said that meanwhile every man must do his duty.'

And on the following night, the night of 20 August 1942, Gerstein, seated on the floor in the darkened corridor of the Warsaw–Berlin express at the side of Baron von Otter, Secretary of the Swedish Legation, could contain himself no longer. The effort to preserve an expressionless face, to utter no incautious word, must have come near to destroying him. Now he burst into tears and the words came pouring out: 'Etwas Furchtbares ... Something appalling.'

## Chapter 12

# THE FRUITLESS BATTLE

'HE called on me late one night when he got back from Belzec,' said Bishop Otto Dibelius, an old friend of Gerstein's who had officiated at his wedding. 'He was in a state of terrible agitation. He talked in a stifled voice. And suddenly he cried out, repeating the words of the women: "Help us! Help us!"'

When Pastor Kurt Rehling went to visit him in Hagen he saw an SS officer's death's-head cap lying on the kitchen table. It looked enormous, and for a moment this was all he saw. Then he became aware of two blank faces on either side of it, those of Gerstein and his own wife. Gerstein had been talking to Frau Rehling, but now they were silent, having nothing more to say. One may act and even die; to talk is more difficult.

Gerstein: 'You must realize that all this is a State secret. Anyone who divulges it, and anyone who listens, is risking death. You and I are now both in danger of our lives.'

Rehling: 'We ought to shout the truth from the steps of the Town Hall. I must proclaim it from the pulpit.'

Gerstein, throwing up his hands: 'Not a newspaper would report it. There would simply be a news item the next day saying that a respected Protestant pastor had had to be hurriedly removed to a mental hospital. And there you'd be forced to give me away, and my friends as well, and we wouldn't be able to help anyone.'

At the Nuremberg trial, Counsel Horst Pelckmann, cross-examining: 'Did you not think it your duty to inform world opinion? Did you not want to ease your conscience by crying murder?'

SS Judge Konrad Morgen: 'Without access to radio or the

press I could do nothing effective. If I had shouted it in the streets people would simply have thought me mad, because this was something beyond human belief. I should have been put in an asylum.'

Rehling: 'Perhaps we ought to be thinking less of our chances of success and more of our moral duty.'

Gerstein: 'There's no sense in being rash and endangering others. This ring I'm wearing contains a poison capsule—cyanide. If I'm caught I shall use it to make sure I don't betray my friends. Under torture a man will say anything.'

The first person to be told, after Baron von Otter, was Horst Dickten. Gerstein telephoned from the station asking him to meet him with a car.

'I found him standing by the wall in a dark corner. He was trembling and he staggered as he walked. When I got him home he just fell on his bed.

'I said: "You're ill. I'll call Doctor Nissen."

'He shook his head and then he began to cry. Fräulein Hinz brought him a cup of tea with a lot of sugar. He lay there in the dark with the curtains drawn. I sat on the edge of the bed and felt his pulse. His heart was beating furiously. He said: "It's not on my own account . . . Leave me alone now." He slept a few hours, and that afternoon he told me. He wanted to read one or two passages of the Bible, but then he said: "What pardon can there possibly be for men like that?" ' '

Before his visit to Belzec, Gerstein had carried a clothes-brush in his revolver-holster. Afterwards he was never without his automatic. He carried it even when he went to visit Cesare Orsenigo, the Papal Nuncio in Berlin.

That was a fateful errand. At this crisis in his life Gerstein the Protestant turned to Rome. In the convulsed world of 1942 there was no higher authority than the Pope. Weaponless he might be, but his word prevailed over many hundred millions of consciences; his hand could hurl the thunder of the Church Eternal.

So, thought Gerstein, let him rise and act and root out Belzec, even if he should destroy himself in doing so, and his brothers in Christ.

Horst Dickten (1968): 'When he got back he asked me to come into his room. There was something he wanted to say, but at first he couldn't tell me. He was sobbing. He asked me for a cigarette and he drank a little brandy, which was very unusual. I kept trying to find out what the trouble was, although he was a man it was better not to question; he liked to say things in his own time.

' "Kurt, has someone given you away?"

' "It's worse than that," he said. "I've lost my last hope."

'He had called at the Nuncio's residence without an appointment. When he told me this I said: "Well, in that case it's no wonder you got a chilly reception."

'He said: "If I'd asked for an appointment they might have refused. I didn't want to give them the chance. As it was, I did at least see the Nuncio."

' "You actually saw him? Well, then . . ."

' "People are all swine. I gave some underling a hefty bribe, and he got me an audience at once. Yes, I saw Orsenigo . . ." '

The Berlin Nuncio was a Lombard, sixty-nine years old, titular Archbishop of Libya, a solidly built prelate with strongly marked features who looked much like the country priest he had been for many years. He had never attended the Pontifical Ecclesiastical Academy, the training school for Papal diplomats. Pope Pius XI, a Lombard himself who had known him since they were boys, had appointed him to be an internuncio in Holland, and when the appointment was criticized he had said: 'I am sure he will never report anything inaccurately, and where I am concerned that is all that matters.'

Orsenigo had gone from Holland to Hungary; he had written two lives of obscure saints and founded a home for scrofulous children. An unremarkable career, if in 1930 he had not been appointed Nuncio to Germany. Here he succeeded Cardinal Pacelli, who in 1939 became Pope Pius XII. Pacelli left Orsenigo where he was. At the time of concluding his Concordat with Hitler he had come to appreciate the value of a submissive and dutiful subordinate.

Since the outbreak of war Orsenigo had performed his duties admirably. He was not the man to go importuning the German Foreign Office about persecuted priests and Polish Catholics—or about the Jews, concerning whom he had heard, and even seen, a great deal. He simply carried out instructions. Pius XI had been perfectly right when he said: 'He will never report anything inaccurately.'

'The Nuncio started by asking me in French who I was. I said that I was a member of the Confessional Church and that I had joined the SS. I was watching his face. This seemed to make no impression. He simply asked:

' "What can I do for you?"

'And so I told him. I told him what I'd seen at Belzec—everything. And nothing happened. He seemed to be scarcely listening. Until suddenly he cried:

' "Go away! Get out!" '

So Gerstein went away. (One may picture him tight-lipped, with his face whiter than ever. Perhaps he was even carrying the suitcase containing his uniform that he had had with him when he called on Pastor Mochalsky—the suitcase that symbolized his longing to escape, to take refuge in a monastery, in the catacombs, anywhere out of this world: precisely what the Nuncio would have liked him to do.)

As he left the building a man lounging by the wall went after him. The approaches to all foreign official residences were kept under observation by security agents. Gerstein, experienced in these matters, soon realized that he was being followed. The first man was presently relieved by a man on a bicycle, a matter of routine. Gerstein released the safety catch of his automatic.

'Thou shalt not kill.' He had no intention of shooting at his pursuer, but he was prepared to do what, in his personal theology, was permissible to a man in desperate straits: to kill himself. But having drawn level with him the man on the bicycle rode away, leaving Gerstein amazed. Had he been terrified by the look of desperate resolution on Gerstein's face, or was it a case of divine intervention?

'What could be required from an average citizen to do against the Nazism when the very representative on earth of Jesus refused even to hear me although tens and tens thousands people were to be murdered every day, although to wait even some hours seemed to me to be criminal. Even the Nunzio of Germany refused to be well informed on this monstrous violation against the basis of Jesus' laws: "Thou ought to love the other man like thyself." So, what could do any citizen who, mostly, had hardly heard of these crimes, who, like millions foreigners (such as Dutch Resistance), thought this kind of things were much exaggerated. Most of the time they never occurred to hear the foreigner broadcasting.' (Gerstein, *Report*—see p. 294.)

He was never to recover from that visit to the Nuncio. Although he continued to harass neutrals and persons of influence like a washing-machine salesman, it was with a growing despair. More often than not the doors remained closed, and if one opened it was upon a refusal to listen. 'Thank you. We don't need anything.' He saw Doctor Winter, coadjutor of the Catholic Church in Berlin, and through this channel the Pope was at least informed, as were, directly or indirectly, the leading German Protestants: Dibelius, Wurm, even Pastor Niemöller in his concentration camp. But what was the use?

*Berlin. August 1967.* Alexandra Bälz, a connection of Gerstein's living in Berlin:
'It was a fine day in the summer of 1942. I was alone in our house in Grunewald. My husband at that time, Heinz Nebelthau, was in Berlin, having been transferred to the Luftwaffe. Gerstein telephoned and asked: "Can you come and see me at once, Frau Nebelthau? I'll send a car to fetch you." I accepted immediately, thinking of all the good things one was offered at Gerstein's

apartment. An orderly came in a service car and drove me to Bülowstrasse.

'Gerstein was looking very pale and upset. We had dinner. After his housekeeper had withdrawn Gerstein took me into the living-room and we sat on straight-backed chairs facing each other across a low, oval table. The room was very badly lighted, so that we could scarcely see each other's faces. Gerstein told me that he had just got back from a concentration camp where he had seen the most unspeakable things: Jewish men, women and children being killed with exhaust gases. He had been forced to watch these scenes, and a senior officer had ordered him to turn his wits to finding a more efficient and quick-acting gas.

'He said that since he was back in Berlin he had knocked at a number of doors trying to tell people what he had seen. He'd been to the residence of the Papal Nuncio and had literally been turned out. He cried: "My God, we've got to do something to stop it! But what? In God's name, Frau Nebelthau, can't you advise me?" . . . He broke down and sobbed in a way I've never known a man to do in the presence of a woman. We sat there till four in the morning. It was beginning to get light and the birds were twittering in the trees. I asked endless questions because I had not known anything about all this.

'Finally he rang for the car and had me driven home. I couldn't sleep for nights afterwards.'

Helmut Franz (1967): 'About a fortnight after he got back from Belzec he asked me to come for a walk with him. He needed to talk. We strolled through the streets for two hours and he talked from between tight lips with his eyes half closed. Now and then he stood still. "I've seen unbelievable things," he said, and clapped his hands to his head. He talked about the very beautiful girl who had been at the head of the column—"Help us!" The worst thing of all had been not being able to answer, having to stifle the impulse to do something. He knew that he was the only man, the only anti-Nazi, who had seen what he had seen and could describe it. He told me about his meeting with Von Otter and how he'd been to the Papal Nuncio and been thrown out. He was terribly bitter about that. "That Church has forfeited the right to represent Christ on earth," he said.

'He knew there was nothing he could do. He said to me: "Helmut, you must tell people." '

Herbert Eickhoff, another friend from his Bible Circle days (1967): 'In August or September 1942, he picked me up at my quarters and took me to his apartment. He talked quite openly about the concentration camps and he referred to Hitler as "that swine." He was full of shame and fury and horror. "We've no right to win this war," he said. "If we do, I shall never again believe in justice."

'But there's something else I've just remembered, and it's important. In 1941 I went to the Engineering School in Hagen. He wrote to me in the spring of 1942 suggesting that I should enlist in the SS and go to Oranienburg. The idea was to get me posted to the Waffen SS Institute of Hygiene to work under him. Well, I applied to the SS but they wouldn't have me. When I saw him this time I'm telling you about, in September 1942, he said: "Thank God! I can never tell you how thankful I am that you didn't get into the Institute of Hygiene." '

Gerstein went to Munich to see the architect Otto Völckers, whose acquaintance he had made on his Mediterranean cruise in 1938. Both Völckers and his wife were shocked by the change in him; he looked old and haggard. 'He had urged someone in foreign diplomatic circles to try to persuade the British Government to have leaflets dropped during air raids, describing these atrocities. He was trying to arrange to go to Sweden, to make contacts there under cover of a service mission. He felt that what mattered was not simply that public opinion abroad should be aroused, but that the German people should be made to realize what was being done in their name. I asked how it was possible for a man like himself, a man of honour and a sincere Christian, to stand by and watch these horrors. He said: "The machine has been set in motion, and I can't stop it. It's something to have seen it with my own eyes, so that some day I can testify to it."

'That he was guilty of high treason in the eyes of the regime was perfectly obvious. He knew he was not only risking his own life but those of his wife and children as well; and he was wondering whether he should get a divorce in order to protect them.'

Elfriede Gerstein, in Tübingen, knew nothing of all this. On one occasion, some time later, he let fall a few words that were almost meaningless to anyone who did not hold the key. 'I can't take you into consideration. You're three or four people, but I'm thinking of hundreds of thousands. I've got to *do* something. I've got to *do* something! . . .'

Life was not easy for Elfriede. Their small daughter, Adelheid, was ill for a long time, and a third child, Olaf, named after Von Otter, of whom Gerstein had had such high hopes, was born in December. She grew exasperated with the shadowy husband whom she so rarely saw and who seemed to have no conception of married life. Perhaps, also, some echo of the strange things he sometimes said at the Institute had reached her ears. 'That woman wants me to have the kids baptized. I'd rather divorce her.' These were the ways in which he sought to safeguard her.

'I saw Gerstein again after our meeting on the train,' said Baron von Otter in 1966. 'It was in Berlin, in the autumn or winter of that same year. He'd been waiting for me in one of the streets near the Legation. He was in civilian dress, not very elegant. He hadn't wanted to call on me openly, or write or telephone. He wanted to know if I'd done anything. I said that I had informed my superiors of what he had told me, but that I did not know if this had had any result. I said that I was afraid it was unlikely.

'He looked downcast and miserable—in fact, he looked utterly despairing. He had obviously overestimated the wisdom of foreign statesmen and their freedom of action. He felt that he had failed. I think he may even have muttered something about committing suicide at the front.'

He had failed. He scarcely understood why. If he himself could gain access to high places, to the Pope or the King of Sweden, to Churchill or Roosevelt, then surely his first-hand account of what he had seen, his flaming eloquence, must change everything.

So he believed; but in that same year of 1942 a Polish officer named Jan Karski, a member of the Polish Resistance ostensibly working for the Germans, had occasion to visit the Warsaw ghetto and Belzec. Later he escaped to England and thence to the United States. His account of what he had seen was as circumstantial as that of Gerstein, and his Polish nationality, and the fact that he was known to be a member of the Resistance, predisposed everyone in his favour. He was most warmly received. The British Foreign Secretary, Anthony Eden, said to him: 'It seems that everything possible has happened to you in this war except one thing—you have not been shot by the Germans. I am proud to have met you, M. Karski, and I wish you all good fortune.' Roosevelt also received him and questioned him as to the truth of the reports concerning 'the measures being employed by the Germans against the Jews.' But there the matter rested. Nothing came of Karski's eloquence except expressions of goodwill. The actor was of interest, not the drama.

At this point we may turn to the other side of the picture and look at it not through Gerstein's eyes but through the eyes of some of those who listened to what he had to say.

'You're lying,' said a friend to Armin Peters, an old associate of Gerstein's then in the Luftwaffe and one of the first people he talked to. Peters never saw his friend again.

'Your friend is mad,' a Protestant pastor and opponent of the regime said to Helmut Franz.

'Allied propaganda,' Heinz Nebelthau said to his former wife, now Alexandra Bälz. He was a lukewarm Nazi.

Her second husband, an army officer, said: 'Germans would be incapable of anything so atrocious.'

Four men whom we may assume to have been of good faith. They did not know. But then, what does 'knowing' imply?

The following is an extract from the proceedings of an American military court at Nuremberg:

'The argument generally put forward by the defence is that the crimes committed by the Reich were under the cover of professional secrecy and that the accused could not know of them. Hitler's famous decree on secrecy was invoked by nearly all the accused. They laid emphasis on the strictness of press censorship, the ban on listening to foreign broadcasts, the oath of secrecy sworn by all persons released from concentration camps ... in general on the ignorance of the German people as a whole concerning what was taking place. All this is true.

'But it is in the nature of things that absolute secrecy, or anything resembling it, cannot be indefinitely maintained. It was not possible to camouflage the huge convoys of slave-labourers transported from the east to the concentration camps. It was not possible to keep the public demonstrations against Jews a secret. Streicher's infamous paper, *Der Stürmer*, had a circulation of 600,000. Himmler talked openly about the "Final Solution" of the Jewish problem. It is impossible to believe that all the people released from the concentration camps kept their mouths entirely shut; and it is probable that Germans on leave from Poland or Russia or the Ukraine told their own people something of what they had seen. No one could fail to see the columns of smoke rising from the furnaces of Auschwitz. Foreign broadcasts were listened to despite the ban. The systematic extinction of millions of human beings over a period of five years was something that could not possibly remain unknown because of its very extent.'

Professor Georges Wellers (1967): 'When the Germans say, "We did not know," there is some truth in it, but in a very narrow sense. For example, they may have known nothing about gas chambers or the methods employed; but that something was being done to the Jews, in fact that they were being exterminated, this I am convinced they knew ... So far as we were concerned, those of us who were sent to the camp at Drancy, we had heard about gas chambers but we did not believe it. But we saw the convoys go off, old men who couldn't walk, and obviously they weren't being sent to work. Postcards reached us, which was reassuring. We had not heard of Auschwitz but only of Pitschepoï, and I imagined for a long time that this unknown land where we were to go was a tale invented by children. I have only recently learned that it is a Yiddish folksong.'

'When people realize . . .' said Gerstein.

He was still thinking of the leaflets to be dropped by Allied aircraft over Germany, hearing the voices of preachers denouncing abomination from a hundred pulpits, feeling the stir as the knowledge spread and the crowds poured out into the streets to besiege the doors of government offices and the Chancellery itself with the outraged cry, 'Cease murdering the Jews!' Love of their fellow-men would erupt with the force of an explosion from the hearts of the noble German people, briefly led astray, to sweep away evil and atone in a single dramatic instant for all the sins of mankind, from Cain to Hitler . . . So he believed. But no one spoke. The voice that had thundered against the euthanasia programme was silent on the subject of the Jews. Those Germans who knew said nothing, and the rest preferred not to know. A voice murmured here and there, but in an undertone, in discreet letters to the authorities. These were so rare that to quote them, deserving as they are of honour, would be to distort the picture, as though they represented a chorus of voices, which, in truth, did not exist. Ten years of anti-Semitic bludgeoning and three years of the tribulations of war had done their work. The Jews were no longer fellow-men to the Germans of 1942.

During that year the Allied Powers and neutral countries began to realize something of the enormity of what was happening. Reports were coming in from secret agents, Resistance movements, religious orders (especially the Jesuits) and Jewish organizations—the latter based on the testimony of persons who had escaped or been rescued. Gerstein was not working alone.

Pastor Georges Casalis (theologian and a friend of Karl Barth): 'I can affirm that from 1933 onward we knew of the existence of the concentration camps; that before 1940 we knew what was happening to interned German Jews, and that from 1941 on we were informed of the mass exterminations and their attendant horrors. I further declare that at Lyons in 1942 I received detailed information of the manufacture of soap from the fat of murdered Jews ... The civilized Christian conscience does not care to be confronted with the hideousness of torture ... The most solemn official denials do not afford the shadow of an excuse.'

In March 1942 Doctor Rudolph B., a Swiss physician who visited the German eastern front, sent in a report to his Government.

In July 1942 the Polish Government in Exile, in London, stated that 700,000 Jews had been massacred since the beginning of the war. The figure was repeated over the air on 8 July by Cardinal Hinsley, who said: 'Great is truth and it shall prevail. I will give you here and now a few details of the truth concerning this murderous business ...' Gerstein listened to this BBC broadcast.

In August 1942 a German industrialist whose name is still buried in the Allied archives informed Gerhard Riegner, the Swiss representative at the World Congress of Jews, that Hitler had ordered the extermination of all Jews who could be captured. There was mention of prussic acid, also of Belzec.

Riegner at once cabled America. An official in the State Department minuted his cable as follows: 'It appears to me inadvisable, in view of the incredible nature of these allegations, and our complete inability to give assistance in the event of their being true, to circulate the information in the manner proposed.' Two half-truths: 'incredible nature' glosses over the fact that the truth was becoming known, and 'complete inability' disguises the resolve to do nothing.

The resolve was not a new one. In the summer of 1938 representatives of thirty-two countries had gathered in Evian-les-Bains to discuss plans for helping the German Jews to escape from persecution. 'I can only hope,' Hitler said in Königsberg, 'that the outside world, which expresses such deep sympathy for these criminals, will have the generosity to convert its sympathy into effective aid. Where we are concerned, we shall be delighted to hand them over to any other country, even if it means embarking them on luxury liners.'

But neither the United States nor the British Empire was prepared to open its doors to an unrestricted flood of refugees. The talk was all of quotas, so many a year and no more. Only the Dominican Republic, ruled by a dictator, announced that it would accept 100,000 persons.

The attitude of the Great Powers was to play an important part in Hitler's decision to exterminate the Jews.

In May 1938 the British Government issued a White Paper in which the number of Jews to be admitted to Palestine during the next five years was limited to 75,000. It was a political crime inspired by the fear of unsettling the Arabs at a time when war was imminent; and it meant that one of the few possible outlets for the Jews was virtually closed.

In June 1938 the liner *St Louis* sailed for Cuba with 930 Jewish refugees on board, the last to leave Germany. Cuba refused to admit them. So did the South American republics and the United States. The *St Louis* was obliged to head back to Germany. Some of the passengers took poison, others opened their veins. A special committee for the prevention of suicide was formed by the more strong-minded refugees. The children invented new games, one of which was described by the ship's captain to the American writer, Arthur D. Morse. Two little boys with scowling faces stood on guard at a barrier made of chairs, while the rest queued up and asked to be allowed through.

'Are you a Jew?'

'Yes.'

'Jews aren't admitted.'

'Oh, please let me in. I'm only a very little Jew.'

At the last moment four European countries—Belgium, Holland, Britain and France—agreed to share the unhappy shipload.

In 1940 a ship that had escaped from occupied France reached the shores of the United States. The US Secretary of State, Cordell Hull, delivered himself of an astonishing pronouncement to the delegation of American Jews who implored him to grant the refugees right of sanctuary. Pointing to the Stars and Stripes, he said that he had sworn to protect the flag and to obey the laws of his country, which he was now being asked to break.

The leader of the delegation, Nahum Goldmann, suggested that a message be sent to the passengers advising them to jump overboard. They could then be rescued from drowning by the coastguards and brought ashore.

Hull replied that he had never heard a more cynical proposal, and Goldmann countered by questioning which of them was the greater cynic—Goldmann, who wished to save these defenceless people, or Hull, who was prepared to send them to their death.

The reasons for the American attitude, both then and later, have never been clear. But Arthur D. Morse[1] cites a remarkable eighteen-page memorandum drafted by a group of Protestant civil servants and submitted to President Roosevelt in 1944. Entitled 'Report to the Secretary on the Acquiescence of This Government in the Murder of the Jews,' it contains the following passage:

'Officials of the State Department have not only failed to use the Governmental machinery at their disposal to rescue Jews from Hitler, but have even gone so far as to use this Governmental machinery to prevent the rescue of these Jews.

'They have not only failed to co-operate with private organizations in the efforts of the organizations to work out individual programs of their own but have taken steps designed to prevent these programs from being put into effect.

'They have not only failed to facilitate the obtaining of information concerning Hitler's plans to exterminate the Jews of Europe but in their official capacity have gone so far as to surreptitiously attempt to stop the obtaining of information concerning the murder of the Jewish population of Europe.

'They have tried to cover up their guilt by:

(a) concealment and misrepresentation;

1 In: *While Six Million Died*. New York, Random House, 1967.

(b) the giving of false and misleading explanations for their failures to act and their attempts to prevent action; and

(c) the issuance of false and misleading statements concerning the "action" which they have taken to date.'

In the spring of 1944, Joel Brand, representing the Hungarian Jews, whose turn it was to be exterminated, appealed to Lord Moyne, British High Commissioner in Egypt.[1]

Lord Moyne: 'What will we do with those million Jews? Where would we put them?'

Brand: 'If there's nowhere on earth for us to go we may as well let ourselves be wiped out.'

Stalin's Russia knew nothing about the Jews.

In an official memorandum dated 28 April 1942, Molotov refers to 'summary executions among the peaceful Soviet population committed by the Hitlerites ... which clearly reveal the criminal and blood-thirsty intentions of the Fascists, whose purpose is to exterminate the Russians, Ukrainians, White Russians and other peoples of the Soviet Union.'

The 'other peoples' included the Jews, but these were never named except in documents intended for foreign circulation. The word was surrounded by an inviolable taboo. 'They were the etcetera,' writes Léon Poliakov, 'the ghost people.' Stalin's anti-Semitic policy, later to become the 'anti-Zionism' of his successors, was beginning to show itself. Why take any special action on behalf of the Jews, whether by propaganda or the bombing of Auschwitz? How could the Jews be exterminated when they did not exist?[2]

The Swiss doctor, Rudolph B., who told his colleagues what

1 Lord Moyne, an honourable man who was simply carrying out his Government's policy, was murdered by Jewish terrorists. The murderers were hanged and later avenged by their compatriots – and so on ...

2 On 16 April 1967 I was present at the unveiling of a memorial erected at Auschwitz to the victims who had died there. The Polish Premier, Doctor Cyrankiewicz, won a bet by delivering a long address without once uttering the word 'Jew.'

he had seen on the German eastern front, was reprimanded for having violated his pledge of secrecy, thereby 'imperilling Swiss neutrality.' Like the Swedes, who did not divulge what Gerstein had told Von Otter until after the war, the Swiss were in mortal terror of offending their German neighbour. Von Steiger, a Federal Councillor, justified the closing of the Swiss frontier with the words, 'The lifeboat is full.' It was far from being the case; but the authorities were afraid to listen to the words of men like Karl Barth who were outraged by the contradiction between the supposed ideals of their country and the lamentable truth.

In 1943 Councillor von Steiger was directly addressed from the pulpit at a church service: 'We have refused to grant foreign refugees the protection of our frontiers ... In the persons of these desperate people we are rejecting Christ himself ... Councillor, do not seek to absolve our conscience; you will be doing a great disservice to our country!'

Deposition by the German diplomat, Von Kessel, at Nuremberg:

'In Geneva I met a member of the Committee of the International Red Cross who said to me: "We're in a terrible dilemma. A woman member of the Committee is urging us to issue a solemn protest against the persecution of the Jews in Germany. But how can we? If we were to protest, Hitler would denounce the Geneva Convention and we should have to give up all our work in favour of the Allies and on behalf of prisoners of war, the occupied territories, civilian internees and so on. It's a hideous position." A few days later I met this gentleman again and he said: "Thank God, after hours of discussion the majority rejected the idea of an official protest. It was a very hard decision, but it means that at least we can carry on our work." '

Yves-Guy Bergès, writing in *France-Soir*, August 1968:

'First we must denounce the scandal of the International Red Cross ... Because it clung to its own regulations stipulating that all aid must be concerted in agreement with both belligerents, and because Nigeria refused to accept this and said that its air-craft would be fired on, the International Red Cross suspended all flights. These were only resumed last week, on a scale of two flights a night when at least ten times as many are needed. Thousands of tons of food and medical supplies—some perish-able and by now useless—are awaiting delivery at São Tomé and Fernando Po, less than two hundred miles from Biafra.'

There remained the tall, pale, ascetic figure in a palace in Rome: Eugenio Pacelli, Pope Pius XII.

When in September 1942 the United States Ambassador to the Vatican delivered the dossier prepared by Gerhard Riegner, he was told by Cardinal Maglione, speaking in the name of His Holiness, that similar reports had been received but that 'it had not yet been possible to establish their accuracy.'

(Whether it was due to anti-Communism, irresolution, fear of annoying the German Catholics or of provoking some greater evil, the Pacelli line remains a mystery.)

'At the time of the crematoria the only sufficient Christian reply would have been a solemn pronouncement in all churches urging all Christians to wear the yellow star, the symbol of opprobrium and of the glory of the sons of David. I am among those who believe that such an act of faith on the part of all Christians would have caused the Nazis to draw back.' (Pastor Casalis.)

'If every Christian in Europe had followed the example of the King of Denmark and worn the yellow star, there would today be neither confusion nor despair in the Church, and we should not be talking about the death of God.' (Emile L. Facken-heim.)

The Paris students, May 1968: 'We're all German Jews!'

But at least there were the allies of Germany.
The Italians protected the Jews in their Zone of Occupation.
The Spaniards under Franco took special measures to protect the

descendants of the Jews who had fled from Spain in the fifteenth century. The Finnish Minister for Foreign Affairs said: 'Finland is a decent country. We would sooner die with our Jews than hand them over.'

And what of Gerstein, peering vainly into the sky for the great shower of leaflets that was to arouse the conscience of the German people, looking helplessly to Rome, to London, any-where; haunted in his dreams by the nightmare marble statues, mottled white and blue, with staring eyes; telling his story where he dared and hearing no responsive voice? If there were any moments of relief, a handclasp, a friendly arm around his shoulders, a consoling word, the records contain no trace of them, nor does the testimony of later witnesses. He was a man in the cold, cut off from the world.

Armin Peters said in 1948: 'I had in my possession a letter dated 1942. He gave it to me "on the off-chance." It had been written at a time when he felt the whole world was against him, including his wife and the members of his family. When I was sure he was dead I opened it. It was addressed to his brother Fritz, the Hagen lawyer. He talked about the Niemöller case and the efforts he had made to get it reviewed; and he described the threats and the attempts at blackmail to which he had been sub-jected by persons close to him, and the consequences to which these might lead. The letter is eloquent enough in itself. It sheds a vivid light on the tragedy of Gerstein and the hopeless battle he fought.'[1]

The Allied leaders, those responsible for the conduct of the war, were too absorbed in matters of high policy to descend to the level of those at the foot of the pyramid.

There was one small, false gleam of hope at the end of the year. On 17 December 1942, the Allied Governments issued a declara-tion (considerably modified by Cordell Hull and his advisers) in which they affirmed their resolve 'to ensure that those responsible for these crimes shall not escape punishment, and to expedite all

1 Armin Peters sent this letter to Fritz Gerstein, who says that he lost it.

measures necessary for the accomplishment of this purpose.' The guilty were to be punished, but nothing was said about saving those victims who were still alive. If these, too, died the guilt of the Nazis would be to that extent increased—and surely this was an excellent thing!

At Christmas Pope Pius XII decided that he must add his word, and he did so by referring, in the course of a twenty-six-page document, to 'persons condemned to death solely for reasons of nationality or race.' The word 'Jew' did not occur. His Holiness was never to be more explicit that this.

Twelve days after the Allied declaration, and five days after the pontifical utterance, the Swiss strongly reinforced their frontier guards. 'All foreigners entering the country by illegal means are to be deported ... A particularly close watch is to be kept on all fugitives awaiting deportation so as to ensure that they do not, directly or indirectly, communicate by telephone with any person in the country (relatives, acquaintances, lawyers, embassies, consulates, etc.).' They might, perhaps, have shed tears over the telephone! ...

A voice raised here and there could not disguise the apathy of hearts. The Western world to which Gerstein looked beseechingly for help was a waste-land of seeming indifference, its eyes steadfastly averted, intent upon other matters. But its conscience was not wholly dead. Now and then a fugitive slipped through the guarded frontiers, even one or two from Auschwitz; and these, being solitary cases, could be welcomed and made much of, treated as heroes, restored to health with food and vitamins, listened to and condoled with—'Don't worry. As soon as we've won the war your brothers will be set free.' If there were any left to be set free ...

*Orly Airport, November 1968.* Lufthansa flight 260 was late in arriving. I was to have identified Horst Dickten, Gerstein's collaborator and 'spiritual son,' by his hat and briefcase. In fact, when he eventually arrived, I knew him by his light blue eyes. He was tall and heavily built without being fat, bald in the fashion of blond men, his skull shining pinkly through the sparse fair hair, with a rounded forehead and affable manners. His present connections with a large German concern took him to all parts of the world, and in his prosperity, which was the reflection of all West Germany's prosperity, he might have forgotten everything that happened during the war. But Gerstein and his folly were things not easily forgotten, and Dickten remembered a great deal. He had not, however, known everything; and it may be that he put his own interpretation, with embellishments, on things that Gerstein, from the depths of his despair, had been unable to communicate in words . . . It was shortly before Christmas when we met, and the street decorations were going up, garlands of coloured lights strung between the trees of the Rue Custine. And Christmas was the first thing Dickten remembered. Christmas 1942, the year of Belzec, Baron von Otter and the Papal Nuncio.

In Berlin it had been a gala season. The Government had released a special ration of such rare commodities as sugar, coffee, pastries and spirits. There were Christmas trees in every window, and the air was filled with the voices of carol singers over the radio.

Christmas Eve was also an occasion of festivity at the Waffen SS Institute of Hygiene, where a long table had been set up in the big downstairs reception room. There were some forty people present, laboratory assistants, two secretaries, Frau Virk and Suzanne Dumont, and officers of all ranks up to the Chief, Colonel Mrugowsky.

'I arrived with a load of turkeys. As soon as he saw me Gerstein got up from the table and came over to me, scowling. "Where have you been? Why are you late?" I explained, and he turned away abruptly and left the room. I asked Frau Virk what was the matter with him and she shrugged her shoulders. "He's been like that all evening. Something's wrong."

'Presently someone said to me: "What's happened to Kurt? He's been gone a quarter of an hour." I went out to look for him in the ground-floor offices and laboratories. There was no sign of him, but I saw that a cupboard had been broken open. It was a poison cupboard. I went back into the reception room and asked

Suzanne Dumont, who was responsible, if she had left it open. She said: "Certainly not. I'm positive I locked it." We told Mrugowsky and he said we had better look upstairs. Kurt wasn't there either. Mrugowsky said: "Something must have happened to him. We must give the alarm." I went round to Bülowstrasse, but no sign.

'And then, between two and three in the morning, when the party was nearly over, he turned up again in the reception room, as mysteriously as he disappeared. I rushed up and asked: "What have you been doing?" and he stared as though he didn't see me. "Kurt, have you swallowed something?" He shook his head. But Doctor Ziezold, who lived in a villa nearby, decided that we'd better take him there to keep him under observation.

'When we got him there the doctor said: "Let him be quiet. Don't try to question him. Perhaps he'll tell us of his own accord." Kurt just sat there, not moving or saying anything. After a long time, it must have been about ten in the morning, he got up as though he were walking in his sleep and left the room. We thought it better not to follow him, but after about ten minutes I got scared. I went into the hall, and the first thing I saw was that Gerstein's pistol was missing from its holster, which was hanging on the hallstand. The front door was open, giving directly on to the woods. Ziezold and I rushed out, shouting at the top of our voices, and presently we found him standing with his back against a tree and his head a little on one side. He had his pistol in his hand. I flung myself on him and snatched it away. We took him back to the villa and then to Bülowstrasse, having warned Fräulein Hinz that he was ill.

'After a time Ziezold left, and it was only when we were alone together that Kurt broke down and cried: "I can't go on! I can't go on!"

'I asked him what had happened and he said: "I can't tell you."

' "Did you break open the poison cupboard?"

' "Yes."

' "What did you take?"

' "Cyanide."

' "Where is it?"

' "In my pocket."

'I took that away from him, as I had taken the pistol, and after a time he fell into a deep sleep.

'The next day he was much better. The crisis was over. "Listen," he said. "You've got to forget everything that happened yesterday. And tell Ziezold to keep his mouth shut." But it was too late for that. Ziezold had telephoned Mrugowsky, and Kurt was ordered to report to him. The interview lasted two hours, and no one has ever known what was said. But when he got back Kurt ordered me to "burn everything." '

They had codified lists in their office files, names of foreign contacts (only bare indications, as much as could be written down) and information about the concentration camps that Gerstein was not supposed to possess. As to the reasons for this whole business, one can only guess that someone had betrayed Gerstein so completely that it should have led to his suicide or liquidation. Mrugowsky, however, did not use his full powers. What price did he exact in return? When he joined the Institute Gerstein had planned to 'draw his chief's claws.' Perhaps it was his own claws that had now been drawn. A double defeat: by the Powers of Darkness as well as by the neutral Powers.

But if Gerstein failed to commit suicide, there was another who succeeded.

When Jan Karski, the second of the two first-hand witnesses of Belzec, arrived in London he saw Szmul Zygielbojm, one of the leaders of the Bund, the Jewish Socialist Party. Zygielbojm listened with great attention to what Karski had to say, seated with a hand on each knee, his eyes wide and staring. He wanted to know everything, and he was told.

'A few weeks later,' said Karski, 'the telephone rang while I was resting in my bedroom in Dolphin Square. In the whirl I'd been living in I had forgotten all about Zygielbojm. I let the phone ring a few times before reluctantly picking up the receiver. A voice said: "M. Karski, I am instructed to inform you that Szmul Zygielbojm, member of the Polish National Committee and London representative of the Bund, yesterday committed suicide. He left a letter saying that he had done everything in his power to help the Polish Jews but his efforts had failed. Since his fellow-Jews were all destined to perish he intended to die with them. He gassed himself." '

## Chapter 13

# THE LIVING GHOST

GERSTEIN was named one evening in a BBC German broadcast.[1] He was, said the BBC, one of the Nazi criminals running the concentration camps and concerned with experiments on human guinea-pigs. Mention was made of his work at the Institute, and he was described as a key figure in the extermination of the Jews, who would one day be called to account.

This was passed on to the Institute of Hygiene by the official monitoring service. Gerstein, being in the habit of listening to foreign broadcasts, had probably not needed to be told about it. Nevertheless, the charges levelled against him were like a blow in the face, bringing him, in his profound despair, to a state bordering on frenzy. Not only had the neutrals failed him and the powers of darkness strengthened their hold over him, but now the Allies, broadcasting his name to half the world, had made of him an object of execration and abhorrence.

The sequel is related by Horst Dickten, in an account based on Gerstein's own words, or on his waking nightmare—an inextricable mingling of facts that can be verified and others that perhaps never will be.

'Kurt wondered how the English had got hold of his name. He came to the conclusion that it must have reached them through the manager of a machine-tool factory in Berlin, an anti-fascist who detested him for personal reasons. Anyway, he was horribly upset. What worried him most of all, apart from personal considerations, was that this was going to make his struggle very much more difficult. He looked round for a way of warning the

1 'Our records for the period October 1942 to March 1943 have been most carefully examined. We have unfortunately been unable to find any reference to Kurt Gerstein.' Margaret Sampson, publicity officer, BBC, 1969.

English of their mistake—which, incidentally, was never repeated. He had influential friends in Helsinki, in particular the Director of Finnish Waterways, who had contacts in Sweden and Great Britain. Kurt decided to go and see him, and he asked me to requisition a plane in the name of Reichsführer Himmler, using forged papers. I was able to do this without difficulty.

'But then things went wrong. The plane developed a mechanical defect and had to make a forced landing at Riga. Thinking Himmler was on board, a special reception committee turned out on the landing strip to welcome him, and when only Gerstein emerged the commander of the airport telephoned Berlin. He was ordered to send the Untersturmführer back immediately under police escort.

'Mrugowsky was awaiting him at the Institute, and there was a heated scene between them. It was a serious matter which could have led to severe disciplinary action. In the meantime Kurt was placed under close arrest.

'From what he told me later, the matter went up to the highest SS level. Walter Schellenberg, the head of the Secret Service, talked to Himmler about it, and Himmler sent for Kurt and kept him standing for a long time in front of him without saying a word, just looking at him. By now, with the help of Mrugowsky and his adjutant, Dötzer, Kurt had managed to work up a case for himself. His story was that he had had to go to Finland because the problem of drinking-water in that country was becoming extremely serious; the rivers were heavily polluted with dead bodies. He had worked out a scientific method of dealing with the matter and had taken the liberty of borrowing a plane in order to avoid administrative delays and lose no time in putting his scheme into operation. Himmler seemed to swallow this, and they went on to discuss the great moral and religious problems of the day. Kurt was kept there for two hours before being dismissed. "He has hard eyes," he said of Himmler, "but he's a weak man at heart."

'Thanks to Mrugowsky, and perhaps also to Schellenberg, Kurt got off very lightly. So far as I remember he was forbidden to wear his uniform for a time, or to leave the country without Mrugowsky's written permission.'

But the echoes soon died down, and Gerstein had no trouble in obtaining leave to pay another visit to France. It would have been absurd to allow this valuable source of supply to dry up. Everyone stood to gain by his trips abroad.

Second Lieutenant Gerstein was now to surpass himself.

When he got back from Paris he invited all the senior staff of the Institute to what he called a '*soirée française*' in his father-in-law's apartment, where he had assembled a truly remarkable collection of things he had bought: furs, shoes, shirts, preserves, boxes of cigars, cases of wine and liqueurs, books, artistic bric-à-brac. Mrugowsky, Ding, Krantz and Dötzer were among the guests, with several ladies of the secretarial staff. So was Horst Dickten, on whose story this account is based.

Gerstein raised his hands for silence.

'My friends, ladies and gentlemen, life is so drab these days that I have sought to make it a little brighter for you. In the next room you will find a few gifts which I am happy to offer you. But I have not attempted to decide who shall have what. It is for you to choose. So I propose a game—a treasure-hunt. When I blow this whistle you will go next door and pick whatever you fancy. But when I blow two blasts the game will be over. You will at once come back in here with whatever you have chosen—or with nothing at all if you have chosen nothing.'

There was a murmur of delighted applause. What a splendid idea!

Gerstein, who kept Horst Dickten at his side, took his time about blowing the whistle while the high functionaries of the Waffen SS Institute of Hygiene—the Chief, the learned professors, the colonels and majors, the cultivated ladies—stood breathless, poised on their marks like sprinters waiting for the gun. And when the whistle blew the whole place shook. It was a stampede. The room next door became a scene of what was not far short of mob violence, jostling bodies and thrusting elbows, army tunics and stockinged legs, iron crosses and ear-rings, flushed, heated faces and furious voices: 'That's mine! I saw it first!' . . . Gerstein gave them plenty of rope. 'Look at them,' he said to Dickten. 'A sweet sight, isn't it?'

When at length he blew the double blast which ended the battle they returned like a victorious army, clutching their loot to their bosoms, clothing disordered, hair dishevelled, but faces bright with triumph as they displayed their trophies.

Then the champagne went round. (Gerstein did not touch it. He was abstinent, but he was also prudent. Sergeant Weigelt once saw him drink a whole bottle of champagne at an SS gathering, after which he let fall one or two remarks that had been better left unsaid. It was a salutary warning. He was not given to repeating his mistakes.) The party went on into the small hours, a drinking orgy worthy of the game they had played, in which the true nature of the players was shamelessly manifest, their secrets, their private relationships one with another. And by the light of dawn they went off with their parcels followed by Gerstein's cold gaze.

'The swine,' he muttered. 'The swine.'

In September 1943 Herbert Eickhoff, on leave from the front, stayed with Gerstein on Bülowstrasse. This was the young man, a member of a Westphalian Protestant community, whom Gerstein had advised to join the SS the previous year, afterwards thanking Heaven that he had been rejected.

Gerstein asked Eickhoff to accompany him to the railway station, where he had arranged to meet an important gentleman who was leaving for Poland. 'I'll say you're my orderly,' he said. The gentleman was Professor Pfannenstiel, who seemed to be sorry that he was travelling alone.

'Why not come with me, my dear Gerstein?' he suggested. 'You'll be able to see the kind of work we're doing.'

'Delighted,' said Gerstein. 'If you can get me a sleeper.'

Eickhoff was struck by the sarcasm in his voice; and when the train had left, Gerstein turned to him and said in a tone of unspeakable disgust: 'The swine! How can he do these things?' And he added: 'Herbert, we mustn't win this war.'

They went together to visit Frau Niemöller at Dahlem, and she gave them coffee while they were waiting to attend the service in the Church of St Anne—where once, an eternity ago, Gerstein had called upon Pastor Mochalsky, carrying a suitcase.

Another pastor was preaching. The Moabit district had been heavily bombed by the RAF the night before, and the preacher, referring to this, made no bones about calling it a judgement upon them. Eickhoff reflected in amazement: 'How does he dare? It's a deliberate provocation.' Two army officers seated in the front row rose furiously and left the church. Gerstein nudged Eickhoff and went after them, while the bewildered young man followed.

Gerstein was in civilian clothes. He caught up with the two officers and introduced himself, saying that he was a member of the SS central office and would personally attend to the matter. 'Oh, well, in that case ...' They beamed at him and departed, and he murmured as he stood watching them go: 'Just as well. They'd have made trouble.'[1]

On their way back to Bülowstrasse on the metropolitan railway they passed through the Moabit district, which was still burning. Heedless of their fellow-passengers, Gerstein suddenly exclaimed in a voice of intense sarcasm:

'We are about to witness *atrocities*!'

It was a typical Gerstein send-up. A young woman in Party uniform seated near them turned crimson with indignation.

'How dare you! Who are you to ...'

'Ah,' said Gerstein. 'If only you knew who I was!'

His manner instantly silenced her, and Eickhoff reflected: Yes, if she only knew!

On Sunday, 5 September, Gerstein and Eickhoff attended service at the church in the Dennewitzplatz, adjoining Bülow-strasse. There were two shabbily clad young men, evidently

---

1 The pastor, Karl-Friedrich Stellbrink, had been arrested in Lübeck the year before for talking about 'the judgement of Heaven' after an air raid on that town. A year later he was hanged.

labourers, in the congregation. Gerstein studied them with care and when the service was over he went up to them.

'You're Dutch, aren't you?'

'Yes.'

'Will you allow me to offer you lunch?'

'You're very kind, but there's a meal waiting for us at the place where we're quartered.'

'Then go back and say you won't be needing it, and then come to my apartment. It's that house there, first floor. My name's Gerstein.'

Their names were Henk de Vos and Miel Nieuwenhuizen. They were twenty years old. They had been rounded up in July for forced labour in Germany: it was either them or their parents. They were now quartered with other labourers in a building on Lützowstrasse, condemned to a life of hunger, fatigue and home-sickness—and now a German had invited them to lunch!

They were there at 12:30 sharp, the door of the first floor, left. But when they entered the apartment they recoiled in terror, for hanging in the lobby were an SS tunic and a death's-head cap.

'They were scared out of their wits,' said Eickhoff. 'Gerstein had great difficulty in reassuring them. They thought it was a trap.'

'Well, what else could we think?' said Nieuwenhuizen. 'We thought it was a friendly invitation and it turned out to be an SS officer! Naturally, we thought he was going to try to force us to spy on our friends. But then he opened his arms to us and said: "Brothers in Christ!"'

The meal that followed was so splendid that they remembered every detail after twenty-five years: soup, roast, vegetables, apricots, all the cigarettes they could smoke; Leokadia Hinz had done them proud. When it was over Eickhoff had to leave, but the other three sat talking. To be more exact, Gerstein talked. With him food always had to precede confidences, as though it added to the credibility of the revelation or to the credulity of the audience. They were still talking when, at four o'clock, Leokadia served tea. The young Dutchmen were ill at ease for a long time, feeling that there must be some ulterior motive behind this lavish entertainment. But by degrees, as they listened, their mistrust of Gerstein vanished. Instead, they were overtaken by a different fear. Why was he telling them these hideous things, laying upon them this burden of unspeakable knowledge? What did he expect in return?

After tea he took them with him to Dahlem, where he delivered a basket of provisions to Frau Niemöller, including a bottle of cod-liver oil for her imprisoned husband. De Vos noted his extreme caution while they were out of doors. He was constantly on the alert, frequently changed direction and hurried them on to a subway compartment an instant before the doors closed. They were back on Bülowstrasse soon after six.

He then questioned them about themselves, their homes and family background; and finally, having set his own doubts at rest as well as theirs, he told them why he had confided in them, two total strangers accosted in the street.

'There have got to be witnesses,' he said. 'The murderers have got to be punished. If anything happens to me it is people like you who will have to tell the story.'

But he impressed upon them the need for present secrecy. Nothing must be said at that time, or written to their friends in Holland.

'I don't want you to be heroes or spies. All that matters is that you should come through this war alive. And then you'll testify. The whole world must know what was done to the Jews.'

While he was saying these things an old man was sitting fretfully in another room in the apartment. Judge Ludwig, Gerstein's father, was on his way through Berlin. He felt that he was surrounded by mysteries and he wanted to know what was going on. His son told him nothing. 'Never once,' he was later to say with bitterness, 'did I manage to have a serious talk with him.'

As evening fell, Gerstein got out his Bible with its worn cover and read aloud from it in the gathering darkness of the room. His voice trembled as he read, no longer the voice of an SS officer but of a man mortally wounded, clinging to the only hope he had left. And at eleven o'clock the young Dutchmen left to return through the darkened streets to their barracks, with minds grievously oppressed, having lived through the most extraordinary day of their lives. They said very little on the way.

As to what Gerstein did, we can only surmise. Perhaps he went to bed, or perhaps, since he slept so little, he set out on one of his solitary pilgrimages through the streets of the town. Perhaps he telephoned to someone, or perhaps sat silently refuting the charges levelled against him by the family and friends from whom he was more estranged, at this stage of his life, than he was from those two youngsters who now shared his secret.

In the previous year, when he had talked to people, he had said: 'You must pass it on—spread the news!' Now he did the opposite. It was the duty of the young Dutchmen to keep quiet. They were the repositories of a secret to be passed on to a later generation. In a sense Gerstein was doing what the Jewish historian Emmanuel Ringelblum did when he collected all the documents he could lay hands on concerning the agony of Warsaw, packed them in sealed containers and buried them. Having done so, he could meet death with a quiet heart. He died, and after the war those archives were dug up from under the rubble.

*

A huge and hidden struggle was in process during those years between the German need of secrecy and the Jewish need to expose. At the Eichmann trial counsel asked a Jewish witness: 'What was it that gave you the will to live?'

The witness, Wells, replied: 'A sense of responsibility. Someone had to tell that ghastly story, someone had to live to do it. We wanted the strongest to come through. It wasn't personal, we simply wanted people to live to tell the tale.'

'Keep your eyes and ears open,' the historian Simon Dubnov shouted to the Jews of Riga as they were being taken away for execution. 'Remember everything that happens, every name, every word! Anyone who survives must forget nothing!'

Documents were buried at Auschwitz, Chelmno, Warsaw and Vilna—letters, diaries, photographs. Children in the Terezin ghetto made drawings and wrote poems, some of which have been preserved.

> Little baby soft and new
> Like a bud that's opening;
> But when the flower should be in bloom
> Little baby will be gone.
> (Frantisek Bass, 1942.)

At the Maidanek camp Alexander Donat was seriously ill. He went to one of the Jewish leaders of the camp and 'blurted out' that he was a professional journalist and thought it his duty to live so that he could tell the world how their people were being exterminated. 'Go back to your block,' the man said. 'I'll help you all I can. Don't worry.'

Extract from *Les Clandestins de Dieu* by Suzanne Loiseau-Chevalley: 'There was a constant stream of visitors to the curé's house in Douvaine. An eight-year-old boy was brought to me, handsome and sensible, with a determined manner. He was Hungarian and his parents had been deported. All his possessions were in a very small case and he had hidden his papers in the lining of the lid. He said heart-rendingly: "I've lost my parents; without my papers I shan't be anything at all. I shan't even have a name." I sewed the papers carefully into the lining of his jacket and he was very pleased.'

In this battle of the *name* against the *secret* Gerstein's attempts had failed, and, like the Jews, he knew it. It took one more setback to convince him. In February 1943 his Dutch friend J. H. Ubbink called on him in Berlin.

'Are you in radio contact with the British?' Gerstein asked.

'Yes.'

'Then use it. Tell them everything I've told you.'

Ubbink said later: 'I did so. But they simply refused to believe anything so atrocious.'

And Gerstein said later: 'The Dutch Resistance sent me a

message through Ubbink. They asked me not to invent atrocity
stories but to stick to the exact truth.'

On 19 April 1943, the day of the Warsaw rising, a last and futile
international conference on the refugee problem opened in
Bermuda. It ended a few days later without having adopted any
resolutions.

'It is strange to note that the countries where public opinion is
most vocal in favour of the Jews are those which refuse to admit
them. They say that the Jews are the pioneers of civilization, with
a genius for philosophy and artistic creation, but when they are
asked to find room for these geniuses they close their frontiers.
"No, no, we don't want them." I think it must be the only case
in world history of a refusal to accept genius.' (Joseph Goebbels,
March 1943.)

'Tell them,' said a leader of the Jewish Resistance to an emissary
from London, 'tell them that the earth will have to be shaken to
its foundations and then perhaps they'll wake up.'

\*

The great dispute over the technical means of achieving the Final
Solution was never settled. Captain Wirth clung to his method
while Lieutenant-Colonel Höss pursued his own. But by the end
of 1943 all the Wirth factories had gone out of business (Belzec
in the autumn of 1942). The gas chambers were demolished; the
charnel pits were dug up, the bodies drenched in heavy oil and
burnt on huge grills made of railway lines. All traces were carefully effaced, for the Führer had come round to the view of
Doctor Linden, that there should be no bronze tablets to celebrate
his victory!

The work continued normally at Auschwitz, however, using
Zyklon B. All Europeans subject to the Law were dispatched in
cattle trucks to the tall gates of Birkenau.

Armin Peters (1948): 'Some time after his visit to Belzec, I
don't remember the exact date, he came to see me at my apartment in Rangsdorf. He was in utter despair. He showed me a top-

secret document which had just reached him by special messenger. It was an order from the SS Chief of Police for the Lublin district (Odilo Globocnik) requiring a monthly delivery of 500 kilos of prussic acid, "for the destruction of vermin," which Gerstein was personally to procure . . . Gerstein showed it to my wife. He told me later that he had had it photographed and that a copy had been passed to the British Secret Service.'

We do not know how many orders of this kind there were, or how many consignments were delivered. The story at this stage is shrouded in mystery, relieved only by a hint here and there from later witnesses.

'As I remember,' said Armin Peters, 'he got the first consignment from Degesch and himself drove it in a truck to Lublin. He staged an accident in which he was slightly injured, but which rendered the consignment unusable.'

Pastor Kurt Rehling, 1967: 'I remember him telling me how he drove the truck while the others were asleep. He ran it into a ditch, and after getting out and examining the damage he said: "Too bad! The consignment's ruined." '

He travelled back and forth between Berlin and Auschwitz, being present, in his expert capacity, at the visits of high Nazi functionaries to that nameless land with which a particular word was later to be associated: 'genocide.'

\*

*Waffen SS Institute of Hygiene, 19 February 1943.*

'SS Untersturmführer Kurt Gerstein, certified engineer, has been a member of the SS since 10/3/1941 and on the staff of the Institute of Hygiene since 1/6/41. While still an ordinary soldier he was placed in authority on 9/11/1941 as a specialist officer.

'Gerstein built up the technical section of the health service out of very small beginnings. The development of decontamination methods and fresh-water units, now in use by the SS divisions, is due to his energy and personal initiative. The activities of his section have been extended far beyond the tasks originally assigned to it. Of all the branches of the Wehrmacht, the Waffen

SS is the only one that has its own research organization and that is therefore not dependent on private commercial enterprise. Its advantage in this respect over other parts of the Army is evident, and the principal credit must go to Gerstein.

'In the course of his duties he has collaborated with an exceptionally large number of high civil authorities and with many branches of the Wehrmacht. It is generally agreed that the perfecting of the necessary apparatus was a task of great complexity. The difficulties have been overcome by Gerstein, who . . . etc.'

On 20 April 1943 Gerstein was promoted Obersturmführer (Lieutenant).

By this time he was no longer rendering the outstanding service he had done at the beginning. His section ran itself. Despite the smoke screen of often contradictory activities with which, as usual, he surrounded himself in order to cover his tracks, he was no longer indispensable. Why, then, this lavish praise? Why the promotion?

It seems that a strange, secret game had come to be played by Gerstein and Joachim Mrugowsky, a contest—or compact—in which the stake was nothing less than the personal future of each of them. The defeat at Stalingrad meant the end of Hitler's Reich, and both men knew it. Whether it took months or years, the final collapse was inevitable, and each man had to consider his eventual position. So for the present, bound to each other and dependent on each other, they preserved the appearance of friendship, watching each other like players in a deadly poker game. Mrugowsky's sidelong 'Polish' glance—had Gerstein ever grown accustomed to it? Which of those two was the snake and which the rabbit? All that can be said is that in his dealings with his commanding officer Gerstein alternated between anxiety and defiance.

Günter Dickten (1967): 'He was on edge whenever he had to see Mrugowsky about anything. It was nothing to do with the work on hand, he knew that thoroughly. But he was always tense and uneasy.'

Fritz Krantz (1968): 'One day in July we went together to report to Mrugowsky. One was sometimes kept waiting a couple

of hours, but one always had to be there on time. The fall of
Mussolini was given out over the radio while we were waiting,
and Gerstein did something unbelievable—it could have cost him
his neck. He scribbled a note on a scrap of paper and handed it to
me. Something like this: "The departure of Mussolini is an
excellent thing. The ex-mason will perhaps help in the rebuilding
of Europe. The question is, when will the house-painter do the
same?" I stuffed the note into my pocket and whispered: "Are
you crazy?" Then I went out to the toilet and got rid of it.'

There were no concealments between Gerstein and Mrugowsky,
no cards up either man's sleeve. It was an equal contest. Mrugowsky knew all about Gerstein's anti-Nazi record and had got
him out of trouble whenever the need arose. He had 'buried' the
Welzheim and Helsinki episodes. At the time of the Christmas
Eve episode he had probably held his life in his hands—and he
had let him live.

Gerstein, for his part, knew all about Mrugowsky's past and
present crimes. The learned doctors of the Robert Koch Institute
and the bacteriological department of the Farben–Behring
factories still came to Mrugowsky when they needed human beings
for their experiments, and he was still supplying them with
victims. In August 1944 Mrugowsky himself proposed a series
of experiments in typhus therapy and human tolerance of a serum
containing phenol; and he sent gangrenous cultures to his
vivisecting colleagues at Ravensbrück. In his passion for experi-
mentation he even sometimes assisted in executions—'thus
pursuing the barbarous premises of Nazi thought to their terrible
and logical conclusion,' in the words of Telford Taylor at
Nuremberg.

'On 11 September 1944, in the presence of SS Sturmbannführer Doctor Ding, Doctor Widmann and the undersigned,
projectiles containing aconitine were tested on five subjects
under sentence of death. The projectiles consisted of 7.65 mm
bullets containing the poison in the form of crystals. The bullets
were fired into the left thigh of the subjects while they were in a
recumbent position. In two cases the bullet passed clean through

the thigh and no reaction to the poison could subsequently be detected. These two subjects were discarded . . .

'The symptoms of the other three were surprisingly similar. At first there was no especial reaction, but after a period of from twenty to twenty-five minutes muscular disturbances were manifest, together with a slight flow of saliva. Both symptoms ceased after a short time. From forty-three to forty-four minutes later there was a fresh, very copious flow of saliva. The subjects swallowed continuously, but eventually the flow became so abundant that it was impossible for them to swallow it. Foaming saliva poured out of their mouths, and symptoms of suffocation and vomiting were noted.

'In the case of two of the subjects the pulse became imperceptible after fifty-eight minutes. The pulse-rate of the third was 76. Arterial tension was 90/60 m/ms Hg after sixty-five minutes. The heartbeats were extraordinarily feeble. Arterial tension fell rapidly.

'During the first hour of the experiment the pupils remained unchanged. At the end of seventy-eight minutes a moderate dilation of the pupil was noted, together with a sluggish reaction to light. At the same time there was very deep breathing, which grew slower, however, after a few minutes. Then the pupils grew larger still and reacted better to light. After sixty-five minutes the patella and achilles reflexes failed to function in all three subjects.

'In two of them the abdominal cutaneous reflexes also disappeared, in the third subject the reflexes still functioned in the upper abdomen but could not be activated in the lower.

'After ninety minutes one of the subjects again began to breathe very deeply and was again overtaken by muscular convulsions which tended to increase. Breathing became rapid and shallow, and at the same time the subject had powerful sensations of nausea.

'One of the subjects tried unsuccessfully to vomit. He put his fingers down his throat, but without result. His face was congested.

'The faces of the other two subjects, on the contrary, very rapidly grew pale. All the other symptoms were similar. The jerking of the muscles gradually became so powerful that the subjects straightened up, let themselves fall back, rolled their eyes, made uncontrolled movements with hands and arms. Gradually this agitation died down, the pupils were enlarged to the fullest extent, the subjects lay peacefully. One was seized with cramp. A flow of urine was observed. Death supervened in respectively 121, 123 and 129 minutes after wounding.

'Summary. The projectiles, loaded with approximately 38 m/mgrs of nitrate of aconitine, had a mortal effect in two hours despite the insignificant nature of the wound. The major symptoms were: flow of saliva, change in the pupils, disappearance of reflexes, muscular convulsions and fruitless attempts to vomit.

'(signed) S S Obersturmbannführer Mrugowsky, physician in charge.'

This experiment was conducted on Russian prisoners of war at Sachsenhausen Camp (Oranienburg). Doctor Ding stated later that a soldier had managed to get hold of a knife and had flung himself on Mrugowsky. After being overpowered he was used as a subject.

When the war was over Gerstein would have Mrugowsky at his mercy; but he himself was no less compromised. He had been drawn into the network of the Final Solution; he had visited the gas chambers; he had been promoted. The man who had wanted simply to know had been compelled to take part, and it is difficult not to suppose that Mrugowsky, who had good reason for mistrusting his subordinates, had deliberately contrived this state of affairs, shrewdly neutralizing Gerstein in order to protect himself. The precarious balance between the two men was one in which, while the war lasted and the grim machinery of the Gestapo was still intact, Mrugowsky had the whip hand. Clearly it was to his advantage to get Gerstein ever more deeply involved.

In June 1943 a certain Gerhard Peters, a member of the firm of Degesch (no connection with Armin Peters, Gerstein's friend), was asked by Mrugowsky to call on Gerstein, who had been ordered by the controllers of the Final Solution to procure a very large consignment of prussic acid. Doctor Peters, who was a

Sturmbannführer and a man with a high sense of patriotic duty, was unable later to recollect the exact amount, but it was of the order of 1,200 or 1,500 kilograms.

The following is a reconstruction of the conversation between him and Gerstein, based on his account.

Gerstein: 'The consignment is to be delivered directly to me, without going through your distributing company, 'Testa.' This is a matter of high policy in which the utmost secrecy must be observed. The acid is not intended for ordinary decontamination purposes but for use against men.'

Peters: 'I quite understand. At the beginning of the war I was asked by the Wehrmacht to organize tests for the stabilization of prussic acid with the idea of using it as a combat gas.'

Gerstein: 'You're mistaken, Doctor Peters. This is not a matter of war gas. By order of the Reichsführer a large number of people have been liquidated—criminals, mental cases and so on. But the methods used have been extremely cruel, not to say barbarous. Recently attempts have been made to humanize the operation by the use of prussic acid. Unfortunately, the acid used by the SS is scarcely less barbarous. The victims suffer appallingly.'

Peters: 'So I gather. A colleague in Frankfurt showed me some horrifying photographs of men like skeletons struggling in their death-throes. It seems that they were being killed with Zyklon. Well, of course, it's perfectly legal. Orders are orders. But what exactly do you want me to do, Doctor Gerstein?'

Gerstein: 'As I understand it, the suffering is caused by the irritant[1] contained in Zyklon. Don't you think pure liquid prussic acid would make death less painful?'

Peters: 'I really don't know how I can get hold of pure liquid prussic acid. But it is perfectly possible to manufacture Zyklon B without the irritant, if that is the main cause of the suffering.'

Peters was a businessman, a technician and a specialist in the

1 The irritant was a form of tear gas, a safety precaution designed to warn personnel of the presence of Zyklon in premises that had not been sufficiently ventilated after its use. By having it removed, Gerstein rendered Zyklon undetectable, which meant that whenever he chose he could declare that there was a dangerous leakage and have the consignment destroyed.

use of gas. (As he still is. He is said to have invented a new type of release valve.) How far his testimony, which is so damaging to Gerstein, may be relied on is anyone's guess. The evidence is scanty. So many men have died or are keeping their mouths shut; so many documents have gone up in smoke. We cannot disregard what Peters has said. But if it is true that Gerstein was actively concerned in the large-scale supply of poison gas to the operators of the Final Solution, we may at least ask ourselves whether, in the circumstances in which he found himself, he could conceivably have done anything else, short of committing suicide. And we may adduce two further items of evidence.

The first is from a medical report of the effects of Zyklon B, administered in the form of small blue crystals scattered through a hole in the ceiling over the naked victims packed like sardines in a room that was then hermetically sealed: 'The victim is reduced to a state of acute mental anguish, precordial anxiety and oppression, while retaining all his faculties. Nervous convulsions ensue, with dilation of the pupils, followed by the phase of asphyxia, the slowing down of respiration, pulse irregularity, cyanosis of the face, chilling of the extremities and eventually death.'

The second is the fact that later consignments of Zyklon B bore the warning: 'Attention! No irritant!'

This, if we accept the evidence of Doctor Peters, may be attributed to Gerstein. He could not save the life of a single victim, even at the cost of his own, but it may be that in some degree he mitigated their last agonies. It was something.

'The man who will not act or speak except in total righteousness achieves nothing. He does not enter the path of progress and he is not true because he is not real ... The man who seeks to be true must run the risk of being mistaken, of putting himself in the wrong; he must carry things to their conclusion, balance them on a knife-edge so that they may be truly and realistically decided.' (Karl Jaspers.)

*

At Auschwitz the tall, haggard figure of Gerstein occasioned a good deal of speculation. Doctor Wilhelm Münch, a former SS doctor, acquitted by the Polish High Court at Cracow, had this to say in 1968:

'The SS doctors at the camp openly discussed the problem of exterminating the Jews. They all accepted the Final Solution in principle, but could not agree about the best means of carrying it out because of the technical difficulty of killing and disposing of an increasingly large number of people every day. It was in this connection that I first heard of Gerstein, although I never met him. The SS doctors talked of him as a sort of amateur, a bluffer who was trying to rationalize the extermination process by the use of Zyklon. They said he carried out secret experiments in developing his method, and that he held aloof from the rest of the qualified staff and made shameless use of his standing with Himmler, who had taken a particular fancy to him.

'Some of the doctors went still further and hinted that he had deliberately wormed his way into Auschwitz in order to work against them and sabotage the Final Solution. One of them even suggested that he wanted to blow up the camp.'

From the Frankfurt *Abendpost*, 17 May 1955: 'At the gas trial in Frankfurt the engineer Armin Peters, aged thirty-six, who had known Gerstein from the time of the Protestant Youth Movement, stated that at the end of 1944 he was planning to kill Himmler and his closest associates by exploding a new type of decontamination plant, which was to be demonstrated to Himmler and his staff in Berlin. Gerstein had invited all the SS leaders concerned in the concentration camp mass murders to witness the demonstration. The plan fell through because the military situation made it impossible to go ahead with it.'

To those who knew him, Gerstein, so mystifying to his fellow-members of the SS, presented a picture of solitude which no friendship or affection could break down.

Horst Dickten (1968): 'He knew that he had been rejected by his family and he did not wish it otherwise.'

Karl Gerstein (1964): 'We were living in Berlin but he hid himself even from me.'

Günter Dickten (1967): 'Before, there had been some gaiety in him; he had been in tune with life. But all this vanished. There were times when his nerve cracked; he flew off the handle and shouted and bellowed in a sort of Teutonic fury. There had been a time when one felt he was proud of being a German, but later he didn't seem to want to belong to any country . . . He would take me aside and tell me of things that had been left undone.'

*

On air-raid nights the shelter under 47 Bülowstrasse was filled with people in their night attire. There were no longer any doors between the basement booths; there were chairs and folding beds everywhere.

The terrified occupants of the house were now able to get a clear view of Gerstein, 'the SS officer on the first floor,' the distinguished personage who had a car, an orderly, any amount of food, and who was said to be high up in the Order of Blackshirts. He was to be seen on those nights of holocaust as though it were his function always to appear in the depths, here as elsewhere.

Not many are now left of the people who remember that vanished house, and for the most part they are aging women who know nothing of Gerstein except that he was once their neighbour.

Frau Gruhn (the widow of a shopkeeper): 'It's a terrible time to remember . . . Our only daughter was killed in the Battle of Berlin . . . The three of us lived directly above Gerstein. When our girl got engaged I went down to apologize in advance in case we made a noise. He couldn't have been nicer. He sent me up some chocolate and some real coffee.

'He and his SS men kept cases with tin cans in a locked cupboard in the basement. Some people said that the tins were really filled with explosives, but Walter, my husband, didn't believe that. They said that Gerstein was one of a special group working under Himmler. He looked very impressive in his uniform.'

Fräulein Klonek (librarian): 'I got to know him by sight,

mainly because of the nights we spent in the shelter. He'd fixed up
a corner for himself, and that's where he and his SS men went
when there was a raid on. Sometimes he invited one or two people
to join them, particularly Frau Hoeflich, the hairdresser, who
came from the Rhineland. She was a very lively, healthy-looking
woman, and this seemed to please him. The other people used to
say: "Gerstein's holding court." . . . I knew his housekeeper, an
old woman who thought he was marvellous. I didn't care all that
much for him because I didn't like the SS and in particular I
didn't like having them in the house. One of the other tenants
was a dentist called Weigandt. He and his wife were both fanatical
Nazis, he especially; he always wore Party uniform and he seemed
to get more ferocious than ever after his son was killed at Stalingrad.

'Gerstein was always very polite but he didn't talk much. I had
a big closet in my basement, a sort of lumber-room. He asked if
he could use it. One day when I went down there I found him
and another SS man and two girls listening to the radio. They'd
plugged it into the ceiling light. I imagine they were listening to a
foreign station. Gerstein was making sarcastic remarks and the
others were laughing; but they all stopped when I appeared . . .

'I blame the wretched man for being the cause of the destruction
of our house when the Russians arrived . . .'

Frau Hoeflich, the hairdresser, said as she looked at his photograph: 'Yes, it's he, just the way he used to be, with that far-
away, melancholy expression. He lived alone in a five-room
apartment. I only once met his wife, when she came to visit him
with two children. She was a very German type of woman. I
know they were Catholics.

'I often went to his private shelter in the basement. When he
came down he always greeted everyone with a proper *Heil Hitler*.
He was very quiet, very thoughtful, with nice manners. He didn't
drink or smoke. During the raids he often handed round hot
punch or candies. He sat in his corner listening to the radio.

'He was tall and looked well in uniform. But his face was
generally sallow. He never carried a pistol in his holster—perhaps
he kept it in his trouser-pocket. The SS men who were with him,

about a dozen of them I think, were all nice boys and I got on well with them. Gerstein liked me, and when I cooked him his favourite dish—a good stew with peas to which he added a big lump of bacon fat, which was a rarity in those days—he would say: "Frau Hoeflich, if you're ever in any kind of trouble don't hesitate to come and tell me."

'I got the impression that he was a man with bad troubles of his own, but who didn't want to talk about them. He never said anything about the war or world politics.'

The alerts grew more frequent, the air raids heavier; phosphorus from incendiary bombs streamed down the streets of Greater Berlin. And when a clouded sky made people hopeful of a quiet night, Gerstein would say: 'Don't fool yourself. The British have instruments that enable them to bomb through cloud.' The dread God of the Old Testament was visiting His lightnings upon the criminal town! . . .

A deacon's wife, carried away with enthusiasm after listening to Goebbels, exclaimed in his presence:

'Our splendid Führer will put an end to all this.'

'You bet he will,' said Gerstein brutally. 'And when our splendid Führer has put an end to the Russians and all the rest, he'll put an end to you too, my good woman.'

In the autumn of that year he went to see his old friend Von Bruch, in Gevelsberg. He drove up in a large car with a uniformed chauffeur.

'I haven't much time. I'm just back from Paris and tomorrow I leave for Prague. How are you, and how are all our friends?'

'How are you yourself?' asked Von Bruch.

'I'm one of the most unhappy men on God's earth,' said Gerstein.

Pastor Mochalsky (1967): 'I was on the train that runs from Dahlem to Schoeneberg through the centre of the town. An SS officer got on at Friedenau and I stared at him, knowing that I'd seen him somewhere before. The hair showing under his cap was turning white, but his face was still comparatively young. After a time I remembered who he was. It was the man carrying a suitcase who had come into my vestry and shown me an order for prussic acid. So after all he hadn't committed suicide, as I had thought he might do. He had carried out the order instead—and how many others like it? "Well," I thought, "so that's why he looks like a ghost." . . . I don't know if he recognized me. He looked at me, but his eyes were terribly empty.'

## Chapter 14

# THE SHRINKING WORLD

ON a day in 1944 Leokadia Hinz, Gerstein's housekeeper, came downstairs in a state of alarm to ask Frau Hoeflich for help. At this time Fräulein Hinz was living alone with her employer, Horst Dickten having been sent to the front. And Gerstein was not at all well. Frau Hoeflich went up to find him stretched out on a couch in the sitting-room, gasping for breath, with a high temperature and apparently delirious.

'Everything is so cruel, Frau Hoeflich,' he said. 'I've got something in this apartment with which if I chose I could destroy the whole world. But I shan't do it.'

She murmured indulgently:

'No, no, of course you won't.'

But perhaps there was an element of truth in his delirium. At the beginning of 1944 Lieutenant-Colonel Günther, Eichmann's assistant, had come to Gerstein with an order for a really enormous quantity of prussic acid, to be delivered as soon as possible. According to Pastor Rehling, who was told by Gerstein, the amount was 8,500 kilos—enough to annihilate the 3,000,000 population of Berlin twice over. The consignment was to be stored in a warehouse near Günther's office on Kurfürstenstrasse, so as to be available for instant use.

Günther did not, however, say what it was to be used for.

It could hardly have been for the Jews. Apart from a pocket of 400,000 in Hungary, whom Eichmann was shortly to send to the 'mills' of Auschwitz, the supply of these was almost exhausted. There were the concentration camps and the POW camps. Or could it be for use on the German people themselves, who had proved incapable of winning the war?

The Russians, having relieved Leningrad, were driving irresistibly towards the frontiers of the Reich. The Allied attack in the west was imminent. Germany's sky was no longer her own; Allied bombers pounded her cities by day and by night. The Führer was frantically pressing on with the manufacture of new weapons, but these *Vergeltungswaffen*, the V-1 and the V-2, were, as the name indicated, simply reprisal weapons which could not affect the final outcome of the war.

The nihilism at the root of Hitlerism was gaining ground, the feeling that destruction might be carried out on so grandiose a scale as to wear an aspect of victory. Neither the Führer nor his circle, each provided with his capsule of cyanide, could endure the thought that Germany might survive them. And did the German people themselves desire it? The death-wish was spreading through the country as a whole. As the Russian armies came closer there was an epidemic of suicides: 500 in Schoenlanke (9,700 inhabitants), 1,000 in Stolp (50,000), 600 in Lauenburg (20,000); and in Breslau, in March 1945, the suicide rate averaged over 100 a day.

During the summer of 1944 a woman leader of the Nazi Party sought to improve the morale of the Bavarian peasants by telling them that 'the Führer in his great goodness has arranged for all the German people to die painlessly by gas if the war should end badly.' And an old woman in East Prussia said to Graf Hans von Lehnsdorff: 'The Russians will never get us. The Führer won't allow it. He'll gas us first.' Even Karl Gerstein asked his brother for a supply of poison, which Kurt gave him on the understanding that it was to be used only if the whole family was wiped out . . .

So the question of what use was to be made of this huge consignment of prussic acid was one of considerable moment. But Günther was not saying. Gerstein got the impression that it was a matter of killing off officers and priests—'anyway, people of education'—in 'clubs and reading-rooms.'

Invited to inspect the warehouse where the consignment was to be stored, Gerstein declared it to be quite unsuitable. How could he possibly accept the responsibility for keeping this great quantity of poison in an unprotected building in a town that was subject to daily and nightly air-bombardment? He suggested that it should be stored in the reinforced hangars in the concentration camps of Oranienburg and Auschwitz. This was expert advice—and Günther and his kind still deferred to the experts.

Eduard Calich, Yugoslav, former inmate of Oranienburg (1967): 'Gerstein was well known at Oranienburg. One of my fellow-prisoners called him "Gasman No. 1." He was typical SS, always gave the Hitler salute. The stock of prussic acid got to be so enormous after 1943 that someone said there was enough to kill off all the camps if Germany lost the war.'

Storing the acid at Oranienburg and Auschwitz meant to Gerstein that he could keep it under his own control and possibly, *possibly*, being out of sight of the masters of the Final Solution, get rid of it altogether. He had the consignments sent to the camps with specific instructions that they were intended for decontamination. Those who worked under him knew Gerstein well enough to know that if this was what he said, it was what he meant—in other words, that it was not to be used for any undefined *special purpose*. In this way the acid was taken out of the Final Solution pipeline.

From the findings of the Frankfurt Court in the case of Gerhard Peters (May 1955): 'None of the witnesses at Auschwitz saw the boxes of 500 grams in which the Zyklon was delivered by the accused at Gerstein's request. Witnesses have referred to a great many sizes (200, 1,000, 1,500 grams) but none has mentioned 500 grams. Even the boxes marked "no irritant" found at Auschwitz were not of 500 grams.'[1]

If Günther had inquired after the Zyklon, Gerstein could have covered himself by saying either that there had been an error in handling (because of the need for ultra-secrecy to conceal the real

1 Peters owed his acquittal after the war to the fact that the acid delivered by him and handled by Gerstein did not, in principle, reach the gas chambers. His present freedom and prosperity are thus due to the shade of Gerstein and to nothing else.

purpose for which the stuff was intended) or else that for technical reasons he had had to make use of the stuff immediately.

He wrote to Doctor Peters in May 1944: 'I should be obliged if you would inform me of the effective life of the special deliveries to Oranienburg and Auschwitz. If there is any doubt as to how long they may be stored without deterioration, we shall have to use the first deliveries for decontamination and only keep the more recent consignments in store. So far no use has been made of any of these consignments. But it is possible that a considerable quantity—indeed, the entire stock—may have to be used at short notice. The most important thing is to know how long it can be stored. *Heil Hitler.* (signed) Kurt Gerstein, Lieutenant, SS.'

The reply to this letter, if it had been what he hoped for, would have provided Gerstein with an argument justifying what he planned to do. He hoped that Peters, who knew from the previous year the 'special purpose' for which the Zyklon could be used, and who was now warned that the danger might be imminent, would as a matter of conscience reply that the acid could only be stored for a short time. Acting upon this assurance, Gerstein would be able to get rid of it quickly through the normal decontamination channels.

But Doctor Peters did not take the hint. What did it matter to him? He passed the letter on to the technical director of his firm, who replied calmly that the product was perfectly sound. 'We can give a guarantee of a year, and are confident that in fact it will last longer than that.' Two further details indicate how easy it would have been to help Gerstein, if anyone had wanted to do so. The technical director went on to say that owing to the air attacks it would be impossible to produce any further supply of acid for some months; he also mentioned that the containers might be subject to corrosion: 'Small perforations may develop through which the prussic acid could escape.'

This reference to corrosion made the reply usable.

Gerstein also took another precaution. 'The Bills of the suppliers . . . had been, on my request, made out in my name— allegedly to keep the secret better—in fact to destroy the poison more easily. For this reason, too, I avoided to present for payment the numerous current bills, in order not to remind constant the SD and the RSHA of the large quantities of poison, supposedly available. I let the suppliers wait for the payment of their bills.' (Gerstein's *Report,* see p. 295).

Some of the invoices have since been recovered—as well as evidence that Gerstein did not pay. 'I made repeated attempts to collect the money due,' Peters was to write to his Board, who were anxious to get the company's books in order. As early as 1946 Degesch and its directors, shaking themselves free of the dust and ashes, were soaring to new heights of efficiency and productivity.

As to whether all the prussic acid ordered by Gerstein was used for the purpose of normal decontamination, or harmlessly disposed of, we have no means of knowing. The plain and heart-rending fact is that, whatever he did or failed to do, the 'mills' of Auschwitz continued to turn.

'When Himmler decided upon a human sacrifice,' wrote Eduard Calich, 'he thought in terms of Security planning, not of the amount of gas that was available. Even if Gerstein managed to conceal cases of prussic acid, as he claimed, the factories produced an ample supply to make good the deficiency. If there had been any real shortage the people responsible for it would have lost their jobs and—at the least—have been sent to the front.'

*

It was about this time that Gerstein wrote to his father in a despairing attempt to bridge the gap between his family and himself. (see p. 20). 'I was greatly shocked by something you said, or rather wrote, to me at a difficult period in my life, when I was wrestling with problems of the utmost gravity—'Hard times call for hard measures.' No! Sentiments of this kind cannot justify the the things that have happened. I cannot believe that, in the face of so many outrageous events, that this is the last word of my aging father, who must not be allowed to take such thoughts with him into the next world. It seems to me that all of us who have still a little time to live will have sufficient reason to reflect on the practical possibilities and limitations, but also on the consequences of the casting away of all moral law . . .'

To this the unrelenting reply was: 'You are a soldier and a servant of the State, and it is your business to obey your superiors. The responsibility lies with those who give the orders, not with those who execute them. No insubordination can be justified. You have simply to do what you are ordered to do. That, at least, is what I learnt as a servant of the State and a Prussian officer.'

In the autumn of 1944 Gerstein wrote again:

'. . . My thoughts are often with you, and more than ever, it goes without saying, during these weeks. But that is the trouble. Our respective attitudes are so radically opposed that it seems to me practically impossible to reconcile them. I have had occasion to reflect deeply, in the light of all the implications, on the distinction between black and white, between good and evil, and—believe me—to suffer from it in the very depths of my soul!

'But nearly everything one can say about these things needs to be said in speech. I knew this when you last visited me in Berlin, but I refrained from saying anything and shall continue to do so. Whatever our relations may be in other respects, our ideas are so diametrically opposed that, in the present state of affairs, we cannot hope to understand one another. Nor can we suppose that we may find a way through to one another, or that we have simply failed to explain ourselves clearly. No; we hear each other speak, but our thinking is on totally different lines. It is no use trying to ignore this; we must simply have the courage to wait until time and history have supplied the answer to present events . . . In any case, if you look around you will see that many families have been divided in this fashion and that close friendships have been broken. I do not regard this too tragically; but the fact remains that for the time being the possibility of a dialogue is as it were in suspense. Contrary to what you say in your letter, I do not believe that a conversation between us would improve matters. On one point, moreover, you are mistaken in your facts. I have never lent my hand to all that. When I have received orders of that kind I have never carried them out and I have diverted their execution. Where I am concerned I come out of this business with clean hands and a clear conscience. This enormously consoles me—and not for opportunist reasons! What does death matter, after all? It is principles and conduct that matter . . . It is the destiny of brave men to risk all they possess, even life itself, for love of a purpose that may never be achieved . . .

'But I think it better to say no more. We will adjourn this debate until we can pursue it with the frankness that is essential.'

That time was never to come.

Obersturmbannführer Günther was to harass Gerstein only once more. He sent for him and asked if it would be possible to kill off the remaining Jews in the Terezin ghetto by showering acid over them from the top of the fortifications. Gerstein's answer was: 'Quite unworkable!'

That was the last time. The masters of the Final Solution decided that they had had enough of the delays and technical objections raised by this unimportant officer. They did without him.

His Dutch friend Nieuwenhuizen said in 1968: 'Gerstein told me: "The SS think I'm too slow in delivering. They don't want to have any more to do with me. They're using another channel." '

In June 1944 a member of the Swiss Legation accepted Gerstein's invitation to dine in Bülowstrasse. He was the Cultural and Press Attaché, Paul Hochstrasser. A retired German officer of his acquaintance had said to him: 'There's an SS officer who wants to talk to you.' It might be a manoeuvre of some kind, but Hochstrasser nevertheless decided to go.

His German acquaintance, who was already there, introduced him to his host, who was in civilian clothes. Gerstein seemed to be in a highly nervous state. 'Before talking,' he said, 'we must eat properly.'

An old woman, whom Gerstein addressed in the harsh, peremptory tones of an SS officer, served them a memorable meal. Duck, among other things. And then Gerstein talked for several hours, 'like a man vomiting,' as Hochstrasser put it.

He talked about the forcible Germanization of Poland and the visits paid to the villages by commissions of young S S doctors whose business was to decide which of the inhabitants should live and which should die. He described what had happened in Belzec, Sobibor and Treblinka. Paul Hochstrasser had heard a good deal over his radio, but never as much as this. 'I began to realize why he'd given us such an excellent meal.'

He asked Gerstein how many deaths National Socialism was responsible for, and Gerstein replied: 'Between twenty and twenty-two million. Tell your Government.'[1]

Hochstrasser did so—and his report went to join others in the files for the benefit of future Swiss historians. In any case, Gerstein had not expected anything to come of the conversation. He was simply passing on his knowledge to another witness.

\*

'The opposition is grouping round Goerdeler. Something will happen before long.'

Gerstein wrote this to Pastor Rehling in May or June 1944. But he talked with some detachment about what has become known as the 20th July conspiracy, as though he were not involved in it.

For the first time since National Socialism had come into power there was a body of organized resistance in Germany, extending from the traditional Right to the Christian Democrats and Socialists (the Communists were still making up their minds). Karl Friedrich Goerdeler, who had resigned his office as Mayor of Leipzig in protest against the removal of the statue of the Jewish composer Mendelssohn, was at the heart of it. His own

1 The figure, according to Hochstrasser, was composed of 15 million Jews, Poles and Russians, 4.5 million German soldiers, and 1 million Germans killed in air raids. It has been claimed that this was an exaggeration, but in fact, as Hochstrasser himself has said, it was probably an underestimate. He himself put the figure of German soldiers and civilians at 6–7 millions. As for foreign civilian populations, the official figure for Poland and Russia alone is between 14 and 15 millions.

sympathies were with the Western Allies, but there were others, notably among the members of the Prussian aristocracy, who leaned towards Russia. But the real split between them was of another kind. The conspirators were divided into those who were resigned to the defeat of Germany and those who refused to accept it. Therein lay the tragedy of these men, all of whom were so soon to die.

According to Sergeant Weigelt, Gerstein was acquainted with Goerdeler. Horst Dickten says: 'He was in touch with members of the Kreisau Circle.'

Kreisau was the Silesian estate of the descendants of Field-Marshal von Moltke, the victor of Sadowa and Sedan. The present Graf Helmuth von Moltke, a giant of a man, deeply religious and with eccentrically radical ideas (he had divided up his land among his tenant farmers), had gathered round him a circle of aristocrats, ecclesiastics and socialists who attached more importance to reflection than to action. They had religious faith in common, and a belief in moral values. They hoped, not for the disappearance of Hitler but for a change of heart in Germany. The thought of a Nazi Germany without Hitler was the threat that restrained them.

'Only certain members of the Kreisau Circle took direct part in the various plots to kill Hitler. A majority of the Circle originally opposed resort to assassination and a coup d'état. They felt that the virus of Nazism had permeated the body politic of Germany so deeply that the removal of the leaders would not in itself suffice. Also, they feared a "stab in the back" legend, a myth that some day could fertilize a rebirth of Nazism. They were particularly apprehensive about this in the early years of the war, when defeat was not yet apparent to the German people.'[1]

On 20 July 1944 Colonel Klaus von Stauffenberg placed his briefcase with its explosive charge under the table in the Führer's headquarters and left the room. The failure of that attempt on Hitler's life, as the world knows, was followed by a wave of arrests, suicides, trials and savage executions. The Army General

1 Allen Welsh Dulles, *Germany's Underground.*

Staff was decimated, as were the aristocracy and the upper bour-
geoisie. Goerdeler, who was arrested, lived only a few months
longer than Stauffenberg, Moltke, Kluge, Rommel and several
thousand others. Whole families were wiped out. Children were
taken away from their mothers to be kept in hiding under false
names. Stauffenberg and three of his associates were favoured with
total extinction. 'I have ordered the bodies to be burnt and the
ashes to be scattered. We do not wish to preserve any trace of
those people, or of the ones still to be executed. Tilled fields are
too good for them; their ashes are to be scattered over sewage
land.' (Himmler.)

In August 1944 J. H. Ubbink, in Holland, received a cryptic
unsigned postcard which conveyed to him that Gerstein had in
fact been involved in the conspiracy but had come through unscathed.

He had been involved, but without ever believing in it.

Later Gerstein explained his position to Helmut Franz. His
view was that the men of 20 July had failed to grasp the essential
truth of the situation, namely, that the German problem could not
be solved except from outside. Both ends of the movement, the
Goerdeler and Stauffenberg factions alike, had blinded themselves
to the fact that the overthrow of the Nazis could be achieved only
by the military defeat of Germany. In the early stages the opposition had said: 'First we must win the war and then we'll get rid
of the Nazi hoodlums.' Later they had said: 'We must destroy the
Nazis but at the same time try to win the war.' It was necessary
to look further, to envisage, however bitter the prospect, a defeat
as total as the one that actually occurred.

Gerstein thought that for Hitler to meet with an honourable
death by assassination was altogether too good for a man 'whom
the rats should devour.' The scriptural violence of the phrase
affords an indication of what was in his exalted and prophetic
mind. The end of the regime in Germany must be something
more than a matter of historical record—it must be an apocalyptic
event. The outrage against Heaven could be expiated only in a
calamity as monstrous and overwhelming as the offence itself, in

the fiery reduction of Germany to dust and ashes, utter squalor, utter shame, so that the very sound of the word 'German' would cause Germans to regret that they had not been Jews ... 'The end will be terrible. A whole world will perish,' Gerstein wrote to his sister-in-law.

But the time was not yet, and therefore Stauffenberg, the crippled, one-eyed man, had failed. The issue was no longer in the hands of men. It was God, and God alone, who had spared Hitler. Another man besides Gerstein took this view—Hitler himself.

*

Meanwhile there ensued a period of suspense.

Gerstein contrived with the help of the chaplain to smuggle food and cigarettes in to the condemned prisoners awaiting execution in the prison at Plötzensee. He used all his contacts, in particular his friendship with Ernst Zerrer, who had done so much for him at the time of Welzheim, to help people who were still only under suspicion. He burned the list of anti-Nazi officials which he and Councillor Walter Eckhart had compiled together, and severed connections with everyone whom he might otherwise compromise.

Kurt Rehling was one of these. At their last meeting, in May or June 1944, Gerstein said with the concentrated fury that had possessed him ever since his visit to Belzec: 'These things must be known and judged. And they will be, even if I have to be crucified for it.' And he added: 'I shan't survive.' They never met again.

During those last months of Hitler's Reich all the 'bearers of secrets' went in danger of their lives. Himmler, in the modest hope of succeeding Hitler, was cleaning up for the future after his own fashion. We have seen how careful he was to destroy all traces of the disused extermination camps and the charnel pits. He now proceeded to deal with the people who knew too much about them.

Execution orders went out to prisons and camps. A good many SS personnel with compromising knowledge were sent to fight against the Yugoslav partisans, where death 'on the field of honour' was of particularly frequent occurrence. One of the first to be killed was Captain Wirth, who had said to Gerstein: 'Fewer than ten people have seen what you have seen. The foreign auxiliaries will, of course, eventually be executed.'

Gerstein, it goes without saying, was on the list of those who knew too much. Everything about him, including his doubtful past, was calculated to attract Himmler's notice. The decontamination expert had become a suitable subject for decontamination. His life was imperilled at this stage not by his opposition to the regime but simply by the fact that he was a Blackshirt. Such was the logical end of the course he had pursued, as though destiny had decreed that, having voluntarily enlisted in the SS, he could never again divest himself of its uniform.

And still Mrugowsky was his protector. The wary pact between them still endured, growing ever more complicated and insecure. An incident during that year shows its precarious nature.

A sum of 4,500 marks reached Armin Peters from Gerstein, derived as usual from some unknown source, to be paid into Peters's bank account pending further instructions. Peters in a moment of absent-mindedness endorsed the cheque with his telephone number instead of the number of his bank account, the two being rather similar. No great harm would have been done if he had not also stamped it with an Institute rubber stamp. A week later, finding that the money had not been credited to him, he made inquiries and was told that owing to the incorrect account number the cheque had been returned to the sender at the Institute. Decidedly perturbed, he went to the Institute the next day. He saw Gerstein, who, however, did not speak to him (Mrugowsky having forbidden him to do so), and he found a written order instructing him to report to the commanding officer immediately.

Mrugowsky started by asking quietly how the anti-malarial pumping vessels were getting on. Then suddenly he demanded: 'Will you kindly tell me how it is that you're able to pay a large sum of money into your personal account bearing our endorsement?' Peters, very much taken aback, stammered out a confused story about provision for contingencies, uncompleted paper-work and so on. Mrugowsky cut him short: 'Well, see that it doesn't happen again. It's only because I value your work that I'm overlooking it this time.' He pressed the bell and an assistant came in and counted out the money to Peters, who by now was in a state of acute alarm. Gerstein, too, must have been decidedly unhappy. If Peters had lost his head and mentioned his name it might have caused Mrugowsky to bring to a drastic end the tacit agreement that had existed between them since Christmas 1942.

Frau Gerstein said in 1969: 'Professor Mrugowsky had for a long time been anxious to meet me and the children. He and Kurt had to pay an official visit to a place near Tübingen some time about the middle of 1944, and Kurt did not see how he could avoid inviting him. He warned me of it in a very worried way, telling me in particular that I must go carefully through the bookshelves in the room where we were to have our meal, to make sure that there was nothing there except "works of piety." And we had to be careful not to use the Swabian form of greeting *Grüss Gott* instead of *Heil Hitler*. Fortunately our oldest boy, Arnulf, who was then four and a half, had got into the habit of saying *Heil Hitler* from hearing it so often in the shops, so there was no danger where he was concerned. All the same, we were uneasy the whole time.

'I'm quite sure, thinking it over, that if we had decided to live together in Berlin either our children would have had to be brought up quite differently and trained to be always on their guard, or else Kurt would sooner or later have been found out and arrested. So perhaps after all it's a good thing we stayed in Tübingen.'

The threat of Mrugowsky hung endlessly over Gerstein's head. The smallest incident, the least breath of suspicion, might cause the card house to collapse. Any day might be the day of Mrugowsky's wrath—and the eve of Gerstein's death. Fear haunted him. The shrinking world in which he lived, the death of his friends at the front, in prison or in concentration camps, was a constant reminder of the precariousness of his own hold on life.

'He was a man of extraordinary courage,' said Niemöller. 'More courage than his body could contain.'

Indeed, it was partly a physical problem. The appalling mental tensions to which he had for so long been subject, together with insomnia, overwork and many bitter frustrations, had so undermined his constitution that he was in danger of a total breakdown. For ten years his life had been a constant battle with ill-health. At the root of the trouble was his long-standing hypoglycemia, the abnormal wastage of his reserves of energy which caused him to devour great quantities of sugar. It was now severe, and it led to frequent crises—even to a 'pre-coma condition,' in the words of the doctor who had been caring for him since 1941.

How he must have despised the body that threatened to fail him, knowing as he did that if he weakened he was done for. By the age of thirty-nine every vestige of youth had left his face. People who met him after even a short interval gazed at him in consternation, scarcely able to recognize him, the tall, pale man, his hair whitening, his features haggard and twitching, his breath coming in gasps, and his gaze, which had never been communicative, seeming now to be withdrawn into some dark chamber of its own.

*I am like a pelican of the wilderness: I am like an owl of the desert. I watch, and am as a sparrow alone upon the house top.*

*Mine enemies reproach me all the day; and they that are mad against me are sworn against me.*

*For I have eaten ashes like bread, and mingled my drink with weeping,*

*Because of thine indignation and thy wrath: for thou hast lifted me up, and cast me down.*

*My days are like a shadow that declineth; and I am withered like grass.*

(Psalm 102.)

Karl Gerstein: 'He'd had enough. He couldn't stand it any longer. He was sick in his soul.'

Robert Weigelt: 'At the end he shivered constantly.'

Franz Bäuerle: 'As time passed he showed more and more signs of distress.'

From a letter to his wife written in hospital, 8 October 1944 '. . . Clearly everything is taking its course, although rather slowly. Patience has never been my strong point . . . I should so like to be able to write more frankly to you, but what can I do? It seems to me certain that it will all be over before very long. Attempts at reconciliation reach me from Hagen [where his father was living], but what's the use? We are more than worlds apart.'

Herbert Eickhoff: 'He had changed so much. He never made jokes any more. The only familiar thing about him was his way of shouting "Hinzchen" to call his housekeeper.

'I asked him: "Kurt, are you in danger?"

' "Why, what can happen to me?" he said. "I can't fall an inch lower than into the hands of the living God." '

On 26 December 1944, Leokadia Hinz took final leave of him. She died in hospital of heart disease.

Gerstein's grief at her death was amazing to his colleagues at the Institute—a mere housekeeper! He personally saw to every detail of the funeral. There was difficulty in securing the services of a priest, and so he appealed to the Protestant Bishop Dibelius and persuaded him to officiate. Leokadia was buried near Nauen 'in the most lovely country churchyard one can imagine, where tombs can lie for centuries in the beautiful pale sand.' Six farmworkers carried the coffin Gerstein had bought for her—a white coffin, since she was unmarried.

'She was buried like a princess,' he wrote to his wife.

But this did not satisfy him. As though it were necessary for the world to know of Leokadia's death, he inserted an obituary in the local press:

'On the evening of the day after Christmas, at 8 : 30, our faithful housekeeper, my friend and second mother

LEOKADIA HINZ

—born on 20 December 1883 at Lesno, died on 26 December

229

1944 at the Elisabeth Hospital, Berlin—trusting in God and submitting to His will after a brief and cruel illness.

'A noble friend has left us, warm-hearted, understanding and filled with the spirit of self-sacrifice. She wore herself out in her devotion to those in her care. Her life was service and love of her neighbour. She died in absolute faith in our Messiah and Saviour.

'We shall treasure her memory with profound gratitude for her goodness of heart, her love, tact and delicacy.'

The devotional phrasing was in itself a declaration, as though from the depths of his grief he were proclaiming: 'Do not forget, you who read, that S S Lieutenant Kurt Gerstein is still a Christian.' He signed his name at the head of those of his family, and followed them with the names of Leokadia's former employers, Leo, Olga, Kurt and Ilse Berger. They were Jews.

This was Gerstein's last act of defiance, magnificently dedicated to a servant.

\*

Darkness now finally enclosed the apartment on Bülowstrasse. Sometimes its ghostlike occupant set up the row of photographs of his friends in the Bible Circles who had fallen in the war, and gazed at them as though passing them under review. 'I would have preferred you to continue with your studies,' he had written, 'but no one can rob you of a "hero's death." '

'Are you sure no one followed you here? Were you watching out?' he asked Pastor Mochalsky.

Mochalsky had the impression that the man stretched on the couch was either crazed with grief or drunk. But if Gerstein had been drinking it had in no way dulled his mind. The pastor explained what he had come about. Pastor Niemöller's youngest daughter had just died in Bavaria, and Frau Niemöller was anxious that he, Mochalsky, should conduct the funeral service. But how was he to get out of Berlin? The Russians had reached the Oder and civilians were no longer allowed to leave the city.

'I don't know of anyone who can arrange it for me, except you.'

Without even leaving his couch Gerstein drafted an official order requiring the bearer to visit an establishment connected with the Institute in Munich. While he was doing so Mochalsky gazed about him at the 'weird' disorder of the room, which was filled with almost forgotten luxuries—cigars, canned food, liquor bottles. Gerstein glanced at him and said: 'Help yourself to anything you want.'

Having completed the order, he got heavily to his feet, opened the front door of the apartment and, after making sure that the coast was clear, allowed his visitor to depart.

Thanks to the order, Mochalsky reached Bavaria without trouble. SS law was still supreme in Germany—four months before the final collapse.

*

Scarcely a sound from the streets penetrated the silence of that sombre apartment—only the wail of sirens, the fury of anti-aircraft fire, the crash of bombs. Although the house had been shaken, its sturdy structure was still largely intact. But in the intervals between air raids Gerstein must surely have listened for another sound, the heavy tread of feet on the stairs, the warning that the game was up. And what way out would he take? The window, like so many Warsaw Jews? (But a first-floor window was too low.) Poison, like Rommel? His service automatic, like Beck? But after all, why should they trouble to come for him, why not simply ring up? A polite feminine voice on the telephone: 'Obersturmführer Gerstein? This is the Waffen SS Institute of Hygiene. Herr Obersturmführer, you are hereby instructed to make use of the cyanide capsule so thoughtfully provided by a management which foresees all contingencies. I am speaking on behalf of Oberführer Professor Doktor Mrugowsky, who is busy on another line. The order is on the personal instructions of Reichsführer Himmler, since you are a bearer of secrets. You have only to bite the capsule. There is no pain. The method has been thoroughly tested on prisoners at Dachau. A slight tremor and that is all. The order is to be carried out immediately. You have quite understood, Herr Obersturmführer? Thank you.

*Heil Hitler!*' ... As for the other thoughts and memories flooding through his fevered mind in the gloom of that empty dwelling encumbered with the bric-à-brac he had collected all over Europe, we may conjure them up for ourselves in the light of what we know of the strange, tormented life that was now nearing its end ...

But for the present life still went on. A young man appeared one day in his room at the Institute.

'Kurt, have you forgotten me?'

It was Günter Dickten, the insubordinate 'son' whom he had virtually disavowed for joining the Army. When, in November 1967, he described this last meeting between them, Dickten had risen to the rank of Major in the Bundeswehr.

'You see,' he said, as Gerstein rose to greet him, 'I've become an officer in spite of you.'

'I'm glad you have,' said Gerstein. 'In this life it's better to be the hammer than the anvil. But the fact that you ignored my advice makes it difficult for us to be friends.'

'Can't we forget that, Kurt? You always said that if I married you would want to meet my wife. She's in Berlin now.'

The three of them went to Bülowstrasse, and little Louise Dickten was dismayed as much by the atmosphere of restrained panic that pervaded the almost empty building as by the sight of Gerstein's ravaged countenance. The luxuries lay scattered indifferently around him, the bottles, the cigarettes ... Dickten took one and began to smoke furiously.

Gerstein: 'So you're hooked. I thought at least that I had taught you self-control.'

The harshness of his manner caused Louise further dismay; but then he gave her a vase as a wedding present and, regardless of principle, he gave her husband three boxes of cigarettes.

Gerstein: 'You're just back from the front? Tell me what's happening.'

Dickten: 'You probably know more than I do. If we can't make a separate peace with the West the war will end in a shambles.'

Gerstein: 'That's precisely how it will end.' Later he said:

'My name's been mentioned over the British radio. They know exactly who Gerstein is.'

Louise: 'But, Doctor Gerstein, how are you going to get out of that?'

Gerstein: 'You'll know when nobody speaks of me any more.'

On their way downstairs Louise clutched her husband by the arm and murmured:

'You mean to say that's the man who brought you up?'

## Chapter 15

# ACROSS THE RIVER

*March 1945.* The snows of winter were melting, spring was coming and Gerstein was still alive. He could stand at his window and reflect on what might lie before him in the coming months.

'I do not move. I await the tempest and the new beginning.' (Kierkegaard.)

Since the beginning of the year the thought uppermost in the mind of every member of the Institute of Hygiene—each one separate, since none dared confide in his neighbour—was, 'How am I to get out of it?'

The smoke of bonfires mingled with the many other conflagrations in Berlin: documents were being burned. Even the most hard-boiled Nazis in the Institute were rediscovering the piety of their youth and praying to Providence that their names might be obliterated—everything except the memory of their good deeds. The crust of bread given to a prisoner of war, the refusal to carry out a particular order—'Surely, Herr Obersturmführer, you have not forgotten that?'

Gerstein as he moved through that apprehensive world seemed to have doubled in stature. They felt convinced, and murmured to one another, that he would be all right. He had the Church behind him, contacts everywhere, even relatives in America. Instinctively the innocent ewe-lambs of the SS turned to him for comfort and protection, envying his look of assurance.

Hauptsturmführer Fritz Krantz was worried about his wife and children, who had been evacuated to Austria. The Russians were very close.

'What will happen if they get in there?'

Gerstein: 'Nothing. According to the inter-Allied agreement

they can't occupy the sector where your family are. If they do go in, they'll come out again. You can believe me—I have it on good authority.' And he added cryptically: 'I'll help you, Krantz, when the time comes.'

Certainly he meant to do what he could for Krantz if he came up for judgement, and there were perhaps half a dozen others. But what about Mrugowsky? Had it not been for Mrugowsky, Gerstein himself would be dead and unable to testify in anyone's favour. On the other hand, had it not been for Mrugowsky, many men now dead might be still alive. Mrugowsky: a man with whom he had been in daily contact for several years, not a friend but not a stranger either; a human being with bloodstained hands, but shaped, like other men, in the image of God. 'It is almost impossible to believe that Christ died for these gangsters, and yet it is so: He died for them as well.' (Gerstein to Helmut Franz.)

It seemed scarcely to occur to him that he, too, was a member of the SS. When Helmut Franz, meeting him in Tübingen in March: asked: 'How do you expect to clear yourself?' he answered impassively: 'Don't worry. Gerstein has more than one trick up his sleeve.'

His brother Karl asked him if he had any plans for the future and he replied no less calmly: 'I'm thinking of becoming a pastor.'

Armin Peters reports him as saying in a tone of profound pessimism: 'The older I get the better I understand the words of the Lord's Prayer—"Thy will be done." '

At the end of March the Russians launched their final assault on the 180 German divisions massed against them. Surrender in the West, resistance in the East; a change of alliance. Hitler was playing his last gambler's throw before he blew his brains out.

Gertrud Klonek, Gerstein's neighbour (1967): 'I blame that wretched man Gerstein. He was the cause of our house being destroyed on 28 April, when a handful of SS men held it against the Russians. One of them told me that Gerstein, whom I'd seen leaving in civilian clothes some time in March, had left a whole armoury of weapons in his apartment. When he was leaving the

SS people carried out several laundry baskets for him. I don't know what was in them.'

Frieda Hoeflich: 'They were French SS men brought in from Kreuzberg and commanded by a General. In the end they set fire to the house. The General was killed and the Russian soldiers took his beautiful shiny boots. As for Gerstein, I saw him leave in civilian clothes a few days before the attack on Berlin began. I remember saying to him, half-joking: "Well, Herr Doktor, so we're clearing out?" He smiled but didn't answer.'

Elfriede Gerstein (1967): 'He arrived in Tübingen on 26 March. He thought the Allies were nearer than they really were, and he was disappointed. It was too soon for the things he wanted to do. He was worried about the children. He said: "I hope the Americans will be here very soon." I was certain it would be the French, but he said no, the Americans. But he only said that to reassure me, because, as Germans, we had less to fear from the Americans than from the French, whose country we had occupied. He went off again without knowing exactly where he was going. He didn't want to go back to Berlin or to stay here. He said: "You wait! You'll be amazed at all the things I've done!"

'Before he left he did something that was very unusual for him. He suddenly bent down and kissed me.

'I never saw him again.'

We do not know what happened to Gerstein during the next two or three weeks. There is no evidence that he went back to Berlin, and it seems more likely that he drifted through the chaos of Germany, witnessing the apocalypse he had predicted and held to be necessary. But on 19 April he was in Metzingen, a few miles from Tübingen, which was now occupied by an advance unit of the French First Army. He was there for three days, stopping with the wife of a university friend. Then he vanished again when it was reported that an SS force was on its way from Urach to attempt to drive back the French. 'Nothing could be worse for me,' he said, thinking perhaps of the documents he had with him (invoices for the supply of gas; the order for his arrest in 1938, and so on). Or perhaps he was afraid, as a 'bearer of

secrets,' that a last-minute order for his execution had been issued.
On 22 April he got on a motorcycle and went through the front
line near Reutlingen.

It was his final departure from Germany. He had entered the
post-war world.

Reutlingen was in the hands of a combat formation of the
Fifth French Armoured Division, composed of units of the First
Chasseurs d'Afrique and the Foreign Legion. Gerstein surrendered
to the first soldier he encountered and asked to be taken to an
officer. He was interviewed by the commander of the shock
battalion, Lieutenant-Colonel Gambiez. Gerstein introduced
himself, showed his credentials and told his story, making great
play—as he was to do everywhere—with the name of Pastor
Niemöller, which was a kind of universal passport with the
Allies.

It was here that the great misunderstanding began. The French
Army listened to Gerstein and were disposed to believe him; but
they were still fighting a war; they had no time to spare for all
the talk about Belzec and the Judgement of History. Their
immediate preoccupation was with Werewolf, the last-ditch
resistance force which the Nazis claimed had been organized to
operate behind the Allied lines. (In fact it had no existence except
in the fevered imaginations of the men in the Chancellery bunker.)

Gerstein seemed to be exactly what they were looking for.
Colonel Gambiez promptly enlisted him in the 'anti-Werewolf'
section and furnished him with a pass that stated: 'The bearer is
not a genuine member of the SS and should not be treated as
such; on the contrary, he is to be given every assistance.' In a
matter of minutes the Obersturmführer SS had been transferred
to French Military Intelligence.

It was not precisely what he wanted, but at least he had crossed
over, and everything could be straightened out later. He drove
off in an army car with other French security officers, having
obtained leave to call at Tübingen to see Elfriede and the children
before entering upon his duties in the sector to which he had
been appointed.

It was lucky for him that he left Reutlingen, where the atmosphere suddenly changed. On the night of the 22nd a French sergeant was shot dead in the main street. Was this the work of Werewolf? A curfew was ordered and a few days later four Nazis, having been judged to be responsible, were shot in reprisal.

In Tübingen, however, he was unfortunate. Elfriede was not there. The French military commander had that day ordered the families of SS personnel and other Nazis to evacuate their dwellings. The neighbours had been delighted to let the French authorities know that Frau Gerstein was the wife of an SS officer. She had had to go with the rest, and she did not return until the next day. A neighbour then called out to her: 'Your husband was here yesterday with some Frenchmen.' Elfriede at once began a search, being certain that Kurt would not have gone without leaving some trace of his passing. Eventually she found, hidden under the cloth on the hallstand, a sum of money and a sheaf of papers, including the order for his arrest. It was the last evidence Gerstein was to give of his skill in contrivance, his ability to do what he wanted when he wanted, even when he was under surveillance.

Rottweil, a small crossroads town and communications centre in the Neckar valley, was occupied by the administrative services of the French First Army. No sooner did Gerstein get there than he was locked up. Military Intelligence was only moderately persuaded of the *bona fides* of an attested SS officer who might be working for Werewolf. It was not until the next day, and after numerous protests, that he was allotted a room on the third floor of the Hotel Mohren, which had been commandeered by the French Army. His window overlooked the main square, congested with military convoys.

He was allowed restricted freedom of movement with orders to report daily to the authorities. It was understood that he was to produce a written account of his experiences. Much was expected of this, names especially—names which would assist in the hunt for Werewolves.

So Gerstein sat down in the small, low-ceilinged room and wrote his testament while the battle raged in Berlin and Hitler prepared to stage a testament of his own.

Frau Beck, at the Hotel Mohren (1967):
'He seemed absolutely shattered. He told us about the concentration camps and the things he had seen. We sometimes invited him to coffee because he was all alone, without news of his family. He often went to pray in the Catholic church because the Protestant one was closed. It was an old Dominican church that had been used as an assembly centre for prisoners; he volunteered to have it cleaned out, and the work was very well done. Having made the acquaintance of Pastor Hecklinger, he borrowed his typewriter to do his writing on, and he was always going to the stationer's shop for paper, but at that time there was very little paper to be had.'

Gerstein's first account of his life and his visit to Belzec, dated 26 April,[1] was written in French—a makeshift French that lent his words an extraordinary power. But this was something that he did not realize. Since his meeting with Von Otter he had made repeated efforts to tell his story and had repeatedly failed, as though he had lost all power of expression. The fact is that Belzec was inexpressible, as in a sense Gerstein himself was—and more so than ever in April 1945, with no one to confirm what he said or to interpret his reasons. It was not a matter for words on paper, but for speech, with pauses in between, fragments of memory, half-truths to make the truth more bearable. He must have suffered agonies as he sat there wrestling with his inadequate French.

And one can imagine how it must have seemed to the French Intelligence officer who had been instructed to supervise his labours, as the latter in growing exasperation flicked over the newly typed sheets.

'This is very interesting, Herr Gerstein, but it isn't what we're looking for. We want to know about Werewolf. Our forces are

1 See Postscripts.

still in action. We've got to keep the occupied territory under control. For the time being that's our problem.'

It was not Gerstein's.

On 5 May a jeep driven by a Negro G.I. brought two Allied officers to Rottweil: an American, John W. Haught, employed by Du Pont de Nemours, who had been given the temporary rank of Colonel, and an Englishman, Major Derek Curtis Evans, of British Army Intelligence. They were the first representatives of CIOS (Combined Intelligence Objectives Sub-Committee) and their task was to find out where certain combat gases that had been developed by Nazi scientists were being manufactured. It was growing late when they arrived, and so they decided to stop at the Hotel Mohren.

In July 1968 Mr Haught wrote to me as follows from Chadds Ford, Pennsylvania:

'As I recall, Major Evans and I were taking a stroll around the village of Rottweil in the early evening when a stranger approached us and said he would like to give us a record of his experiences. He had tried to interest others in his experiences but with little success . . . After all these years any description I would give would be purely imagination. I would not recognize a picture of him at this time . . . The only impression remaining after all these years is that Gerstein was very sincere and anxious to give his records to persons who might get them in the hands of those who might be able to prosecute those people who had tortured and killed so many innocent people.'

I talked to Major Evans in London in February 1968—a very English-looking Englishman of sixty-five. In 1961 he had been asked to furnish a written statement for use at the Eichmann trial, and it was only then that he had discovered that Gerstein had been a person of some consequence and was now dead.

'Whilst sitting in the lounge of an hotel in Rottweil,' ran the relevant part of his statement, 'an individual came over to us, introduced and identified himself as Doctor Kurt Gerstein, handed over a batch of papers, stating that they were of great importance, and asked us to ensure their safe delivery to the appropriate authorities in London.

'Having read these documents and listened to his story, we decided that they appeared to be of considerable interest, and that Gerstein was probably telling the truth; we, therefore, agreed to take them from him, with a promise that they would be duly forwarded as requested. My colleague and I subsequently drew up and signed a report in manuscript of this meeting, attached Gerstein's papers to it, and handed it in to our Field Head-quarters.'

It was the lack of interest on the part of the French that now most distressed Gerstein. He was not worried about Werewolf, but he was decidedly worried about the S S, which, though it had gone under cover behind the Allied lines, was still capable of retaliatory action. Having burnt his boats by openly fraternizing with the French, he was an obvious target. Haught and Evans, indeed, had passed on his statement with a recommendation of their own: 'There is reason to consider whether Doctor Gerstein should not be protected against the local Nazis.' But who was to protect him against incredulity and indifference?

Hitler destroyed himself and Germany surrendered. There was no news of Mrugowsky, although there were many rumours of suicide. It was said that General Doctor Grawitz, the head of the S S Health Service, assembled the whole of his staff in the Institute for a 'farewell party,' after he had mined the basement with explosive charges. When they had drunk and eaten handsomely, and had had a ceremonial speech, he blew the place up with everyone in it, himself included. No one, it was said, had escaped alive . . .

Raymond Cartier, writer, formerly officer in the Deuxième Bureau (1970): 'It was in the very last days of the war, perhaps one or two days before the German capitulation. I was attached to the staff of General de Lattre (1st French Army) and I was touring the territories which we had just conquered. I arrived at a small town in Württemberg, where the military commander—an infantry captain, as far as I remember—had just set up his headquarters. This good man was in a state of great confusion for two reasons. The first was that there was at Rottweil a Russian POW camp and an alcohol factory, and the liberated Russian POWs were drinking raw alcohol with predictable results. As for the second reason, the good captain told me: "My dear friend, something extraordinary is going on here. I have a man who boasts of having killed, I don't know exactly how many, but something like a million people."

' "This I'd like to see!" I said.

'The man in question had so impressed the authorities that, despite the fact that he bore the SS tattoo, he had not been put in the camp where the Nazis were sent. He had been given a room at the Rottweil Hotel . . . I went up and found myself in a small room facing a tall fellow, very sallow, very pale, with almost colourless hair. I said to him: "Who are you?"

'He then told me that he was a Christian chemical engineer from Westphalia, that he had wanted to expose the atrocities of which he had heard, and had accordingly joined the SS; he had asked to be assigned for duty in the extermination section of a death camp, and there, as chemical engineer, he had been put in charge of the chamber in which the unfortunate inmates were gassed. And he told me that he had killed something in the order of a million of them. Naturally I did not believe him, because at that time we had no knowledge of the extent to which the Jews had been exterminated. Naturally we had seen a few deportation camps, but in fact we had no idea of the scale and the horror of this unprecedented phenomenon. I said to the man:

' "You are a murderer certainly! But in addition you are a lying murderer. You have committed crimes but you are proudly claiming the commission of crimes even greater, out of all proportion, in order to prolong your miserable existence."

'And the man replied with a sort of extraordinary passion; he told me something like this (I had threatened to have him shot on the spot, but only to impress him, of course):

' "If you knew how little life means to me after what I've seen! But I would not like to die before knowing what happened to the reports I transmitted to the Swedish Red Cross and to the Catholic Church at the Vatican."

' "Now really! This is just another excuse, a way of gaining time. You are a murderer, a miserable wretch." I swore at him in a most violent and coarse manner. But he stood by what he had said.

' "I repeat," he said, " I am a Christian!"

'And I can see him now taking a piece of paper and working out his calculations:

' "$x$ number of men entered the chamber . . . I made it work so many times . . . I watched the agony through a small window and after 20–25 minutes, when everything was finished, I would give the signal, the doors were opened, the bodies were removed and preparations were made for the next lot."

'And he did his multiplication sums again, telling me: "Let's see, that made, say, 1,223,425 people . . ."

'I then told myself that the man was probably mad. After all, it was no business of mine, it wasn't my job, I wasn't supposed to track down war criminals. I remember having simply reported my encounter when I got back to Lindau.

'Then I did hear him mentioned once more, a few months later. I don't remember the exact circumstances, but someone told me: "Yes, it is true, that man did manage to hand out some reports on the extermination camps." '

Gerstein remained miserably in the Hotel Mohren, in a state of semi-captivity (very suited to a man who all his life had steered a course between 'black and white, and good and evil') and without news of his family, uncertain of everything and able to trust no one. He produced two other versions of his statement, more detailed than the first and written in German, but both bearing the impress of the man who wrote them—a man neither a prisoner nor free. He gave one of these to the proprietor of the Hotel Mohren, who passed it on to his wife. The third turned up later, although whom he gave it to is not known.

None of these three statements seems to have interested the French Army Command in Rottweil. Only the one handed to

Major Evans eventually reached its destination—the International Tribunal at Nuremberg.

The French were now wondering what to do with Gerstein, since he had proved useless for their purpose. On 26 May two French Security officers arrived at the Hotel Mohren with orders to transfer him elsewhere. He had just time to tell the pastor and write a hurried letter to Elfriede:

'After having spent five weeks in Rottweil at the disposal of the Military Governor I am today being taken by car to somewhere in the neighbourhood of Constance—I don't know exactly where—to appear before a higher authority. They kept me under lock and key for an afternoon and a night, at which I protested, and since then I've been lodged in this hotel. I left my papers on the hallstand at 24 Gartenstrasse because I'm sure you'll need them. Let me give you one piece of advice: stand up for yourself. Don't let them push you around. It goes without saying that people like you—like us—should be treated differently from the rest. Everything I did in the Waffen SS was done as an agent of the Confessional Church. I told you as little as possible, because they might have tried to get information out of you. Security would have twisted my neck if they'd known that in my distress I told the Swedes and the Swiss everything.

'If you have any trouble go to the Military Governor with the attached statement. Mind you keep the orders for my arrest and the letter of expulsion from the Party, etc. You can show them if necessary, but don't give them away to anyone. Fräulein Doctor von Huene[1] (Zeppelinstrasse) may also be able to help you. I would advise you also to go to the Mayor.

'I don't know when I shall be back. So far I've been allowed my freedom, and I hope it will be the same when I appear before the higher authority. I have also been very lucky in the matter of board and lodging. That is all I can tell you at present. A great deal of interest is being taken in my case, and I shall have to

1 The daughter of a university professor, Fräulein von Huene, on Gerstein's advice, had gone to Ernst Zerrer of the Gestapo, to get help for a friend of hers who was implicated in the 20 July conspiracy.

appear before the International Court of Justice as a material witness against the war criminals.

'I send you and your father and the children my fondest greetings.'

Punctilious as ever, even in that crucial moment, he not only dated the letter but added the time—10:58.

At Langenargen, near Lindau on Lake Constance, Gerstein was taken in charge by French Army Intelligence. He was interviewed by Captain Paul Engelmann, head of the local section of ORCG (Organe de Recherche des Criminels de Guerre), an offshoot of the French Secret Service, who told him that he was to be sent to Paris.

He still imagined, as he had written to Elfriede, that he was to be called upon to give evidence against the leading war criminals. The French rated his importance less highly. Captain Douchez, another ORCG officer, wrote as follows on 28 May to Lieutenant-Colonel Mantout, the head of the organization: 'I enclose the dossier compiled by local Army Intelligence regarding Karl Buck, formerly commander of the camp at Schirmbeck, who is being sent to you under the escort of Second-Lieutenant Joos... The man named Gerstein, who is also being sent to Paris, may be useful as a witness in the case of Buck.'

The man named Gerstein . . .

# Chapter 16

# THE END

'The door opened and he came into the cell. He had no uniform. His hair was white. He sat on the floor on a blanket and didn't say a word. He sat clutching his head in his hands. For a long time— a day or two, I don't remember—he remained prostrate and silent, In the end we asked him: "Who are you, and why are you here?" ' (Karl Buck.)

The house was on the corner of the Rue de Villejust and a side street just south of the Avenue Foch: a rich man's mansion with a portico, balconies, an elevator and a garden. It had been commandeered in 1940 by the Gestapo to serve as the headquarters of a branch of the service entitled the *Intervention Referat*, in which members of the PPF (Parti Populaire Français), and later the French militia, worked hand in glove with the Germans. It was from this bloodstained Bastille that the killers and torturers went out in search of their designated victims. Countless cries of anguish must have been heard on the broad stairway of that haunted house, and in its rooms with their high moulded ceilings. Sometimes bodies fell into the garden from the upper windows.

In 1944–45 it had been taken over by ORCG, the French organization for the investigation of war criminals. Suspects arrested in Germany were brought here before being passed on to the Military Tribunals, and dossiers were compiled for transmission to UNWCC (the United Nations War Crimes Commission). ORCG had inherited from its French parent body, the DGER (Direction Generale des Études et Recherches), a fondness for adventure and secrecy which was to prove its undoing. Before the end of the year it had ceased to exist and its personnel had been dispersed as casually as it had been brought together.

There were all kinds in ORCG: career officers, secret agents, heroes of the Resistance, professional politicians, lawyers, amateurs, socialites. The successive accretions from London, Algeria and Paris could almost be distinguished by the naked eye. Few questions had been asked in the zeal of setting up the organization: all applicants had been welcome. The strange collection included an investigator who aped the SS (boots and whip) and a car driver whose over-enthusiasm aroused suspicion. Both were eventually arrested. And there was the lady who took particular pains to avoid the Luxembourg Legation, going a long way round. This was considered curious, and she too was dealt with.

People thronged up and down the stairs. Officials went to obtain statements at the Hotel Lutétia, on the Left Bank, where the French survivors of the labour camps in Germany waited in long desolate queues. A constant stream of cars drew up or drove off from the mansion, its portico flanked by police or *gardes républicains*—people back from Germany or on their way there. Prisoners were admitted and others were sent elsewhere. It was like a market of Nazis.

The prisoners were housed in the former servants' quarters on the top floor—a dozen small attic rooms on either side of a corridor with enamel number-plates on the doors. Only one or two guards were needed. Very little trouble was given by those highly disciplined dignitaries of the Nazi Party, who clicked their heels even when the food was brought and did not have to be encouraged to start eating. The air rang with their denials. One alone, of all the dozens, had the courage to march into his inquisitor's office giving the Hitler salute.

Lieutenant Blondeau, of ORCG, had the job of interrogating this former concentration-camp commander who blustered and refused to answer. Blondeau rose calmly to his feet, removed his tunic and loosened his tie. 'Get ready,' he said. The German protested and displayed an artificial leg, whereupon Blondeau pulled up his trouser-leg and showed that he had one too—a souvenir of the Maquis. 'Now defend yourself.' After a fight lasting a few minutes Blondeau put on his tunic again and started the interrogation.

The name of the German was Karl Buck.

*Rudersberg (Württemberg), November 1969.* 'We're expecting the doctor,' Frau Buck said. 'If you will call back in an hour my husband will see you.'

My companion, Herbert Weisselberg, had already met Buck. I knew him only by his damning record: volunteer for the Gestapo (1933), head of preventive internment in Stuttgart, creator and commander of the concentration camp at Schirmbeck in Alsace (1940–44), arrested in May 1945, condemned to death, sentence commuted to forced labour in perpetuity (1953), imprisoned in Metz, released two years later suffering from an incurable disease.

'All I want is to be left in peace,' he said to Weisselberg. What sort of peace? Peace of conscience or, which was more common, the peace of comfortable retirement?

It was dark when Frau Buck admitted us to the bright, cosy dwelling where the former camp commander, SS Hauptsturmführer Karl Wilhelm Buck, was living out his days. The place smelt like a drugstore. An aging man with brushed-back grey hair and a red, puffy face received us in the sitting-room and then sank back into an armchair, his leg creaking as he did so. He wore thick glasses which hid his gaze, but when he moved his head, as happened only rarely, one had a glimpse of alert, penetrating grey eyes. With a stiff courtesy he invited us to be seated.

'At the end of May the French transferred me from Lindau to Paris. I was taken there by car with another accused man, escorted by an officer. We were taken to a house that had been used by the Gestapo. There were thirteen of us in one attic room. There were rugs on the floor, two or three mattresses and a table. Food was brought up from the kitchen; it wasn't bad. The door was opened by a guard every morning. One or the other of us had to stay behind to clean up, but the rest went down to exercise in the yard. One day a woman flung herself out of the window. She was the wife of the Gauleiter of Alsace, Wagner, who was later condemned to death and shot. I rescued her powder-puff for him. Every now and then one of us was taken down for interrogation.

My chief interrogator wore a monocle. Another of them was a lieutenant with an artificial limb, like mine.

'A few days after my arrival a new prisoner was brought in. It was Gerstein. I did not know him.'

This was untrue. Buck had been in charge of preventive internees in the Gestapo prison at Stuttgart at the time when Gerstein had been kept there for interrogation before being sent to Welzheim. Weisselberg compared his present signature with the one on the order for Gerstein's release in 1938; they were the same. Desperately ill though he was, Buck had lost nothing of his wariness.

Buck: '. . . After keeping quiet for about two days the new-comer told us that he was SS Obersturmführer Kurt Gerstein. Then he told us that he had met a friend in the SS and had gone to Berlin and had heard things about gas. He had become obsessed with the subject and wanted to find out the truth. He had been to Belzec and had written a report, of which copies had gone to Switzerland and several other countries, and to the Pope. When the war ended he had gone to Tübingen. He had handed his report to the Allied authorities and had been sent to Paris. He was to be the chief witness at a big trial. In Paris he had at first been allowed his liberty and had been lodged in an hotel, which was what they had promised him. But at the end of three days, after he had several times been cross-examined about his report, he had been brought here to share our cell.

'The things he told us were so fantastic that we could hardly believe them. But the man himself made a very good impression, honest and frank, and we were all convinced of his sincerity. He did a great deal to comfort the younger prisoners, some of whom were in despair.

'One morning during the second week he was with us he was sent for and didn't reappear until evening. I don't know whether he spent the day being interrogated or simply cleaning somebody's office. He didn't say anything. Anyway, he seemed to have been well treated, not beaten up or anything like that.'

Why should he have been ill-treated? He had committed his

inexpressible secrets to paper, and all he had to do was to fill in
a few details which his interrogator, Major Beckhardt, seemed to
find of particular interest.

Beckhardt: 'How were you able to join the SS after having
been arrested several times by the Gestapo?'

Gerstein: 'I simply accepted the proposals made to me by the
Gestapo after my second arrest.'

Beckhardt: 'When were you tattooed with the emblem of the
Waffen SS?'

Gerstein: 'In May 1941, and with the letters AB, indicating
blood-group IV.'

Beckhardt: 'Weren't you sent to Belzec to play some kind of
active part in the massacres? Were the SS content for you to be
there simply as a spectator?'

Gerstein: 'I have no human life on my conscience. My work
was entirely concerned with the supply of sanitary equipment
to combat epidemics. My first duty was to make the water
fit to drink, and I was responsible for this to the SS and the
police.'

Beckhardt: 'Are you in a position to prove that you were in
contact with the Resistance?'

Gerstein: 'For the Protestant Resistance I got my orders from
Pastor Niemöller, who had been interned in Dachau since 1937,
through members of his family. My contact with the Dutch
Resistance was an engineer in Doesburg named Ubbink. I was in
touch with the Swedish Resistance through Baron von Otter, of
the Swedish Legation in Berlin, and with the Swiss Resistance
through Doctor Hochstrasser, of the Swiss Legation. In Paris I
made the acquaintance of the proprietor of the Restaurant Louis
XIV, situated on the intersection of the Boulevard Strasbourg
and the Boulevard Saint-Denis. I talked in his presence of my
disgust at the concentration camps and massacres.'

The French reference was a particularly weak one, certainly
not enough to remove suspicion; and the other witnesses were a
long way off, not easy of access.

Gerstein's personality and the hideous nature of his story caused a sensation at ORCG. A rare bird indeed! Even the deputy-director, Lieutenant-Colonel Gilbert Mantout, condescended to take an interest in him:

'Sturmführer Kurt Gerstein, who had been arrested—one might say, at his own request—by the ORCG in Germany, was sent by the Constance section to our Paris headquarters, where he was interrogated before being handed over to the military courts. My attention was drawn to this rather special case, and I remember being present on two occasions when he was questioned. My impression of the man was that he was a mystic in a state of traumatic shock, and desperate because no one, neither the Germans nor the French, would take him seriously. As it were, a discredited Joan of Arc deprived of her funeral pyre.'

Not wholly deprived . . . On 13 June a specific request was forwarded to the Military Government of Paris (legal section) for the indictment of Karl Buck and Kurt Gerstein, those former inmates of Stuttgart, the one gaoler and the other prisoner.

'I have the honour to submit copies of the interrogation proceedings and other documents passed to me by the Organe de Recherche des Criminels de Guerre, 49 rue de Villejust, Paris.

'From these it is clear that formal charges should be preferred against the two men, Kurt Gerstein, a prominent member of Himmler's headquarters staff, and Karl Buck, commander of the Schirmbeck camp.

'The men are being held at 48 rue de Villejust, where, however, they should not be kept any longer. It is important that they should be conveyed without delay to a top-security prison, a matter which I have already discussed by telephone with Major Bertrand.

'The charges are as follows:

'*Gerstein*: That, as head of the technical section of the sanitary service at SS headquarters in Berlin, he issued orders on and after February 1942 (a date which seems to coincide with the invention of the gas chamber as a method of mass extermination) leading to the killing of an immense number of human beings in the said gas chambers, and that he furnished the RSHA with huge quantities of prussic acid for the purpose of poisoning millions of people, thus supplying the means of perpetrating a criminal action on a vast scale, thereafter assisting the perpetrators, or witnessing the perpetration of the crime, in the gas chambers at Belzec, where there were 15,000 executions a day, Sobibor (20,000 executions a day after June 1942), Treblinka (25,000 a day) —acts defined and condemned under Articles 60 and 301 of the Penal Code and Article 2, Paragraph 3, of the Order of 28 August 1944 (conspiracy to poison).

'*Buck*: That as commander and overseer respectively of the camps at Schirmbeck, Welzheim, etc., he was responsible for the internment of civilians under inhuman conditions, and issued orders for the killing of individuals singly and collectively, and for ill-treatment and torture—acts defined and condemned under Articles 60, 296, 310 and 344 of the Penal Code, and Article 2 of the Order of 28 August 1944.'

The terrible document made it plain that Gerstein was under suspicion of having invented the gas chamber. But that was not all. Having worked for years with the object of testifying against the leading war criminals, he found that he was now to be treated not as a witness for the prosecution but as one of the accused!

A list of major war criminals, based on Gerstein's testimony, was forwarded to the United Nations Commission in London. The first names were those of Hitler, Himmler, Eichmann, Günther, Pfannenstiel, Linden, Gundlach, Gebhardt. Then came the names of the 'Belzec group': Globocnik, Wirth, Oberhauser, Heckenholt, Haller and Gerstein—all described as 'organizers of the system of extermination.'[1]

But this was not the worst. What must have seemed to Gerstein most shameful was that, having in good faith given the names of men—colleagues within the Institute and doctors outside it— who had assisted him in his real intention, and whom he thought

---

1 The original document states: 'The second part lists the names of certain German officials, including the author of the report, Kurt Gerstein, who resisted this policy of atrocities.' Someone felt this to be over-indulgent and for 'resisted' substituted 'claim to have resisted.'

thus to exonerate from blame, these men, by his action, were now included in the list of the accused.[1]

Among these latter were the following: Doctor Krantz, who had told Gerstein what was being done at Mauthausen; Sergeant-Major Holländer, who had given him a secret report on the medical experiments on human subjects; Doctor Villing, who had disclosed the massacre of Polish priests; Doctor Focht, Doctor Nissen and others.

It was the absolute reversal of everything Gerstein was and everything he had stood for. Not only was he placed in the same category with Wirth, skipping about among the corpses, or Oberhauser, cold-bloodedly considering how he should liquidate a boyhood friend, but he was treated as a turncoat, an informer ratting on his friends to save his own skin.

On 5 July, after spending more than a month at ORCG headquarters, Gerstein was transferred to the Paris Military Prison on the Rue du Cherche-Midi, a few minutes away from the Luxembourg. As he left the Rue de Villejust he was heard to exclaim in tragic amazement: 'I'm a prisoner!'—as though he still could not believe it and were only now becoming aware of his position.

That same day his name was heard all over Paris. The evening paper *France-Soir* printed a three-column front-page 'exclusive' from Stuttgart signed by its correspondent Géo Kelber. The headings ran: 'Nazi Concentration Camp Executioner Confesses'; ' "I exterminated up to 11,000 people a day" '; 'Engineer Kurt Gerstein tells his French examiners: "My conscience is clear." '

Kelber's article was based on a version of Gerstein's Report passed to the press by an army PRO. The following may be quoted:

' "Before God and before men I take full responsibility for my disclosures, for I am one of the few eye-witnesses of the greatest of Hitler's massacres. I have omitted nothing of what I saw, and I have added nothing. This is the truth, so help me God . . ."

1 The first version simply described them as 'persons who, according to Gerstein, resisted the perpetration of the German crimes.' To this some zealous hand added: 'All having, in fact, assisted in carrying them out.'

'Those are the words of Kurt Gerstein, SS engineer, professor
with diplomas from the Universities of Marburg, Aachen and
Berlin, speaking to Intelligence officers of the French First Army.
He then made his deposition, which afterwards he carefully
revised and signed. It is a recital of the abominations, the mon-
strosities, for which Gerstein was responsible at Belzec concentration camp in his capacity of chief of scientific executions.

' "One day Sturmbannführer Günther sent me urgently to
Lublin in connection with 'an affair of State which I was the
eleventh person to know about, by special favour of the Führer.'
At Lublin I was received by SS General Globocnik . . ." '

The statement was broadcast by the French radio.

Gerstein was put into a cell in the Cherche-Midi prison with
three other SS men, Karl Buck, Heinrich Birnbreier and Walter
Koehler.[1] The cell was typical of that ancient prison, built in
the reign of Napoleon III, which in 1945 housed as many
French prisoners as Germans.

Pastor de Billy (1967): 'Things were chaotic at that time . . . I
had been appointed Protestant chaplain to the Cherche-Midi. I
held separate services for the Germans and French on Sunday
afternoons. I very seldom went into the cells, in fact never. I
hadn't the time. I was doing this duty in addition to my normal
parish work, which was heavy. My Catholic colleague, Abbé
Lacour, and I took in food for the prisoners, the gift of American
and French people with Christian feelings. Some of the prison
warders did not much like it, they thought we were overdoing it.
But I never noticed any brutality on their part.

'Did Gerstein attend the services? I've no idea. He certainly
never asked to speak to me or I should have remembered him. But

1 Birnbreier, aged 31, was handed over to the Americans, convicted of
murder and hanged at Landsberg in 1947. Koehler, aged 20, was passed on
to the Poles and sentenced to six years' imprisonment for the murder of a
woman and child near Lublin; he died in prison in 1950. He once referred to
Gerstein while he was under examination: 'I never heard anything about
camps for the extermination of the Jews while I was in Poland. I first heard
of them in Paris, from my fellow-prisoner, Gerstein, who was in the same
cell with me.'

now I come to think of it, there was one man who looked absolutely broken up. He had been brought from Germany. I remember thinking: "He must have done the most terrible things." Could that have been Gerstein?'

Abbé Lacour (1967): 'French army prisoners were on the first floor of the Cherche-Midi and German war criminals were on the floor above. Abetz was there, and so was General Stülpnagel, who later committed suicide in his cell, and a lot of SS men. The groups were never allowed to mix. Separate Masses were held on Sunday, one in French and the other in German. The prisoners were in bad shape—no beatings but no comfort either. A mattress on the floor, a bucket and that was all. There was no water, nothing but a wash-basin on the ground floor. Only the high-ups had separate cells; the rest were two or three or four to a cell.

'About 7 in the morning they went down in file to empty their buckets in the toilets. There was exercise in the yard at 8, and at 9 they went up again to clean their cells and see their lawyers. The morning meal was at 11. People went from cell to cell with a huge mess-can. The food was clean but not very palatable. The prisoners were allowed to receive cigarettes and parcels. Monsieur de Billy, the Protestant chaplain, and I handed out extra rations on Sundays. In the afternoon they slept or read or wrote. The evening meal was 5 to 5:30, and the lights went out at 9.'

Karl Buck: 'The food was more or less adequate, and we got extra from the chaplain. Gerstein didn't complain. He scarcely ever spoke, just a word now and then. He didn't want a lawyer, he said his report would be enough. He seemed as though he wasn't there, staring into space, not seeing anyone. He obviously suffered acutely from being treated as a criminal. He also suffered from the bugs, which fell in hundreds from the ceiling when we were trying to sleep. Pesticides were useless. They were always with us, and Gerstein had a sensitive skin. For him it was torture. He stripped himself naked, and all night you could see him killing bugs. He never slept at all.'

It was perhaps the culminating irony that Gerstein, the decontamination expert, who owed his job with the SS, and his present desperate plight, to his skill in destroying lice, should at the last have found himself at their mercy. Naked, covered with bites, hungry and ill ... no one procured him the sugar his body so urgently needed. Even if he had asked to see the doctor, what could the doctor have done?

Doctor Jacques Trouillet (1967): 'In 1945 I was appointed chief medical adviser to the Paris military prisons. I went in to Paris every day, lunched at one of the prisons and quite often got back early in the afternoon. I had practically no resources. At that time medical supplies were terribly hard to come by. All they had at the Cherche-Midi was the usual list: aspirin, laudanum, sulphonamides.

'I often saw Abetz, the former German Ambassador in Paris. He swore to me that he had known nothing whatever about the concentration camps. This was when people were beginning to learn the truth about the mass exterminations, the charnel pits and so on. I'm still surprised that there were no reprisals at the Cherche-Midi, which the circumstances would certainly have explained even if they did not justify them ... I never saw Gerstein alive. He certainly didn't ask to see me as a doctor. I should be bound to remember.'

On 19 July Major Matthieu Mattéi, public examiner for the Second Military Tribunal in Paris, had Gerstein brought to his office on the Rue de la Faisanderie for the purpose of confirming and drafting in official form the charges brought against him by ORCG. Major Mattéi, a former colonial magistrate, was a small, brisk man, terse and clear in speech. He was said to be strict but was known to be fair. He gave the individual seated on the stool every chance to speak.

A stool, not a chair: it was an indication of the Major's distaste, and also of the bounds within which he confined it, for the criminals he had to deal with. Gerstein sat on the stool. The examination lasted six and a half hours. Two other persons were present, M. Lehmann, the interpreter, and a young clerk, Jacques Clavel, who wrote down the questions and answers. He noted in his diary: 'A very fine, warm day. Interrogation of a German in the Second Military Court from 9 to 12:15 and again from 3 to 6:15.'

It is not surprising if that particular German had a prejudice against judges. A judge had begotten him, oppressed him in childhood, watched him in adolescence, disapproved of him in his maturity and always failed to understand him. Why should this one, who made him sit on a stool of repentance, be any different?

Major Mattéi had carefully studied the dossier. There were implausibilities in Gerstein's story that exasperated him. He asked questions: 'Why were you specially chosen to convey the cyanide from Kolin to Poland? Why did an officer have to be sent all the way from Berlin, when it would have been a simple matter to appoint one in Czechoslovakia or Poland to take charge of the consignment? Did you have written orders? To whom were you responsible? You say that the driver of the truck was unknown to you. How was it, if as you say you destroyed the consignment, that he did not report the matter to his superiors?'

Gerstein explained endlessly but could not exculpate himself. He talked for hours, but in the end Major Mattéi signed the document charging him with 'having directly or indirectly participated in the murder of numerous persons by supplying 260 kilos of potassium cyanide for the purpose of asphyxiating them in gas chambers.'

Whereupon Colonel Abel Sauzey, the representative of Intelligence on the staff of the Military Governor of Paris, ordered Kurt Gerstein to be placed in solitary confinement 'so that he may not be able to inform his compatriots of the details of his interrogation.'

The order reached Captain Chiaramonti, the officer in command of the prison, on 20 July, the day after the hearing.

Of all the witnesses I interviewed, Chiaramonti was one of the most difficult to find. He had retired and no one seemed to know where he was living. Eventually, after many inquiries, I ran him to earth on an August morning in 1967, in the small town of Villemaur-sur-Vanne (Aube). He was doing repairs to the front

of his house in a thin drizzle of rain, an elderly man in overalls
who did not seem at all pleased to see me. Still under the influence
of military discipline, he wondered if he ought to tell me anything at all. In the event he said very little. 'I remember the case.
A tall, thin German. I wrote an official report on his death which
you've probably seen. I received instructions to place him in
solitary confinement, and I passed the order on to a subordinate,
Sergeant-Major Gascard, I think. He lives at Celsoy, not far from
here.'

Marcel Gascard (1968): 'Acting on orders, I put the prisoner
in solitary, in a cell on the Boulevard Raspail side of the prison.
Later the prison commander asked me why I had put him there
and I said: "Because it's where they used to put spies to prevent
them from communicating with each other." '

The spies' cell . . . Fifty years earlier a French officer had been
confined in the Cherche-Midi prison, possibly in that same cell,
before being cashiered and sent to Devil's Island. He was Captain
Dreyfus, a Jew, condemned because he was a Jew . . .

On 23 July Baron von Otter, then in Helsinki, wrote to his
London colleague, Baron Lagerfelt, strongly urging that something should be done to help a German named Gerstein, and
asking Lagerfelt to bring the matter to the notice of the Allied
authorities.

It was too late. After two or three days and nights of naked
misery spent in that noisome and infested place, its walls running
with the damp of a hundred years; haunted by his shame, his
unspeakable memories, his sense of utter failure; on the morning
of 25 July, a fortnight before his fortieth birthday, Gerstein
ended his life.

\*

Léon Entz (1968): 'I was on duty on the second floor. We went
the rounds at two and checked the prisoners. I knew the one
who had been put in solitary. He scarcely ever said anything
although he could have talked to me because I speak German. I
went round that day at two as usual. When we went in they stood

to attention and clicked their heels. But when I opened the door of his cell there wasn't a sound. I went in and saw his body hanging from the ventilator grille.'

*25 July 1945.* St Christopher's day, the weather fine and warm. The second day of the trial of Marshal Pétain for treason. Churchill, Eden and Attlee were at Potsdam. A gala night at the Paris Opéra, where Grace Moore was singing. A memorial service at the Palais de Chaillot for Paul Valéry, attended by General de Gaulle. Cardinal Faulhaber, Archbishop of Munich, applied to General Eisenhower for permission to build a convent on the site of the Dachau concentration camp, to make it a place of pilgrimage for all the peoples of Europe and to pay tribute to the victims of the Nazi regime.

Alexandre Auer, sergeant in charge (1969): 'Entz shouted to me down the corridor to come at once. I went in and saw that the man had hanged himself. I knew him, a tall, silent man, very depressed. He had said once or twice in German: "I've nothing to reproach myself with, nothing." While I was there Entz did an astonishing thing. He undid the man's flies and said: "He's had an ejaculation. It's all over." I hadn't known that that was how you could tell a hanged man was dead.'

Marcel Gascard (1968): 'I heard someone shout, "He's hanged himself!" and I thought: "Hell!" We disliked suicides as much as we did escapes. Regulations were very strict. It was a bad mark for us. I shouted to the sick-bay attendant, a French captain who had been given a sentence for contravention of security regulations. He came running up. Someone produced a knife and they cut him down.'

Major Chiaramonti (official report, 1945): 'Sergeant Entz, assisted by Sergeant-Major André Ucci, cut him down and started artificial respiration.'

Noël André Ucci (1968): 'That's absolutely untrue. I wasn't there. The only suicides I saw at the Cherche-Midi were Stülpnagel and another German, a young man who went mad—not that one.'

Major Chiaramonti (1945): 'The prisoner had hanged himself with a rope made out of a strip of blanket which he'd tied to the window. His head was turned to the wall and his feet were touching the floor.'

Major Chiaramonti (1967): 'I seem to remember that he hanged himself with his belt, which he had cut off the top of his trousers.'

Marcel Gascard (1968): 'He ripped the belt off his trousers and tied it to the bars.'

Major Chiaramonti (1967): 'I sent for everyone possible, the fire service, the doctor, the police. The fire service brought artificial-respiration apparatus, but it was no use.'

Major Franceschi, of the fire service (1966): 'According to the report, our men were there only a short time. They found that the man was already dead and went away.'

Doctor Jacques Trouillet (1967): 'I remember very little about it—only that they came to fetch me after I had left the prison. I went back and certified death by self-strangulation.'

Doctor Jacques Trouillet (1945): 'At 17:25 on that day I signed the death certificate of the prisoner Gerstein. That the death was caused by hanging was clearly evident from the furrow round the neck and the position of the body when found. It is a form of suicide that cannot possibly be prevented in a prison.'

Marcel Gascard (1968): 'An Intelligence officer who had interrogated him blew his top when he heard about the suicide: "So he went off with all those crimes on his conscience! More than sixty thousand murders. He wouldn't confess. And you let him do away with himself!" '

Karl Buck (1967): 'The prison warder, Entz, an Alsatian who was always very reasonable, told us that Gerstein had left a letter for the examining magistrate, written in his own hand.'

Report of the Police Superintendent of the Notre-Dame-des-Champs district (1945): 'Gerstein left several letters in which he announced his intention of committing suicide. I was told of them. They were presumably passed to Judge Mattéi.'

Letters . . .

Report from Army Legal Archives (1960): '. . . that the commander of the army prison did, on 26 July, send to the Government commissioner attached to the Second Permanent Military Tribunal in Paris a report on the suicide of the subject, together with a letter written by him (probably shortly before his death, intended to justify his action). No trace of this letter has, however, been found on the files of this establishment.'

French National Archives: 'Despite our search . . .'

American Archives (Alexandria): 'No letter . . .'

Polish Delegation to the United Nations War Crimes Commission: 'Nothing . . .'

French Delegation to the same: 'We have searched in vain . . .'

French Embassy, London: 'Regretting that we cannot . . .'

French Foreign Office: 'We do not possess . . .'

Polish Resistance (London): 'This dossier has not . . .'

UNWCC: 'Our researches have not . . .'

French Judicial Police: 'No letter has been . . .'

ORCG (from Security archives): 'We greatly regret . . .'

Major Chiaramonti (1967): 'Certainly. He left a letter which I took possession of. 1 didn't notice that it was addressed to the examining magistrate and so I read it.'

The present writer: 'You read it? Do you remember what it said? Judge Mattéi is dead, and so is the Government Commissioner. You are the only person who knows what Gerstein's last words were.'

Chiaramonti: 'I only remember it in outline. It was quite short. He said that he was innocent of all the crimes he had been charged with and he asked that his body should not be mutilated.'

'Did he write in French or German?'

'I don't know German.'

Léon Entz (1968): 'I was told that he said in the letter that the guards had always treated him properly.'

Pastor de Billy (1967): 'Three services were held in the prison between 5 July and 25 July on the three Sundays—on the 8th, the 15th and the 22nd. So I must have heard what had happened on the following Sunday, the 29th. I don't remember any details except that my Catholic colleague, Abbé Lacour, said to me: "It's mysterious." '

Abbé Lacour (1967): 'I visited the prison on Wednesday afternoon. The 25th was a Wednesday, so I suppose I must have heard about it then. But it's so long ago. I may possibly have said to De Billy that it was mysterious. So many things happened in the Cherche-Midi at that time: attempts to escape, men getting themselves hospitalized in the hope of escaping more easily, particularly the French prisoners. Frankly, I don't remember what I meant when I said it was mysterious, if that is what I said.'

The tall body lay on the floor of the cell, to be taken away when convenient. And the whisper went round the prison: 'A German on the second floor has hanged himself.'

*25 July 1945.* In Tübingen, Elfriede Gerstein, who was not to learn for a long time of her widowhood, heard the shouts of the neighbours outside her windows: 'Dirty Nazi swine!'

In Hagen the thoughts of Judge Ludwig Gerstein went back to 1918: 'We are defeated.' He had put his trust in two great men, Wilhelm II and Hitler, and perhaps it was only his death in 1954 that prevented him from trusting a third. Meanwhile he grieved for Kurt, the most recalcitrant and intelligent of his sons, who had disappeared . . .

Within a stone's throw was Pastor Rehling, whose house had been bombed but who had found somewhere else to live and had already repaired his pulpit, while his wife cooked meals in a cellar for five hundred homeless people.

Niemöller was still living. After eight years of internment he had been released in Austria with a group of other internees which included Léon Blum, the former Austrian Chancellor, Schuschnigg, a cousin of Winston Churchill's and a few survivors of the 20 July conspiracy. Mochalsky, to whom Gerstein had once turned in vain for counsel, was now assistant pastor of a small parish in the Allgau. Nieuwenhuizen was ill in bed at his home in Eindhoven, and his friend De Vos had returned on foot from the

Sudetenland with a pack on his back. Eickhoff was a prisoner of the Russians, as were Günter Dickten, Robert Weigelt and Friedrich Geissert (who escaped and reached the Black Forest by way of Silesia). Horst Dickten was in the hands of the Americans. Frau Marlo Bälz, another person of whom Gerstein had once asked advice, had found shelter in Württemberg. Armin Peters, free in Berlin, was thinking of becoming a watchmaker.

That month of July saw one of the most senseless of all deaths, that of Gerhard Krone, Gerstein's friend since their Bible Circle days. They had seen each other in Berlin during the war. Krone, after serving in the Army, had returned home safely at the beginning of the summer and had taken over his father's drugstore. Driving one evening to see friends in Gevelsberg, he failed to hear an Allied sentry's challenge and was shot.

The leaders of the Third Reich were dead, and so were most of the Belzec team, Globocnik having committed suicide, and Wirth, Heckenholt and other potential witnesses from the 'special commando' having been liquidated by Yugoslav partisans, to Himmler's great satisfaction. But Oberhauser was not run to earth until the 'sixties, when he was found working as a waiter in a Munich café; and much the same happened in the case of Höfle, Globus's adjutant, who became a prosperous shopkeeper but committed suicide when he was arrested. Eichmann, as the world knows, escaped to the Argentine, to meet his death in Jerusalem in 1961. Günther, the errand-boy of the Final Solution, survived and is said to be still living somewhere in Germany.

Obersturmbannführer Professor Doctor Pfannenstiel, captured by the Americans but released for lack of evidence, was destined to become consultant physician at Garmisch, research director of the firm of Schaper and Bruemmer, and member of a long list of learned bodies concerned with nutrition, microbiology, thermal baths, climatology, pest-control, entomology and even architecture.

A man of substance who may be supposed to have taken at least an academic interest in the mass murders at Belzec, Herr Gerhard Peters, the supplier of Zyklon B, also survived without much trouble. Although he was several times arraigned in the

German courts, he got off with the help of his employers, the highly influential firm of Degesch.

Ernst Zerrer, of the Gestapo, spent several years in an internment camp, and so did Doctor Krantz.

Doctor Ding, Gerstein's enemy at the Institute, who had been in charge of the experiments on human subjects at Buchenwald, was never to achieve his ambition of being addressed as Herr Professor: he was another of those who committed suicide. And Joachim Mrugowsky, the Chief, was condemned and hanged without having uttered the name of Gerstein ... That was the end of it.

His Holiness Pope Pius XII had no audience of importance on 25 July. His Berlin Nuncio, Monsignor Cesare Orsenigo, had been quietly replaced, having become an embarrassment. Orsenigo was posted to Eichstätt in Bavaria, one of the smallest bishoprics in Germany. The cardinal's hat which he had so coveted went in April 1946 to Bishop von Galen, who had preached against euthanasia. A sad blow for the diligent servant, who died a month later and was accorded a routine obituary in the *Osservatore Romano*.

From Baron von Otter: 'When Germany surrendered I had been posted to Helsinki. I felt it my duty to do what I could to protect Gerstein. What followed is a matter of infinite regret to me. It was only after some weeks that I wrote to my London colleague, Baron Lagerfelt, Secretary of the Legation. That was on about 24 June. I told him what I knew of Gerstein, and asked him to forward the information to the appropriate Allied authority.

'A few weeks later the US Legation in Helsinki rang up to inquire after a Baron von Otter, who had been Secretary in Berlin. It must have been either my letter, or Gerstein's written testimony, which prompted the phone call. The tragedy is that Gerstein was dead—he may even have died on that day. I'm afraid my letter didn't arrive soon enough to save him. You will understand now why I don't like reading about that business, or even talking about it, except to clear his name. To me it remains a bitter memory.'

*

Major Chiaramonti: 'They brought in a municipal coffin. He was too tall for it and his head had to be pushed sideways.'

Madame Chiaramonti: 'I looked down from our window and watched them put him in the van. It was five or six in the evening. It made a great impression on me.'

From the police records of the Notre-Dame-des-Champs district:

'Received from the Cherche-Midi prison the body of a prisoner named Gerstein, Kurt, to be conveyed to the Institute of Forensic Medicine for autopsy. Paris, 26 July 1945.' (The date has been altered from 27.)

'I, the undersigned, Doctor Piedelièvre, medical expert for the Tribunal de la Seine . . . having been instructed to investigate the cause of death of the prisoner Gerstein (Kurt) and to ascertain whether responsibility is to be attributed to any other person, and if so to whom; and having completed my examination on 31 July 1945, beg to report as follows:

'1. The death of Gerstein (Kurt) was caused by hanging.

'2. There are no indications of violence, no suspect lesions.

'3. In medico-legal terms, it is a case of suicide.'

Comment of a forensic specialist who prefers to remain anonymous (1967): 'You call that an autopsy report? I could show you a real one. They may run to ten or fifteen pages if the job's been properly done . . . This man doesn't even mention the state of the lungs. Nothing said about whether the body was white or blue, or whether or not there was bruising round the furrow left by the rope. Not a word about what kind of knot it was. A report like that is quite worthless.'

On 3 August the body was taken from the Institute of Forensic Medicine to the Paris cemetery of Thiais and placed in the communal grave of the 14th division. Officially it was an 'unclaimed' body. Unclaimed, abandoned of men, robbed even of its name:

for it is entered in the Thiais register as 'Gastein' and no one can dispute the official archives.

'If I were to propose an inscription for my tombstone I would ask for nothing more than "An individual"; and if that word is not yet understood, some day it will be.' (Kierkegaard.)

On 7 August Baron Lagerfelt, prompted by the letter from Baron von Otter, handed the Foreign Office in London an official memorandum relating to a German named Kurt Gerstein, who had given a Swedish diplomat valuable information concerning the camp at Belzec.

Three years too late to help the Jews, thirteen days too late for Gerstein.

The man who only three weeks before had achieved a brief celebrity in the Paris newspapers lay mouldering in a common grave, consigned to a forgetfulness so complete that one would be hard put to it to find a similar instance. All the papers had been signed, no formality had been neglected; and yet, after August 1945 all trace of Kurt Gerstein was lost. Years were to pass before it was rediscovered. Inquiries came from Allied, German and even French authorities: but, whether because they could not or would not, no one mentioned that he had been in the Cherche-Midi prison and had died there. Yet many men had seen him.

And when at length the trail was picked up it was again too late. The remains had been removed to the boneyard, mingled with other bones, like those reposing in the shade of the memorial at Belzec presided over by Dominik Wojtek.

For Gerstein there was no memorial.

# Postscripts

## I

Westphalia: *Where is Kurt Gerstein?*

Judge Ludwig Gerstein: 'I am worried about Kurt. I hope and expect we will have some good news in the course of the next few days.'

Elfriede Gerstein: 'I wait. I listen for the sound of the occasional car in our street. He left in a car with some Frenchmen. He is alive. He is working for the French authorities. I am waiting. Watching.'

## II

### INCIDENT AT NUREMBERG (1946)

Among the mountains of documents collected at Nuremberg was Gerstein's French statement, written while he was at Rottweil, in April 1945. It was to have a strange history.

Delphin Debenest, French advocate general (1968): 'I came across the document in the American files while I was preparing Prosecutor Dubost's brief. The reference was PS 1553. I don't know why they didn't use it. I at once brought it to the notice of M. Dubost.'

Charles Dubost, joint prosecutor general at Nuremberg (1967): 'While I was preparing my account of the concentration camps one of my collaborators told me that among the documents captured by the Americans he had found invoices for the supply

267

of gas to the Oranienburg and Auschwitz camps and also a remarkable statement by an SS officer named Gerstein. At the same time a French journalist, Mme Madeleine Jacob, brought me photostats of the papers in question, the whole constituting Document PS 1553.

'The Americans had made no use of them . . . We did not know why. They were clearly of importance. There was a sheaf of invoices which showed, subject to error, that within a period of less than three months the Degesch Company had supplied 2,263 kilos of Zyklon B to Oranienburg and 1,703 kilos to Auschwitz. Moreover, there was the Gerstein statement, which left no doubt as to the use made of that gas, and of the exhaust gas from Diesel engines, in the gas chambers.

'I decided to use it all. But there are one or two curious points to be noted.

'In the first place, PS 1553 was not reproduced *in extenso* in the report of the trial. The Gerstein statement is not included. Indeed, except for two lines at the bottom of p. 230, vol. 3, of the French arraignment, reproducing the stenographic report of the pro- ceedings, there is nothing to show that I submitted this document in evidence, together with the invoices. My words were: "To file 1553 is attached Gerstein's deposition, together with the remarks of the American official who handled the file."

'I decided after careful consideration that this deposition should be placed before the Court. I discussed it with several of my collaborators; we weighed the consequences and they agreed with me. It was decided to put forward these documents that the Americans had not used, and we considered that the invoices could not be separated from Gerstein's statement.

'But it was not so simple in Court . . .'

*Nuremberg, 30 January 1946.* Prosecutor Dubost, addressing the Court: '. . . as to the inhumane extermination by gas, we have invoices for asphyxiating gases supplied to Oranienburg and Auschwitz which have been placed before the Court, refer- ence RF 350 (PS 1553). Madame Vaillant-Couturier has told us in evidence that these gases, used for the destruction of lice and other parasites, were also used for the extermination of human

beings. Moreover, the great quantities and the number of consignments, as evidenced by the invoices, show that these gases
were intended to serve more than one purpose . . .'

At this point there was a murmur on the bench. The American
Judge, Francis Biddle, said something to the presiding Judge,
Lord Justice Lawrence of Great Britain.

The presiding Judge: 'Are you submitting the originals of the
invoices to which you refer?'

Monsieur Dubost failed to hear the question which the presiding Judge then amplified.

'I want to know what authority may be attributed to the document. Does it come from one of the commissions set up by the
French Republic?'

'It is an American document, numbered PS 1553 in their files.'

Presiding Judge: 'Monsieur Dubost, am I not right in saying
that the note at the end of PS 1553 is not part of the original
supplied to you by the United States?'

After a discussion of the authenticity of the text it was decided
to put the document provisionally aside, pending verification.

Dubost: 'We shall ask our American colleagues for the necessary confirmation. We believe that this evidence, held in their
files, cannot be ignored.'

On the afternoon of the same day the British deputy chief prosecutor, Sir David Maxwell Fyfe, intervened and settled the
matter in a few words.

'I was able, during the suspension of the hearing, to discuss
the matter with my friends Mr Dodd [US advocate general] and
Monsieur Dubost. All the PS documents belong to a series of
captured documents of which the origin and the file-numbers
were authenticated on 22 November by Major Coogan . . . The
PS series has been verified and can be accepted by the Court.'

The presiding Judge: 'Thank you very much. We now understand the position. Let me, on behalf of the Court, apologize to
the French legal representatives. We have just discovered that
the marginal note is on the copy. Monsieur Dubost, please accept
my apologies.'

'Thank you, Monsieur le président.'

The document could now be admitted in evidence. Having been disdained by the French authorities, taken in charge by the Anglo-Saxons, shelved by the Americans and rediscovered by the French, the Gerstein statement had narrowly escaped being ruled out by the Americans. It was 30 January 1946—the eleventh anniversary of Gerstein's protest and beating-up in the theatre at Hagen. The Court at Nuremberg had come near to repeating that event in its own way.

From then until the end of the proceedings at Nuremberg, in October 1946, there was no further mention of the name of Gerstein. No one troubled to inquire whether he was alive or dead.

M. Charles Dubost: 'That incident is beyond me. I still wonder about a number of things.

'1. Why did Mr Biddle try to shelve P S 1553? It cannot have been on account of the invoices, the authenticity of which was not in doubt. Are we to suppose that the Gerstein statement was superfluous? Or that Biddle thought it better to suppress it? In the event that is what happened, because it was not included with the rest of P S 1553 in the printed record of the proceedings.

'2. Why should Gerstein's testimony have been censored in this way? I saw no reason to doubt his sincerity. Did Biddle have particular reasons? Why did he not say what they were?

'3. Was Biddle acting on his own responsibility or on instructions from his Government?

'4. I had not asked for Sir David Maxwell Fyfe's assistance. Why did he come to my support? Was it simply to prevent his compatriot, Lord Justice Lawrence, from making a mistake? Or did the British delegation know something about Biddle's reasons which was not known to us?'

Francis Biddle (1968): 'I do not remember the "Gerstein Report" ... But in any event I would have had no reason to know what caused the Prosecution's decision—that would not have been reported to us ... I do not remember the report or its introduction.'

Judge Boucly (member of the French delegation, 1968): 'The matter of criminal organizations such as the S S came within the brief of the American Prosecutor, Judge Robert H. Jackson Gerstein's statement, which pointed to the existence of "good" SS men, ran directly counter to his argument. His assistants may have suppressed it.'

Serge Fuster (French deputy-advocate): 'A town in ruins. The euphoria of victory. It was a "show" put on to celebrate the end of the killing. There were masses of visitors, great disorder, a plethora of documents, some genuine, some false. You could do what you liked in Nuremberg, even slip Göring a dose of cyanide. The officials didn't seem to realize the procrastinations, although there were plenty. The cold war had already begun, although not yet openly.'

Albert Lentin (French delegation): 'It was the cold war. Churchill made his Iron Curtain speech at Fulton in March. The Nazis in the dock read the US Army newspaper *Stars and Stripes* and roared with laughter. People from the Vatican were bringing pressure to bear on the Americans and MRP members of the French delegation.'

Philippe Bauchard (French delegation): 'Was the Gerstein statement suppressed for reasons of policy, the necessity of placating the Germans in view of the cold war? I wouldn't know. There could equally well have been other reasons. After all, the document condemned the Allies and neutral countries for their failure to take action—and Pius XII in particular.'

## III

### WANTED FOR MURDER (1947)

After Nuremberg, Gerstein was suddenly much in demand. As much energy was spent in looking for him as, seemingly, had hitherto been devoted to not finding him. He was wanted as a witness at the trial of Nazi doctors in November 1946. His family and friends were trying to break through the bureaucratic entanglements of the Allied Occupation authorities. Germans pursued by justice wanted him to testify in their favour. Never was a dead man more sought after. Friends and enemies, lawyers and Gestapo men, wrote to him appealing for help. People of all kinds were asking what had become of him. The replies were no less various. He was alive, he was dead; he had been seen here, there and everywhere . . . he was always somewhere else.

In October 1946 an American called on Frau Gerstein to ask for her husband's address. Armin Peters made inquiries of the secretariat of the Nuremberg Tribunal. Paul Hochstrasser, now Swiss Consul in Frankfurt, received a telephone call from that same source: 'You remember a man called Gerstein? . . . He's here, and he says he told you everything. He claims to be innocent.'

*14 October 1946*. From the Director of ORCG to the Director of the Court of Justice, Baden-Baden: 'I have the honour to inform you that Gerstein, Kurt, whom you have asked me to produce, committed suicide in his cell in the Paris military prison on 25 July 1945.'

*23 October 1946*. Baden-Baden to ORCG: 'I should be obliged if you would inform me if Gerstein, Kurt, born in Tübingen 11.8.1905, SS Oberscharführer FHA, wanted by the US authorities as a war criminal, is at present detained in a prisoner-of-war camp in France.'

*26 October 1946*. 'The Commissioner for German and Austrian affairs desires to know if Gerstein, Kurt, born at Tübingen, wanted by the US authorities as a war criminal, is in France.'

*8 December 1946*: 'Dear Herr Gerstein, . . . I am writing to beg you to help me by testifying as to my conduct during the war . . . Ernst Zerrer.'

*February 1947*. To the Director-General of the Court of Justice, for information: 'Gerstein transferred as a witness by ORCG Lindau to ORCG Paris, 48 rue Villejust, in October or November 1945. Chief of Police, Baden-Baden.'

Administrator-General Laffon to General commanding POW Service, Baden-Baden: 'I am informed by ORCG that this man was not detained in France.'

*22 February 1947*: 'Dear Herr Gerstein, I have often thought of you, and I have now learned by chance that you were mentioned in the *Telegraf*. I rejoice with all my heart in your rehabilitation. It is a great relief to me . . . Irmgard Eckhardt.'

*June 1947.* Gerthoffer, deputy Prosecutor of the French Republic attached to SHAEF, to the Keeper of the Seals: 'The United States Public Prosecutor considers it desirable to hear the testimony of Gerstein, Kurt. I am informed that he has spoken on the radio from Lyons. Inquiry has not so far revealed his address . . . The US Public Prosecutor has since informed me that he was interrogated. This additional information will no doubt make it possible to find him.'

*21 June 1947.* Director of ORCG to Monsieur Gerthoffer, '. . . Gerstein, Kurt, committed suicide on 25 July 1945. According to ORCG records he was at the camp of Belzec, near Lemberg, in charge of the decontamination service, from 1941 onwards.'

*October 1947.* The Rottweil pastor to Elfriede: 'Dear Frau Gerstein, Lieutenant Jumez, at that time a Security officer, said that your husband was passed on to another branch of the Service, he was not sure where, but most probably in Constance. He considers that your best course would be to apply to the French Security Service in Tübingen, thus bringing the loose ends together. I am sorry I cannot tell you anything more definite. Let us hope that in one way or another this mysterious affair will be cleared up. That is the wish I send you; it is time that your trials were ended.'

*December 1947.* Entry in the records of CROWCASS (Central Registry of War Criminals and Security Suspects): 'Gerstein, Kurt, 34893. Wanted in France for murder.'

# IV

## ELFRIEDE

*Mössingen (Württemberg), April 1967*

The word 'family' has a strange ring in connection with a man who always ignored its implications, so extending his duties as a human being as practically to abolish those of the husband and father. 'You are three or four,' he had said to Elfriede, 'but they are thousands!'

They are still living in the modest house near Tübingen: Elfriede, round-faced, white-haired, slow-spoken, a woman whose looks and features betray her deep inward trouble: Olaf, the son, born in 1942, the year of Belzec; and the photograph of Kurt Gerstein in a large frame. One thing about this portrait is immediately noticeable: he is in uniform, but there are no insignia of rank on his tunic.

'When people called on me,' says Elfriede, 'they saw the SS on his lapels and said: "So he was one of those," and then I had to explain and explain, and it was too painful. So I had them blotted out.'

Hanging on the wall of the living-room is a small reproduction of the picture *Jeremiah Weeping for His People*. Elfriede says: 'Kurt wept for the same people . . .

'For a long time I hoped he would come back. They returned his effects in 1949: a pair of braces, a collar, an old wrist-watch, a few papers and some cancelled banknotes . . . Later I tried to find his grave, but it was empty, the remains had been taken to the boneyard. And then I had to find out how he had died, which entailed legal procedures, a long struggle . . . I had to bring up our three children without help from anyone—bring them up to the age when I could tell them who their father was.'

But in spite of everything—her exile in Tübingen while he was so furiously busy elsewhere, denied his confidence and saved by her ignorance, little loved and little helped, her present life an endless farewell to someone who was never really there—in spite of it all she has managed to bring up her children. Arnulf, aged thirty in 1969, is married and an assistant lecturer at Tübingen University; Adelheid, aged twenty-nine and also married, is a certified interpreter in Russian and French; Olaf, who is in trade, is still a bachelor.

# V

## POST-NUREMBERG

On 17 August 1950 nine citizens of Tübingen, constituting the local Denazification Court, passed judgement on Gerstein.

Elfriede Gerstein had applied by process of law for a war widow's pension, which entailed the rehabilitation of her husband since he had been a member of what was now regarded as a criminal organization.

The thing was done in style. The whole of Gerstein's life—as much of it, at least, as appeared above the surface—was passed under review. The evidence of Pastor Niemöller, Bishop Dibelius, Doctor Ehlers, Canon Buchholtz and Pastors Rehling and Mochalsky was heard, and the Court also took note of the testimony of Baron von Otter. In short, all the material was available on which to base an equitable verdict.

The verdict was as follows: Gerstein had been a Nazi and remained one. There could therefore be no pension, no allowance or compensation for his widow. On the other hand, since her husband was dead no proceedings would be taken against her.

This was no hasty judgement. It was confirmed by the same Court three months later, when Elfriede Gerstein appealed. The reasons given at the first hearing were:

'One might have expected of Gerstein that, in view of what he had seen at Belzec, he would have refused with all his might to become an instrument of this cold-blooded massacre. The Court is of the opinion that he did not do everything in his power, and that he could have found additional ways and means of personally divorcing himself from it. It is neither comprehensible nor excusable that, as a convinced Christian who in the previous years had maintained such an upright and courageous attitude towards National-Socialist policies, he should, a year later, have consented to place orders with the firm of Degesch. His earlier experience should have made it clear to him that he was in no position single-handed to prevent the process of mass extermination or to save the lives of even a small number of the victims.'

At the second hearing: 'The execution of a criminal order can be excused only if the person concerned is unaware of its criminal nature, or if a state of "unavoidable necessity," as defined in Article 54 of the Criminal Code, can be shown to have existed. It is apparent from the nature of this case that the subject was not unaware of the illegal nature of his orders and knew perfectly well what he was doing. A state of "unavoidable necessity" would have existed only had he been under the threat of instant and inevitable death, to himself or his family, from which he could escape only by carrying out the orders. Fear of any other kind, regarding the general situation, professional standing or advancement, is not an argument warranting exemption from complicity. While it may be admitted that it would not have been easy for the subject to obtain his release from the SS, in view of what he knew, the Court remains convinced that he would not have been in danger of instant death had he refused to carry out these particular orders. What happened at Auschwitz was so monstrous that it may reasonably have been expected of the subject that he would do everything humanly possible not to blacken his own conscience, even though he could not thereby prevent what was happening.'

Of which the moral seems to be: 'Do nothing in case you dirty your hands.' In 1967 Helmut Franz commented as follows: 'When a post-war Denazification Court shows no comprehension for those solitaries, but persists in regarding them with mistrust and malice because in its view what they did is unbelievable, this is an example of German conformity.'

There is a sentence in the Tübingen summing-up that indicates the nature of the Court's thinking: 'Gerstein would undoubtedly have been tried by an Allied military court *if he had not evaded justice by committing suicide.*' The real reasons for his death, as we know, lie far deeper than that (like Van Gogh, he was a victim of society). As to the assumption that he would have been convicted and condemned to death, for a long time I myself refused to believe it. I believed he would have been released after a few months. But since studying the proceedings of the 'doctors' trial' at Nuremberg in November 1946 I have changed my mind.

The accused in this case numbered about twenty, including Karl Brandt, Reichskommissar at the Ministry of Health, Gebhardt, an SS surgeon, and Gerstein's chief, Joachim Mrugowsky (who was hanged).

There was also a certain Wolfram Sievers, aged forty, who had been on the administrative committee of Himmler's *Ahnenerbe* (Ancestral Heritage Society). Besides 'conducting researches into the localities, the spirit, the acts and the heritage of the Nordic Indo-Germanic race, and communicating the results of these researches to the public in an interesting form,' *Ahnenerbe* also concerned itself with military research and medical experiments on human subjects.

Sievers defended himself vigorously at Nuremberg, claiming that he had been a Resistant, and to the surprise of the judges he produced a witness on his behalf, Doctor Friedrich Hielscher, who informed the Court that he had himself secured Sievers's entry into *Ahnenerbe* with the intention of preparing a coup d'état against the regime.

'Sievers helped me by giving me a forged order for research into German culture which enabled me to travel abroad. I was arrested in September 1944, charged with being involved in the July conspiracy and in danger of being hanged. Sievers used his influence with Himmler to get me off. He gave me valuable information; he was the only one of our group who was really close to Himmler. In conjunction with some young men in our organization, he was planning to assassinate Himmler and Hitler ... The more active he was in his under-cover opposition to National Socialism, the more loudly he had to speak in its favour. He told me in 1942 of Himmler's wish to use *Ahnenerbe* in connection with experiments on human beings. The intention of the SS was quite clear, and the question was whether one was prepared to act as Himmler's instrument in proceedings which reduced men to the level of insects. But even if Sievers had withdrawn, not a single victim would have been saved. By staying he could at least throw a little sand into the machinery, besides continuing his anti-Party work . . . The human experiments were only a part of the hideous Nazi system.'

Prosecutor Alexander G. Hardy: 'Sievers told you about Professor Hirt's collection of skeletons. You knew that people were selected for their size, that anthropometric records were kept, that they were sent to Natzweiler to be killed and then shipped on to the University of Strasbourg? You knew all that?'

Hielscher: 'Yes.'

Prosecutor Hardy: 'A charming position for a member of the Resistance to be in, was it not?'

Had it been Gerstein in the dock, the cross-examination could have been almost identical.

'You knew what was happening in those camps. You knew it so well that, ostensibly for reasons of humanity, you tried to improve the process. By your own admission, you saw thousands of people killed. And you procured and transported supplies of the gas known as Zyklon B?'

'Yes.'

'A charming position, was it not, for a member of the Resistance and a professing Christian?'

The mention of the dread name of Zyklon B would have been enough of itself to offset Von Otter's testimony. The likelihood is that Gerstein would have been hanged along with Mrugowsky at Landsberg in June 1948—the twenty-fifth of the hanged men of Nuremberg. It was only one of the many deaths he might have died.

# VI

## THE GERSTEIN REPORT

A note on the source of this transcript: In April 1945, while at Rottweil, Kurt Gerstein committed to paper everything he knew about the crimes of the Third Reich, not in self-defence but to expose them—and at that time he was virtually the only witness from the SS side. He apparently made two copies of this report in German and entrusted them to the hotel proprietor at Rottweil, who forwarded one of them to Frau Gerstein in 1946. He also made an abridged version in French dated April 26, 1945. This is the version which he handed to Major Evans and Mr John W. Haught, which was used in evidence at Nuremberg, and subsequently disappeared.

The transcript reproduced here is a translation of the original and more detailed German version, identical with that in Frau Gerstein's possession. It is in the US Archives at Alexandria, Virginia, from which Pierre Joffroy obtained a copy.

*Information on the author of the report*:
Kurt GERSTEIN, certified Engineer, attached to the Service of Mines, out of activity, removed from Civil Service for anti-nazi activities in favor of the Reformed Church (Pastor Niemoeller) (27.9.'36).

I am co-proprietor of the firm LINON, FLUHME & Co., manufacture of machinery for automatic lubrificating of locomotives.

Ludwig E. GERSTEIN, my father is former President of the Court of Justice at Hagen (Westphalia).

Clara GERSTEIN, maiden name SCHEMANN, my mother, died in '31.

I married Elfriede BENSCH (Tuebingen, Gartenstrasse 4) on August 31, 1937.

We have three children: Arnulf, aged 5; Adelaide, $3\frac{1}{2}$ years old, and Olaf, aged 2.

*Curriculum Vitae of GERSTEIN*:
From 1905 to 1910, at Muenster (Westphalia)
From 1910 to 1919, at Sarrebrueck.
In 1921, at Halberstadt.
From 1922 to 1925, at Neu-Ruppin, near Berlin, where I took my B.A. degrees.
From 1925 to 1930, practical work in mines, alternatively with

studies in Marburg, Aix-la-Chapelle and Berlin. In 1931, examination and diploma as Engineer.

Since 1925, active member of the Protestant Youth, especially in Bible circles and superior pedagogical Institutes.

*Political Activity*:

Active partisan of BRUENING and STRESEMANN. From 1933, always prosecuted by the Gestapo for anti-nazi activity in favor of the Christian Resistance Church (Pastor Martin NIE-MOELLER, Berlin Dahlem–Dachau) and for holding on the prohibited meetings of the Protestant Youth.

January 30, 1935, I was maltreated and wounded for having protested against the representation of the anti-christian play: 'Wittekind' at the Theater of Hagen (Westphalia).

November 27, 1935, I was appointed deputy-inspector to the Service des Mines; I became after an official of the Administration of Mines of Saar at Sarrebrueck.

September 27, 1936, I was arrested at my office by the Gestapo for having distributed 8,500 anti-nazi pamphlets to all the high State officials. The reason of my arrest was; put into protective custody, for pernicious activity against the State, in spite of many warnings in organizing a systematic attack against Nazism in the literary field.

Having left the Civil Service, I could realize one of my strongest wishes: to study tropical medicine at the Protestant Institute for Medical Missions, Tuebingen. I got every year an income of M. 18,000 from the firm LINON, FLUHME, & Co., and so, I was financially independant. Since 1931 I used to spend a third of this income for my religious ideals. It is at my expenses that I got 230,000 religious and anti-nazi leaflets printed and distributed.

On 14.7.'38 I was arrested again by Gestapo and SD, Stuttgart. I first stayed several weeks in various SD prisons, then I was interned in the camp of WELZHEIM. Previously I had been interrogated and warned a couple of dozen times by the Gestapo and the SD. I was then forbidden to speech within the whole Reich and this prohibition has been maintained until the end of the Nazi government.

Since I knew the slaughter of all the insanes at HADAMAR, GRAFENECK, and other places, I wanted only one thing: to see to the bottom this witch-pot and then tell the people what I would have seen there,—even if my life was then threatened.

I had not to scruple: I had been myself twice betrayed by SD agents, who had infiltrated into the most exclusive circles of the Protestant Church, and prayed close to me.

I thought: "What you are able to do, I can do it better than you do", and I volunteered as SS. I was helped in doing so by the fact that my own sister in law, Bertha EBELING, had been murdered at HADAMAR. I could be introduced by two Gestapo agents, who had been in charge of my case and was easily taken in the Waffen SS. Once a SS man had told me: "Idealist as much as you are, you should be a fanatic member of the Party"; they showed me the way by themselves. I got my basical instruction at Hamburg, Langenhorn, where I had a probation with 40 other doctors, and then at Arnhem (Holland), and Orianenburg. At Arnhem, I got immediately connected with the Dutch Resistance through school-friend, Ubbink DOESBURG, a manufacturer.

My double studies, as a physician and as a technician brought me soon to the E.M. of the SS Section "D", Hygiene. One must admit that this section was organised very broad-mindedly and thoroughly.

I was absolutely free to choose my occupation.

I started building in great quantity local and mobile disinfection installations for PW and concentration camps, for troops in the field, which were badly needed. Without having there any personal merit, I got a great success and from then I am considered—wrongly—as a technical genius. I have simply a great common sense and a very sure instinct. From then, I was entrusted with the carrying out of many projects of the Ministry of Labour and the Ministry for the East. I was charged of improving the very deficient system of disinfection of the O.K.W. But this system had been so spoiled that it was very hard to improve it. Yet, I succeeded in stopping the terrible wave of typhus of 1941, which caused daily tens of thousands deaths in PW and concentration camps. I was soon promoted 2nd Lieutenant, and, later, 1st Lt.

In December, 1941, I was again in danger. The Court of the Party which had decided my execution had just learned that I had got infiltrated into the E.M. of the S.S. But I was protected by my chiefs and maintained, thanks to my successes and to the esteem my chiefs had mostly to me.

In December, 1942, I was appointed head of the technical sanitary section which includes all the system of drink-water and all the technical organisation of disinfection,—even by means of toxic gases.

June 8, 1942, SS Sturmbannfuehrer GUENTHER, of the R.S.H.A., Kurfuerstenstrasse, came to my office. He wore civilian clothes. I had never seen him before. With many mysterious hints he ordered me to get 260 kilogs of prussic acid and to carry it by a car of the R.S.H.A. to a place known only to the driver.

Some time after I went by this car to Kellin near Prague. I could understood more or less what was the nature of this mission; yet I accepted it. Even today I believe that a chance, strangely resembling the providence, put me in a position to look at where I did want to see through. Among hundreds possible jobs I was offered right the post which made the most close to the field I was the most interested in. This seemed as more incredible than, in the past, I had been several times interned by the Gestapo and SD for anti-nazi activity. My chiefs knew this through the denunciation of the Party. Truly, the SD and their chief the RSHA did sleep in this case and took the very wrong man.

However, according to an order, I kept this mission absolutely secret, even at the office. Had I said something to anybody, I would have certainly been put to death after terrible tortures and my whole family would have been executed.

As I was regarded as an authority in the field of prussic acid and toxic gases, it was easy to me to get a whole load destroyed, under pretext of damages or decomposition. So I accepted the mission. I was offered without any scruples, for anybody else would have carried it out for the purposes of the SD. So, I could prevent the use of prussic acid to kill people. Anyway, from then, I manage to carry always on me poison and a charged pistol to suicid if my own feelings were discovered.

The day we drove to Kellin, we were accompanied by SS Obersturmbannfuehrer Professor Dr. PFANNENSTIEL, professor of Hygien at Marburg (Lahn) university.

The staff of the factory of prussic acid at Kellin understood, through my voluntarily awkward technical questions that the acid was made to kill human beings. I was used to do so in order to spread rumors among the people.

While at Kellin, our car was closely watched over.

We were received at Lublin by SS Gruppenfuehrer GLOBOC-NEC, Waffen SS General. He said, about gassing: "This State secret is one of the most important I even may say the most important. Whoever mention it will be shot immediately; yesterday, we have silenced two babblers. At present (August 17, 1942) we have 3 installations:

1. *BELCEC* on Lublin–Lemberg road. The camp is situated at the northern angle of the road, right at the point where the road is crossed by the Russian demarcation line.
   *Daily capacity*: about 15,000 executions
   *Average use*: 11,000 daily since April 1942.
2. *SOBIBOR* near Lublin, Poland; I do not know exactly where.
   *Daily executions*: 20,000 since June, 1942.
3. *TREBLINKA*, Poland, 120 km. NNW from Warsaw
   *Daily executions*: 25,000 since May, 1943.
4. There is another camp not yet built up at MAIDANEK, near Lublin.

Except the last, I visited thoroughly all these camps and was accompanied by Police Capt. WIRTH, chief of all these death factories. WIRTH had, before, been entrusted by HITLER and HIMMLER to put to death the insane at HADAMAR, GRAFE-NECK, and other places.

GLOBOCNEC told me: "Your job is to disinfect the immense quantity of woolen stuff, linen clothes and shoes produced by our factories. We collect every year clothes among the Danes in

order only to camouflage from the people and the foreign workers
the source of so many old clothes. Another even more important
point of your mission is to modify the way our death institutes
work. At present, we have rooms which are run by gases exhausted from an old Russian Diesel motor. This should be im-
proved and work much faster. There must be something to do
with the prussic acid. The day before yesterday (August 15, 1942),
the Fuehrer and HIMMLER went here. I was ordered not to
give a permit to people who must, on duty, visit our installation;
I must accompany them myself."

Thereupon PFANNENSTIEL asked: "What did the Fuehrer
say of this?" GLOBOCNEC answered us: "He said that all the
work must be carried on as quickly as possible. He was accompanied of Dr Herbert LINDEN, Councellor at the Home-
Ministry who has been responsible as doctor of the big execution
of the insane. Dr. Linden suggested that the corpses be incinerated
instead of buried because, he said, we may be succeeded by a
generation which will not understand us very well". GLOBOC-
NEC said that he answered then: "If ever we are succeeded by a
generation who do not understand our great and so imperious
duty, then the Nazism will have been unefficient. My own mind
is, on the contrary, to bury simultaneously with the corpses,
bronze-tablets on which we get inscribed that we did have the
courage to carry out successfully this so important and necessary
task".

Hitler said then: "Well, GLOBOCNEC, this is my own
feeling".

Nevertheless some time later Dr LINDEN's opinion pre-
dominated: even the already buried corpses were burnt with
gasoline or crude oil on grates built up with rails.

The office of these factories were at Lublin at the so-called
JULIUSSCHRECK barracks. On the following day, I was
introduced to the men who worked there. We drove to BELCEC.
A little station had been especially erected near the road, not far
from a little yellow sandy hill. Several buildings wearing the inscription: "Special Commando of Waffen SS, BELCEC" lay on
the southern part of the road.

GLOBOCNEC introduced me to WIRTH's representative: SS Hauptsturmfuehrer OBERMEYER of PIRMASENS.

With a remarkable discretion, OBERMEYER showed me "his estate".

There was a great barrack with the inscription "Vestiary", right after the station; it was all surrounded with thick barbed wires rows. Inside the barrack there was a large wicket on which was written: "Checking room for gold and valuables". Further there was the "hairdressing room" with about 100 stools in it. After there was a tree shadowed allee, about 150 meters long, barbedwired all along, with a sign post at its beginning: "To inhalation and Bathing-Rooms". At the end of the allee we found a building looking like a bathing house, with a wrought iron staircase on the front. A board on the building informed that it was the "Heckenholt Foundation". That afternoon, I saw no more.

The gassing rooms were on the right side of the corridor within the "bathing house". On both sides of the corridor, three rooms looking like garages, 5m. long, 5m. wide, and 1,90m. high.

An unrespirable, pestilential smell of corpses prevailed all around, even up to the road. Millions of flies were humming everywhere. But I saw no corpse that day.

The following day [presumably 18 Aug., trsl.], some minutes before 7 a.m., I was reported that "the first convoy was to arrive in a few minutes". As a matter of fact, at 7 striking, a train of 45 carriages arrived from LEMBERG. Behind the barbed-wired openings of the waggons appeared awfully lean children, and men and women with terrified faces. Two hundred Ukrainians wrested the doors and whipped the people out of the carriages. At the arrival of the train 1,450 people out of 6,700 were already dead.

A loudspeaker gave the following orders: "You have to undress entirely, to take off even spectacles and prothesis apparatuses" (A guardian told a girl: "Do not worry about taking off your spectacles: you will get other ones inside"). "Bring your valuables to the wicket without getting a receipt". A jewish boy (3 years old) was given a handful of strings to distribute to all the people so that everybody ties its both shoes together, otherwise it would have been later impossible to identify the pairs in a heap of boots of several meters.

Then women and girls must go to the "hairdresser", who in 2 or 3 times of scissors cut their hair and put it in potatoes bags.

An Unterscharfuehrer on duty told me: "This hair will serve to special isolation use for submarines". I predicted already then to everybody that the German submarines would soon cease roaming about seas for the most efficient Army in the world must loose its sharpness when soiled of innocents' blood. The events showed me soon after that I was right.

The death's train started then, a lovely girl in front of it. They went down the alley. Everybody was naked, men, women, and children. The cripple had been obliged to let their prothesis apparatusses and went along supported by others.

I standed at the top of the slope with Capt. WIRTH, between the rooms of death. Mothers with their sucklings, naked children, women and men, everybody pell-mell, were toiling up. The first ones entered the rooms of death, pushed into them by standing behind people who were forced by the whips of the SS men.

In a corner of the alley a fat SS man with a bull-dog's face standed; he was surrounded by these unfortunate people. He was telling them with a honey mouthed voice: "Nothing is to happen to you. You will have in these rooms only to breather deeply; these inhalations are necessary to avoid diseases and epidemies and will make your lungs good". When asked: "What will become of us?", he answered: "Of course, men will have to work, to build up houses, to make roads; but the women will not be obliged to work; only if they like, they may help in factories and kitchens."

This dim flame of hope was sufficient to make some of these unfortunate people enter willingly the rooms but most of them had understood what was to happen: the smell had informed them on their fate.

They stepped up the small stairs and saw the whole installation most of them, absolutely silencious, were like a herd of sheep entering a slaughter house. A Jewish woman, looking to be 40 years old, with sparkling eyes appealed the murderers of all these innocent people be damned for their coward crimes. Captain WIRT whipped by himself at her face 5 or 6 times; she disappeared also into the room. Somme people were applying to me: "Oh sir, do help us, do help us . . ." Many others were praying. I could not help them. I started praying with them and, hidden, I shouted toward their God and toward mine. I allowed myself to do so as there was a great noise all around me. I should have willingly entered these death rooms, I should have liked to die there with them. If my corpse in SS Officer uniform had been found in the gassing room, nobody would have believed that I was dead in protestation against these murders . . . My death would have been regarded as an accident and my epitaph would have been: "Dead for his dearest Fuehrer, while on duty".

It ought not to be so. I had not yet the right to fall into the temptation of dying with these people. I knew quite a lot concerning the murders. WIRTH had told me: "There are not 10 living people who have seen or who will see as much as you did; the foreign auxiliary personnel will be executed at the end". I am one of the 5 men who saw the whole installation, and I am certainly the only one to have visited it as an enemy of this gang of murderers.

I must now proclaimed what I saw there, and charge the murders.

The rooms were getting full. "Load them well" ordered WIRTH. The people were treading on each other's feet. About 7 or 8 hundred people in a room of 25,2m. by 45,3m. I resumed: more than a half were children, so the average weight was around 30 kg, i.e. there was in each room about 25.250 kg. "of man". WIRTH was right: it was possible to make enter 750 persons in a room of 45,3m.—with the SS whips.

The doors then were closed.

The others were waiting outside; they were always naked.

Meanwhile a second convoy had arrived.

I was told: "Of course, they have to wait outside, whatever the weather is, even in winter". I had not yet put a question and seemed to be most interested, when a silly word escaped my lips:

"They will get death, waiting naked outside." A SS man answered me in his dialect: "Well they are here for that purpose".

I suddenly understood why the whole installation was named: "Hockelchoc Foundation". HOCKELCHOC was the heater of the Diesel motor the emanations of which killed people in the rooms. According to WIRTH, HOCKELCHOC was a hard-working little technician, he had plenty of ideas; he had already got overlasting merits at the time of the insane's execution.

This day, the Diesel did not work. I was told this was quite unusual.

WIRTH was approaching. He was worried that this happened the very day I was there. I was observing and listening. My watch registered everything: 50, 70 minutes. The Diesel always did not work and people in the rooms were always waiting, in vain. They were heard moaning and sobbing, "like at a Synagogue" said Pr. PFANNENSTIEL who had put his ear against the wooden door. WIRTH whipped the Ukrainian in charge of helping HOCKELCHOC.

After 2 hours and 49 minutes the Diesel started to work. After 25 more minutes, many people were dead. We could watch the operation through a little window in the wall, now and then open to lighten a moment the room.

WIRTH asked me thoroughly whether I thought it was better to let people die in darkness, or in a lighted room. He asked it to me as same as he would have asked: "Do you prefer sleeping with or without a cushion?" or "Do you prefer coffee with or without milk?"

After 26 minutes, very few were stille alive, and after 32 minutes all were dead. I was told this was the usual time to make the people die.

On the other side of the room, the men of the labour commando opened the wooden doors. They also were jews, but they had been promised freedom and a percentage upon found valuables. Three men were in ch. to keep an accurate and up to date reckoning and estimated the percentage.

The deads, like marble statue, stood closely one to another. They had no room to fall down or even to be bent. Even dead, members of one family could be easily recognized: they were still clutched to each other by their stiffened hands and it was difficult to separate them when emptying the room for a next "turn".

The corpses were wet from perspiration, urine, dejections; legs were strained with menstrual bleedings. All people were thrown out; children bodies were cast in the air; there was no time to spend. The Ukrainians whips fell on the backs of the commando men. Two dozen of dentists opened the mouths of the deads with hooks, searching for golden teeth. The golden teethed were put on the right, the others to the left ... Other dentists extracted the golden teeths with tongs and hammers.

WIRTH was jumping all around; this was his field.

Workers checked the genitals and anus, searching concealed gold, jewels or other valuables. WIRTH told me: "Weigh this can, it is filled with golden teeth it is but the crop of the last two days". With an extraordinary vulgarity he added: "You cann hardly believe all what we find as gold and diamonds". He took me to the "jeweller" in charge of all the treasures and showed them to me. Among the lot, 2 big 20 dollars coins seemed to delight particularly WIRTH who put them into his pocket.

I was shown also the former manager of a big Berlin store, and a small violinist, both of them chiefs of the jewish labour commando. The violinist was former captain in the Austrian Army, Iron Cross first class.

The naked corpses were thrown into nearby ditches of 100m. by 12m. and 20m. After somme days, the corpses swoll, then, a few days later, sank down, and so they could be covered of a new lay of corpses; then about 10 cm. of sand were spread on them, and only a few heads or limbs emerged from that. The day of my visit, only two convoys of about 12,500 people arrived at BELCEC.

This "factory" worked since April, 1942, and hade about 11,000 deads every day. When my friends and myself listened London broadcasting, or the "Voice of Amerika", we were often surprised by the innocent angels who talked of hundred thousand deads, while there were already effectively over 10 millions.

In 1943, the Dutch resistance informed me through UBBINK that I was begged not to imagine stories concerning the atrocities, but only to say the right truth.

In August, 1942, the Swedish Embassy in Berlin refused to believe my statements. But I swear the amount I give is true.

According to my trustworthy documents, I estimate the amount of defenseless men and women and children murdered by HITLER and HIMMLER to about 20 millions.

The 5 or 6 millions of European jews who were murdered are not only in question here, of course, there are also all the intellectual society of Czechosloviaquia, and the elite of others peoples, f.i. the Serbians, who suffered the same fate. The Poles suffered much also, and a few Czechs No. 3—i.e. those who were called "the biologically useless ones" who, from the SS viewpoint, had no longer the right to live as they could not work.

Commissions drove from village to village, from town to town; they consisted of so-called doctors who used very nice cars and medical tools; they were dressed in white clothes, with stethoscopes in their hand, and auscultated everybody all around. People designated, after an examination of a few seconds as unable to work were enlisted as "useless". Later on, they were fetched and "given a job".

These "doctors" were the young men dear to HIMMLER. They had not even elementary school instruction, although they greeted each other: "Dear Colleagues, and Eminent Professor".

A sturmbannfuehrer of Lublin told me: "Had not we applied these measures, Poland would be of no value to us for it is overcrowded and two weak. We do but what Nature does in any field and what it unfortunately forgets to do as for the human beings". Even a game-keeper asserted me that the elimination of the weak and the insane is necessary. This conception had become so evident that it was very difficult to argue with most of the elite.

WIRTH asked me to propose at Berlin no change to the present gassing methods, "for they proved themselves efficient". I found strange not to be asked anything concerning gassing, in Berlin.

I got the prussic acid buried.

The next day, August 19, 1942, Captain WIRTH's car drove us to TREBLINCA, 120 kms. N/N-E of VARSOW. The installation resembled, though less important, BELCEC camp: 8 gas-rooms and several high heaps of bags, clothes and linen.

To welcome us, a Himmlerian banquet was served up in the hall in the purest old-German style. The food was plain, but unrestricted deal of everything was available for everybody. HIMMLER himself ordered to give this kommando men as much meat, butter, and especially brandy as they wanted to have. Pr. PFANNENSTIEL in his speech underlined the importance and usefulness of the duty these men had to perform. Turning to me, he spoke of the "most human" methods and "beauty of that work". This seems unlikely, but I assure that PFANNENSTIEL himself, who had 5 children, did not speak either joking or in earnest, but treated the question as a doctor in the most serious way. More than a half of the killed people were children: the right time necessary to kill,—without taking into account the transportation and the so painful waiting—is 32 minutes. PFANNENSTIEL said even to the kommando men: "When we see these Jew corpses, these wretched faces, we still more understand how great a gratitude our duty will provoke".

When going to leave, we were offered several kilos of butter and numerous bottles of liquor to carry away with us. I manage to refuse all these things, pretending to have plenty myself. PFANNENSTIEL was happy to grab my share. We returned to VARSAW by car, when leaving, we could see again a group of Jews in one of the common graves busy with a heap of corpses. Capt. WIRTH explained me: "It had been forgotten to undress these of the newly arrived who had already died a natural death. We must catch it up, on account of the valuables and the clothes". In VARSAW, whilst waiting in vain for a sleeping-car, I met Baron von OTTER, Secretary of the Swedish Legation in BERLIN. Still under the fresh impression of the horrible sights, I told him everything with the pressing request to communicate all this to his Government and to the Allies, as every day of delay meant the death of tens of thousands of people. I told him: "If the Allies sent, instead of many bombs, millions of comprehensive pamphlets and leaflets, showing clearly the German people all that is going on it is likely that within several weeks or months, the people would have been through with Adolf HITLER".

Baron von OTTER asked me for some references, as such a conversation was rather delicate for him, in his capacity as diplomat. I gave him the name of Dr DIBELIUS, Bruederwag 2, BERLIN, a leading member of the Protestant Resistance and close friend of my friend, Pastor NIEMOELLER, at that time at DACHAU.

I saw Baron von OTTER two more times at the Swedish Legation. Meanwhile, he had communicated personally with STOCKHOLM and he told me that his report had had a considerable influence on the Swedish–German relations. Several days later, to relieve my conscience and in order to have done my utmost, I tried to communicate with the Nunzio in BERLIN. At my very first words, I was asked whether I was a soldier; then any talk with me is declined and I was requested to leave immediately the legation of His Holiness.

In Poland there was also another way to kill people: they were ordered to go up the ladder of a blast furnace; they were then killed at a blow of pistol, and thrown down into the blast furnace. Many people are said to have disappeared in brick furnaces, suffocated by gas and buried. But the source of my information on this case is not absolutely reliable.

S.S. Stubaf. HALLER, a chief of the Police of BROMBERG, reported to the Doctor who attended the course with me, what he had seen when in BROMBERG: the Police people were used to take the Jewish children by their feet and to break their heads by striking against the wall of the rooms in order to avoid the firing report. HALLER is said to have ordered to stop this absurdity and to have got that the children be shot. He is supposed to have been particularly afflicted once to see two little girls, 5 and 8 years old, kneeling down and praying. "Of course," continued HALLER, "I had anyway to order them also to be shot". He talked to us of the execution of intellectual Poles. They were obliged to dig their grave, then to lie down in it, the stomach against the earth, and were shot with machine-pistol. The following man had to lie down on the still warm corpses and were shot groups after groups; several, not yet dead, have been shot when trying to get out of the heap of corpses.

One of the Chiefs of the German Government in CRACOW, while carving a turkey, talked to me of specially interesting capture he had made: a Jew, of the Polish Resistance, refused to tell what he knew. After having had his wrists broken, he was still refusing to talk, he was then compelled to seat on an iron-plate warmed to white heat: "You should have seen how talkative he became then", he said.

On a visit to an office of building up of the Waffen S.S. at LUBLIN, the architects told me about a visit they had made the day before to the mortuary of a PW camp, in view to enlarge it. "There were thousands of corpses, mostly dead from typhus, which had been piled there, in a hurry". They noticed that some of the bodies were still moving, the Hottenfuehrer who had the key, asked only very calmly: "Where?" then, he took a round iron-hammer and broke up the skulls of the designated persons. The fact by itself did not surprise these two architects, only the natural manner in which it was done did surprise them.

During my visit to BELCEC, a Jewess who had a hidden razor, hurt some Jews of the labour kommando. WIRTH regretted this woman had already died, because, she should have been most strongly punished for the example. He had ordered the wounded Jews to be very well nursed, so that they may hope to live and get a compensation: "And these silly people believe it", said WIRTH laughing.

An especially disgusting sight at BELCEC was the competition organised between the men and the boys in charge of carrying dresses to the waggons. The one who works the more is supposed to be put into the labor kommando. This was a kind of competition for life or death between the naked people who carried the clothes while the S.S. laughed at them.

I relate this in order only to show how difficult it was even for a German, who was a bitter enemy of the Nazis, to find a way to discredit the criminal Government.

What could be required from an average citizen to do against the Nazism who the very representative on earth of Jesus refused even to hear me although tens and tens thousands people were to be murdered every day, although to wait even some hours seemed to me to be criminal. Even the Nunzio of Germany refused to be well informed on this monstrous violation against the basis of Jesus' laws: "Thou ought to love the other man like thyself". So, what could do any citizen who, mostly, had hardly heard of these crimes, who, like millions foreigners (such as Dutch Resistance), thought this kind of things were much exaggerated. Most of the time they never occurred to hear the foreigner broadcastings.

I left the Legation much disappointed and depressed not to have been advised nor helped at all. I was followed by a policeman; a few minutes later, another policeman on bicycle followed me, too. I went through minutes of immense disappointment and despair. I tok my revolver out of the pocket and got ready mentally for suicide. But something incomprehensible happened: the policeman came quite close to me, as near as about 50 cms., he stopped a moment and . . . went on. From then, risking every hour my life, I kept on informing hundreds of influential persons of the atrocious slaughters: among these people, the NIE-MOELLER family, the Press Attaché of the Swiss Legation in BERLIN, Dr HOCHSTRASSER, the Coadjutor of the Catholic Bishop of BERLIN, Dr WINTER,—to hand information to the Bishop and to the Pope,—Dr DIBELIUS and many others. Thus, thousands of people were informed through me.

I must add that GUNTHER, probably son of GUENTHER of the racial studies Institute, asked me again, early in 1944, to procure big quantities of prussic acid. The poison was to be delivered to his office, in Kurfuerstenstrasse, BERLIN, and held at his disposal. This poison was sufficient to kill several millions of human beings, who, thus, would have disappeared without much noise. GUENTHER told me that he did not know yet when, or in what way, or to what ends, and for what kind of people this poison was to be used. At any rate, it was to be available at any time. I understood from several technical questions of GUENTHER, that at least a part of this poison was to be used to kill a great number of men of clubs and reading-rooms. Scant indications led me to believe that officers and clergymen and, at any rate, cultured people, were aimed at and that this poison was to be used in the very city of BERLIN.

After a thorough examination of the shed, I told GUENTHER that I could not assume the responsibility of stocking at that place such quantities of poison,—(enough to kill twice the number of the inhabitants of the town). With much difficulty I obtained that this poison be kept at ORANIENBURG and AUSCHWITZ, in the concentration camps. I managed to make the poison disappear, pretending it was for disinfection. The bills of the suppliers,—"German Company for the fight against parasites", FRANKFURT and FRIEDBERG,—had been, on my request, made out in my name,—allegedly to keep the secret better,—in fact to destroy the poison more easily. For this reason, too, I avoided to present for payment the numerous current bills, in order not to remind constant the S.D. and the R.S.H.A. of the large quantities of poison, supposedly available. I let the suppliers wait for the payment of their bills. In the course of a talk, Dr PETERS, Director of the Company, told me that he had furnished prussic acid in phials, for use on human beings. I have never known what class of people GUENTHER was still to kill, on orders of his chief, EICKMANN. Judging by the quantities, I thought at first of the internees. For this reason, when JOCHEN, son of Pastor NIEMOELLER, asked me whether he would ever see his father alive again, I answered "no". HIMMLER's order to murder all the inmates of the concentration camps, if need be, could already be foreseen at that moment. It was also clear that at least the Ukrainian teams of the camps would be sacrificed, in order to suppress witnesses of gassings. I also thought it was possible they slaughtered the Pw, as a mean of blackmailing.

When later on, GOEBBELS said that, if necessary, the Nazis would slam the door behind them in such a manner as to shake the world, I ascertained once more that the poison-stocks were actually destroyed.

Some time later, GUENTHER ordered me to come to the R.S.H.A. and asked me how it would be possible to poison the Jews interned at MARIA-THERESIENSTADT, by throwing prussic acid from the high fortifications. I declared this plan unworkable, in order to prevent its execution.

I heard later that he had procured prussic acid from another source and that he did slaughter the Jews, who, allegedly, were having such a good time at MARIA-THERESIENSTADT. These Jews were the fathers of men killed in action or of men having been granted high distinctions or rendered precious services.

The most horrible camps were not BELSEN or BUCHEN-WALD; AUSCHWITZ and MAUTHAUSEN were much worse and millions of human beings perished in the gas-chambers and -cars (mobile gas-chambers). In AUSCHWITZ alone, millions of children were killed, by means of a pad of prussic acid held under the nose.

At RAVENSBRUECK concentration camp I witnessed experiments made on living beings by Dr GUNDLACH Hauptsturmfuehrer, acting on orders of S.S. Gruppenfuehrer Professor Dr GERBHARDT, Hohenleichen.

The experiments on women were, if possible, still more sickening and odious than those on men. To the men they said frankly: "Take care, you are going to have injections and you will die". In the concentration camp for women at RAVENS-BRUECK, they proceeded differently: "Mrs. MEYER", they were used to say, "you have an absess at the liver, we shall make you a few injections and you will be much better" . . . The most horrible was their eyes and their base irony. It was a real compe-tion,—from the Star of David put on the death-chambers down to the humoristic diagnosis.

Daily such experiments were made at BUCHENWALD on hundreds of internees by means of 1 to 100 "pervitine"—tablets, and on another part injections of typhus. HIMMLER himself gave the authorisation to undertake such experiments on people sentenced to death by the S.D. The reports on these experiments were all centralised in my office. The Stabescharfuehrer was used to give regularly to me.

One day, at ORANIENBURG, I saw about a thousand pederasts vanish in an oven.

At MAUTHAUSEN, it was a current custom to throw Jews from elevated spots down into the quarries. These "accidents of labour" were always foreseen by the guardians several minutes before.

S.S. Hauptsturmfuehrer Dr Fritz KRAATZ, chief of mission detached with S.S. Reich-medecine, told me of these facts with a sincere disgust. He made these things known of the people. KRAATZ is bitterly opposed to the Nazis.

At BELCEC, after my inspection I had the impression that, having stayed so long in the gas-chambers, everybody was really dead. Capt. WIRTH, a man without education nor any notion of chemistry or physiology, told me things apparently very strange. WIRTH was particularly fond of carrying out different experiments to bring people to death. Thus, he reported me, how, one morning, a child quite happy and quick was found in a gas-room that had not been cleared the evening before.

WIRTH is told to have carried out particularly interesting experiments on silly people. The different degrees of sensibility can be studied on them better than on normal people. Experiments with compressed air were also carried out; people were put into old boilers filled by a forcing pump with compressed air. At TREBLINCA, it seemed to me that several of the people subjected to this treatment were still living and just swooned, which did not exclude that they could always revive and suffer a new martyrdom till they die. Most of them had opened eyes and were horrible to see. Though my great attention, I could not perceive any motion among them. Most of the murderers took never any trouble in carrying out these executions on a human way, if this word may be used about these facts. All this was done, less with sadism than with a complete indifference, because it was convenient.

Hauptsturmfuehrer Dr VILLING of DORTMUND reported me he had been particularly impressed by this: about 2,000

Polish priests were ordered to dig ditches; after, they had to undress and stand before these ditches, then, they were shot, naked. They had been, right before asked ironically whether they still believed in God, in Mary and in Poland; they had answered with a severe faith that they believed more than ever in Christ, in the Blessed Mother of God and in the resurrection of their nation. VILLING spoke to me about this with trouble.

Other Poles died in the same exemplary attitude, particularly schoolmasters and mistresses. When hearing of all this, I reminded my own jail at Buechsenstrasse, STUTTGART; an unskilful hand had engraved in the metal of the bed: "Pray, Mother of God will help you". It was a great comfort to me in these hard days and my cell appeared to me as a small church. I salute with gratitude this unknown brother who sent me this encouragement in my deep affliction. God bless him.

Naturally afterwards all of them had to go into the gas-rooms; only a few people, very old and sick, who even helped by the others, could not creep along the rooms, were put in a different place and shot.

A few thrilling pictures stayed in my memory: A three years old jew boy was, thoughtful, distributing strings to tie together pairs of shoes. Even this child was rately put into the dreadful HITLER death engine.

I remember also a young girl who lost her little coral necklace about one meter far from the gas-room: a three years old boy found it, picked it up, considered it lovingly, enjoyed himself with the necklace and was then pushed sweetly, I must confess, inside of the gas-room by a guardian who still had a bit of feeling.

S.S. Hauptsturmfuehrer OBERMEYER told me the following story: "In a village in the neighbourhood, OBERMEYER met a Jew coming from his own native town, PIRMASINZ, during the war, this Jew had been unteroffizier, a very nice fellow. When children OBERMEYER and the Jew were used to play with each other and even once the Jew had saved him from death, so OBERMEYER said that he was now to take this man and his wife into his own labour kommando. I asked him what would happen of them later on. He looked at me looking surprised and answered: "What could become of them? the same thing as of the others, there is no other solution: well, maybe I shall get them shot."

Yet, I must confess that I met some S.S. men who blamed strongly these methods and who became earnest anti-nazis; first of all Hauptscharfuehrer HOELLAMOER who has always kept me well informed of all the secrets, and who has always destroyed all what could have become dangerous for me.

S.S. Sturmbannfuehrer Dr FOCHT was also anti-nazi: he was the chief of the inside section of the S.S. Hospital in Berlin and, since 1941, blamed openly these methods, knowing well that he was risking his life in doing so.

Dr NIBSEN, surgeon at ITZCHOF, and Dr SORGUE of JENA, the three chemist Chiefs of the Waffen S.S. did the same; BLUMENREUTHER, BEHNENBURG and RUDOLPHI took part in the officers plot of 20 July. 2/3 of the Dutch and Belgian SS, had been integrated by force or by cunning under pretext of sport training. Had they refused to obey, they would have been shot at once.

Anybody, even people not living in the camp, who, in dangerous gesture touched the trousers of somebody else was immediately shot. This order originated direct with HIMMLER and caused the death of many a very young SS coming right from the HITLER jugend and forced to the SS Force.

Many Navy and Air Force men have been suddenly sent to the SS Force. So, in spite of the hate which the SS men naturally inspire, it would not be just to make no difference. We must say in here that very often, the Police was much worse than the SS between them.

SS Gruppenfuehrer Dr GRAWITZ, president of the german Red Cross, is one of the chief responsible for the dreadful administration of the Concentration Camp.

# VII
## VOICES . . .

Pastor Martin Niemöller: 'He was a very special kind of saint, but perfectly pure and of irreproachable rectitude. He meant what he said and always acted according to his convictions, regardless of the consequences. . . . I am certain that he was the victim of his extreme resolution and of the attitude he chose to adopt, in absolute contradiction of his personal convictions, for the sake of which he was prepared to sacrifice, and indeed did sacrifice, his honour, his family and his life.' (1948.)

Pastor Otto Wehr: 'A figure such as Kurt Gerstein must necessarily, by bourgeois standards, appear in a half-light, or, better, a dubious light; and at the worst it may appear unbelievable. The disturbing mastery with which, simply from a desire to serve, he concealed his deepest Christian feelings under an outward appearance designed to inspire awe, makes it absurd to judge him by any normal scale of values. I had ample evidence of his skill in camouflaging his personal feelings. A judgement truly based on the essence and inner impulses of such a man must run counter to all attempts to explain him in politico-psychological terms.

'During the religious conversations I had with him, when he visited me for that purpose, the unshakable nature of his inner being never seemed to me to be in doubt.' (1949.)

Rudolf Vrba: 'He was a remarkable man . . . The Swedes kept his evidence secret and the work of extermination went on without interference by the free world. Having encountered a similar reluctance after my escape from Auschwitz and the writing of my report, I can guess the extent of Gerstein's disillusion. That he should have committed suicide is understandable.' (1963.)

Léon Poliakov, historian: 'Our personal conviction is absolute. It can be stated in very few words. The German, Gerstein, was "a just man among the Gentiles" and his name deserves to be remembered in history as that of a lofty, tormented conscience.' (1964.)

Doctor Ernst Wilm, head of the Evangelical Church of Westphalia, a former inmate of Dachau: 'Madness or grace? It is something witnessed only two or three times in a century. To join that gang of murderers was an act of near-madness. The huge burden was beyond the strength of any single man . . . A case beyond our power of measurement.' (1967.)

Charles Dubost, French prosecutor at Nuremberg: 'I never saw Gerstein. He figured for a moment in the Nuremberg trial and his testimony caused an unexpected stir . . . I don't know if he was as pure as he claimed to be. You remember he wrote: "Many were praying. I prayed with them. I huddled in my corner and besought my God and theirs . . ."

'To pray is not enough and I do not think he did everything possible, but he is dead. What is there to say? He was a split personality. This present age, which seems to leave man more solitary in the face of his conscience than he has ever been, is rich in them.' (1967.)

Eberhard Busch, writing on behalf of Karl Barth, theologian: 'Professor Barth had no personal contact with Gerstein, nor did he hear of him while he was alive. It was news to Professor Barth when he learned that he had influenced him.

'So far as he can remember, it was reading and seeing Hochhuth's play, *The Deputy*, that first drew the professor's attention to Gerstein. Since then he has heard more about him from various sources. Everything he has heard leads him to believe that Gerstein was a truly remarkable figure such as could only have existed and can only be understood in the context of that time and those terrifying dilemmas—a figure which, in spite of this or rather because of it, can only be evoked in the largest terms (it is not a question of "admiration"!) and which, in spite of this or rather because of it, must be regarded as a portent full of hope in the total chaos of the age.' (1967.)

Eduard Calich, writer, former inmate of Oranienburg: 'Of course in some circumstances one cannot judge simply by a man's actions and their outcome, particularly when it was impossible for him to do anything heroic. We must content ourselves with the degree of hatred he showed for the enemy; his personal suffering atones for the fact that he could do nothing to restrain the criminals. And yet, how are we to account for the fact that a man who so hated the SS, and in 1942 poured out his secrets to Von Otter, did not take the road to the front line and cross over to the side of humanity?' (1968.)

Hermann Langbein, former deportee and Secretary of the International Concentration-Camps Committee: 'I have heard and read a great deal about Kurt Gerstein. I respect the men who joined and ran risks, as happened in his case. On the other hand, there is the doubtful light shed by his uniform and his officer's rank. I came in contact with a great many SS people at Auschwitz, particularly doctors, and I realized that one had to make distinctions between them. Of all the figures with SS ranking who have passed into history, Gerstein is probably one of the most positive.' (1968.)

Horst Dickten: 'Gerstein was undoubtedly an exceptional man, and this in itself made him difficult, incomprehensible to other people. His temperamental make-up often drove him to the extreme limits of sanity. In his deepest self he was a man of faith without affiliations. He had a slight tendency to arrogance. Then again he had a sense of apartness which was almost misanthropic . . . He particularly enjoyed being with intelligent people, and he believed that it was their business to help others. The impulse to help others was very strong in him. He believed that the injustice of life began in the cradle and that it was everyone's duty to remedy this state of affairs so far as possible. He was in a sense a socialist, but he rejected the hierarchy and when he came up against it either tried to get round it or broke away. He recognized nothing but the Fear of God. To him all other things were institutions more or less well devised by men . . . I am convinced that if he had survived the war he would today be in a very prominent position.' (1968.)

He was a character
'like Wallenstein'—Helmut Franz, 1967.
'like Faust'—Ernst Weisenfeld, 1967.
'like Joan of Arc'—Gilbert Mantout, 1967.
'possibly to be understood in terms of the music of Bach. The *Art of the Fugue*, the first five variations'—Robert Weiss, 1967.

# Institutions Consulted

| | |
|---|---|
| Kurt-Gerstein-Haus | Berchum |
| Centre de documentation juive contemporaine | Paris |
| Dépôt central d'archives de la Justice militaire | Meaux |
| Ministère des Affaires étrangères – Bureau de liquidation des Affaires allemandes et autrichiennes | Colmar |
| Gouvernement militaire de Paris – Section de Justice militaire | Paris |
| Tribunal permanent des forces armées | Metz |
| Archives Wast | West Berlin |
| Ministère des Armées – Direction de la Gendarmerie et de la Justice militaire | Paris |
| Ministère des Armées – SIECA | Paris |
| Service historique de l'Armée | Vincennes |
| Royal Ministry of Foreign Affairs | Stockholm |
| Ministère des Affaires culturelles – Archives de France | Paris |
| Institute of Contemporary History | Berlin |
| Institute of Contemporary History | Munich |
| National Netherlands Institute for War Documentation | Amsterdam |
| Ministère de la Justice – Archives | Paris |
| French Embassy | London |
| Association indépendante des anciens déportés et internés juifs | Paris |
| Wiener Library | London |
| World Jewish Congress | Paris – New York |
| The Hoover Institution | Stamford, Conn. |
| *France-Soir* – Archives | Paris |
| Secours catholique | Paris |
| Auschwitz Museum | Oswiecim |
| Der Polizeipräsidium | West Berlin |
| Defense Department | Washington, DC |

# SS Military Divisions

*with approximate equivalents*

| | |
|---|---|
| Gruppe | division |
| Brigade | brigade |
| Standarte | regiment |
| Sturmbann | battalion |
| Sturm | company |
| Truppe | platoon |
| Schar | combat unit |

# SS Ranks

*with approximate equivalents*

| | |
|---|---|
| Reichsführer | field-marshal |
| Oberstgruppenführer | general |
| Obergruppenführer | lieut.-general |
| Gruppenführer | major-general |
| Brigadeführer | brigadier |
| Oberführer | colonel-in-chief |
| Standartenführer | colonel |
| Obersturmbannführer | lieut.-colonel |
| Sturmbannführer | major |
| Hauptsturmführer | captain |
| Obersturmführer | lieutenant |
| Untersturmführer | second lieutenant |
| Hauptscharführer | warrant officer |
| Oberscharführer | sergeant-major |
| Scharführer | sergeant |
| Rottenführer | corporal |
| SS Sturmmann | private, first class (no exact equivalent in British Army) |
| SS Mann | private |

# Acknowledgments

Those mentioned in the text I do not need to thank. They already know my debt. I hope the others will accept this mention of their names as some small expression of my gratitude.

Abensour (Maître P.)
Aymon, J. P.
Barrière (Captain)
Bausset, Ph. de
Benz, W.
Bessy (Mme)
Blet (Rev. Fr)
Buis (General)
Cahen (Rabbi)
Caillau-Lamicq, P.
Cant, de
Chalufour (Mlle)
Chamson, A.
Chapar (Councillor)
Chateauneu, R.
Chateauneu (Mme)
Chiaramonti (Mme)
Conte, A.
Courcel, de (Ambassador)
Cyprian (Professor)
Daboval (General)
David, M.
Delarue, J.
Drappier (Mme)
Faye, J. P.
Feldman, M.
Fournier (General)

Freudenberg (Doctor A.)
Gambiez (General)
Gerthoffer (Councillor)
Giacobbi, Ph.
Glaser (Professor)
Goess, F.
Gouberville, de (Captain)
Hallart (Registrar)
Heinrich (R. P.)
Herzog (Public Prosecutor)
Hessel, U.
Hourtoule, G.
Jumez, M.
Karski (Professor)
Kelber, G.
Klimek (Frau)
Koenigseder (Frl.)
Kronefeld (Engineer)
Laborde (Public Prosecutor)
Laffolay, M.
Laporte (School Superintendent)
Lecœur (Doctor)
Leluc (Police Commissioner)
Lemoine, S.
Lentin, A.
Lequette (General)
Less, A.

# ACKNOWLEDGMENTS

Le Tac, J.
Levi (Maître C. H.)
Levy-Mandel, R.
Löscher (Frl.)
Mady (Mlle)
Malliard, J.
Maloy (Maître F.)
Marbat (President)
Masson (General)
Mattéi (Mme)
Matter, F.
Matthias, G.
Mazor, M.
Meyer, S.
Milliot (General)
Monneray
Mutel (School Superintendent)
Neher (Professor)
Northam (Mrs)
Pelletier, R.
Pilichowski (Doctor C.)
Poggioli, Y.
Portefaix, de (Mlle),
Pottecher, F.
Poutier, J.
Rapinat (Mme)

Raynaud (President)
Richert (Ambassador)
Riegner, G.
Robert (Lieutenant-Colonel)
Roels (Mme)
Rouché (Professor)
Saint-Germain, de (General)
Sanchez, S.
Schirman (Maître L.)
Schmelck (Public Prosecutor)
Schmidt (Frl.)
Schwed, P.
Silianoff, E.
Steinberg, L.
Sydney-Smith, E.
Szerrer (Professor)
Tabouis (General)
Tardrew (Mme)
Telou (Mlle)
Thery, B.
Touffait (President)
Vanlaer, B.
Weliachew, D.
Wilm (President E.)
Wolff (Mme)
Zachayus (Maître S.)

In addition, I gratefully salute the memory of Karl Barth, Professor J. Sawicki, General Gallut, Maître Pierre Stibbe, Major Chiaramonti and M. Guillaume Widmer, who died while this book was being written.

# Bibliography

Franz, Helmut: *Kurt Gerstein*. ABC-Verlag, Zürich
Friedländer, Saul: *Kurt Gerstein: The Ambiguity of Good*. Alfred A.
  Knopf, New York, 1969
Bayle, François: *Croix gammée contre caducée*. Imprimerie Nationale,
  Paris


Amort, C., and Jedlicka, I. M.: *On l'appelait A.54*. Laffont, Paris
Arendt, Hannah: *Eichmann in Jerusalem*. Faber & Faber, London, 1963;
  The Viking Press, New York, 1963
Barth, Karł: *The Germans and Ourselves*. Nisbet, London, 1945
Barth, Karl: *Deliverance to the Captives*. S.C.M. Press, London, 1961
Bar-Zohar, Michael: *The Hunt for German Scientists 1944-1960*. Barker,
  London, 1967; Hawthorn, New York, 1967
Baumont, Maurice: *Aux sources de l'affaire – L'affaire Dreyfus*. Les
  Productions de Paris
Baumont, Maurice: *La grande conjuration contre Hitler*. Del Duca, Paris
Bayle, François: *Psychologie et éthique du national-socialisme*. Presses
  Universitaires de France, Paris
Bevenstein, Tatiana, and Rutkowski, Adam: *Assistance to the Jews in
  Poland 1939-1945*. Polonia Publishing House, Warsaw
Billig, Joseph: *L'Hitlérisme et le système concentrationnaire*. Presses
  Universitaires de France, Paris
Biss, André: *Un million de Juifs à sauver*. Grasset, Paris
Borwicz, Michel: *L'Insurrection du ghetto de Varsovie*. Julliard, Paris
Calic, Edouard: *Himmler et son empire*. Stock, Paris
Casalis, Georges: *Portrait de Karl Barth*. Labor et Fides, Geneva
Cohn, Norman: *Warrant for Genocide*. Eyre and Spottiswoode, London,
  1967; Harper & Row, New York, 1967
Comité international de la Croix-Rouge: *L'Activité du CICR en faveur
  des civils dans tous les camps de concentration en Allemagne*. Geneva
Delarue, Jacques: *Trafics et crimes sous l'occupation*. Fayard, Paris
Delarue, Jacques: *History of the Gestapo*. Macdonald, London, 1964

*Dokumenty I Materialy – Oboz y.* Lodz

Donat, Alexander: *The Holocaust Kingdom.* Secker & Warburg, London, 1965; Holt, Rinehart & Winston, New York, 1965

Donikian-Nazarian-Solakian: *Le Deuil national arménien.* Centre d'études arméniennes, Gardanne

Drawings and Poems of the Children of Terezin, 1942-44. Jewish State Museum, Prague

Dulles, Allen W: *Germany's Underground.* Macmillan, New York, 1947

Dvorjetski, Marc: *Ghetto à l'Est,* Robert Marin, Paris

Fest, Joachim C.: *The Face of the Third Reich.* Weidenfeld and Nicolson, London, 1969; Pantheon Books, New York, 1970

Friedländer, Saul: *Pius XII and the Third Reich.* Chatto & Windus, London, 1966; Alfred A. Knopf, New York, 1966

*German Crimes in Poland.* Warsaw

Heine, Heinrich: *Mein wertvollstes Vermächtnis.* Manesse Verlag, Zürich

Hitler, Adolf: *Mein Kampf.* Hurst and Blackett, London, 1939; Houghton Mifflin Co., New York, N.D.

Hochhuth, Rolf: *The Representative.* Methuen, London, 1963; U.S. title: *The Deputy.* Grove Press, New York, 1964

Hoess, Rudolf: *Commandant of Auschwitz.* Weidenfeld and Nicolson, London, 1959; World Book Company, New York, 1960

Höhne, Heinz: *The Order of the Death's Head.* Secker and Warburg, London, 1969; Coward-McCann, New York, 1970

Jünger, Ernst: *Journal.* Julliard, Paris

Kessel, Joseph: *The Man with the Miraculous Hands.* Farrar, Straus & Giroux, New York, 1961

Lapide, P. E.: *The Last Three Popes and the Jews.* Souvenir Press, London, 1967; U.S. title: *Three Popes and the Jews.* Hawthorn, New York, 1967

Limagne, Pierre: *Ephémérides de quatre années tragiques (1940-44).* 3 vols. Bonne Presse, Paris

Loiseau-Chevalley, Suzanne: *Les Clandestins: de Dieu; Cimade 1939-45.* Fayard, Paris.

Ludwig, Carl: *Die Flüchtlingspolitik der Schweiz seit 1933 bis zur Gegenwart (1957).* Verlag Herbert Lang, Berne

Mazor, Michel: *Le Phénomène nazi.* Editions du Centre, Paris

Minc, Rachel: *L'Enfer des innocents.* Centurion, Paris

Mitscherlich, Alexander, and Mielke, Fred: *The Death Doctors.* Elek, London, 1962; U.S. title: *Doctors of Infamy.* Abelard-Schuman, New York, 1949

BIBLIOGRAPHY

Morse, Arthur D.: *While Six Million Died*. Secker and Warburg, London, 1968; Random House, New York, 1968
Neher, André: *L'Existence juive*. Seuil, Paris
Nobécourt, Jacques: *Le Vicaire et l'histoire*. Seuil, Paris
Perrault, Gilles: *The Red Orchestra*. Simon & Schuster, New York, 1969
Poliakov, Léon: *De l'antisionisme à l'antisemitisme*
Poliakov, Léon: *The History of Antisemitism*. Elek, London, 1966; Vanguard Press, New York, 1964
Poliakov, Léon: *Le Procès de Jérusalem*. Calmann-Lévy, Paris
Poliakov, Léon: articles in *Le Monde juif*, Jan.-Mar., 1964, Apr.-June, 1964
Portmann, Heinrich: *Kardinal von Galen, Ein Gottesmann seiner Zeit*. Aschendorffsche Verlagsbuchhandlung, Münster/Westf., 1953
Pradier, Jean: *Les Kurdes, révolution silencieuse*. Ducros, Bordeaux
Proudfoot, Malcolm J.: *European Refugees, 1939-52*. Faber & Faber, London, 1957; Northwestern University Press, Evanston, Ill., 1956
Rehling, Kurt: articles in *Unsere Kirche*, nos. 14, 15 and 16, 1964
Ringelblum, Emmanuel: *Notes from the Warsaw Ghetto*. McGraw-Hill, New York, 1958
Rossa, Kurt: *La Peine de mort*. Plon, Paris
Rothfels, Hans: Critical edition of the Gerstein Report in *Vierteljahreshefte für Zeitgeschichte*, April, 1953
Schellenberg, Walter: *The Schellenberg Memoirs*. Deutsch, London, 1956; U.S. title: *The Labyrinth*. Harper & Row, New York, 1956
Schmitzek, Stanislas: *Vérité ou fiction?* Zachodnia Agencja Prasowa, Warsaw
Schnabel, Reimund: *Le Dossier des S.S.* Librairie Académique Perrin, Paris
Schneersohn, Isaac: Mémoires in *Le Monde juif*
Shirer, William L.: *The Rise and Fall of the Third Reich*. Secker and Warburg, London, 1960; Simon & Schuster, New York, 1960
von Schramm, Wilhelm: *Conspiracy among Generals*. Allen and Unwin, London, 1956; Scribners, New York, 1957
Ströbinger, Rudolf: *L'Espion aux trois visages*. Casterman, Paris
U.S., Axis Criminology, Office of the Chief of Counsel for Prosecution: *Nazi Conspiracy and Aggression*, vols. IV, 215 (Mrugowsky); VI, 377 (Gerstein); 263, 317 (Mrugowsky); XX, 528-31 (the camps of Lublin); XX, 580, 598-9 (Sievers). Washington, D.C., U.S. Government Printing Office, 1946

Vrba, Rudolf, and Bestic, Alan: *I Cannot Forgive*. Sidgwick and Jackson, London, and Anthony Gibbs and Phillips; Grove Press, New York, 1964

Weissberg, Alex: *Advocate for the Dead*. André Deutsch, London, 1958; U.S. title: *Desperate Mission*. Criterion Books, New York, 1958

Wells, Léon, W.: *Janowska Road*, Cape, London, 1966

Wiesenthal, Simon: *The Murderers Among Us*. Heinemann, London, 1967; McGraw-Hill, New York, 1967

Wild, Herbert: article in *Le Messager évangelique d'Alsace et de Lorraine*, Feb., 1964

Wulf, Joseph: *Martin Bormann, l'ombre de Hitler*. Gallimard, Paris

Zahn, Gordon: *The Life and Death of Franz Jägerstätter*. Holt, Rinehart and Winston, New York, 1964

# Index

# Index